modernism and the
posthumanist subject

modernism and the posthumanist subject

**THE ARCHITECTURE OF
HANNES MEYER AND
LUDWIG HILBERSEIMER**

K. Michael Hays

the mit press · cambridge, massachusetts · london, england

First MIT Press paperback edition, 1995

© 1992 Massachusetts Institute of Technology

This book was set in Trump and Franklin Gothic by DEKR Corporation and was printed and bound in the United States of America.

Library of Congress Cataloging-in-Publication Data

Hays, K. Michael.
    Modernism and the posthumanist subject : the architecture of Hannes Meyer and Ludwig Hilberseimer / K. Michael Hays.
        p.   cm.
    Based on the author's thesis (doctoral—Massachusetts Institute of Technology)
    Includes bibliographical references and index.
    ISBN 0-262-08212-8 (HB), 0-262-58141-8 (PB)
    1. Meyer, Hannes, 1889–1954—Criticism and interpretation.
    2. Hilberseimer, Ludwig—Criticism and interpretation.
    3. Functionalism (Architecture)—Germany. I. Title.
    NA1353.M4H39   1992
    720'.92—dc20   92-1165
                                                              CIP

To my parents, Dorothy and Kenneth Hays

contents

acknowledgments

This book was based on research done for my doctoral dissertation in the Department of Architecture at the Massachusetts Institute of Technology. I am grateful to my dissertation advisors, Stanford Anderson, Benjamin Buchloh, and Anthony Vidler, for their careful readings. The writings of Fredric Jameson have guided my understanding of Frankfurt School critical theory, especially of Lukács and Bloch, and discussions with Benjamin Buchloh have clarified its use in explicating productivist aesthetic practice. A version of the chapter "Reproduction and Negation" was previously published by the Princeton Architectural Press in the volume *Architectureproduction*. I thank those who have commented on that publication; their criticisms, in some part, prompted me to elaborate the arguments presented here. Above all, Martha Pilgreen has guided me through the personal and intellectual traumas as well as shared the giddy highs that must accompany the publication of any first book.

modernism and the posthumanist subject

introduction

It is possible to define humanism's status, and reject
its theoretical pretensions while recognizing its practical
function as an ideology.

Louis Althusser, "Marxism and Humanism"

Modernism, whatever else we may mean by the term, has something to do with the emergence of new kinds of objects and events and, at the same time, new conceptualizations of their appearance, of the changed event structures and relationships between objects, their producers, their audiences and consumers. A history of modernism, then, must involve the concept of the producing, using, perceiving subject as well as the object. The subject is a signifying complex, constituted in the ideological space and categories of possible experience, formed through the very object world it would organize and explain. Thus modernism itself defeats the view that meanings and subjectivities are already formed and existent somewhere outside the work of art and that the critic's and historian's business is to locate them, and forces the recognition that modern aesthetic practice aims to bring into being new meanings and new subjectivities, seeking to figure not only what *is* but what *could be.*

A particular dialectic of subject and object emerges in the buildings, projects, and writings of Hannes Meyer and Ludwig Hilberseimer, each of whom, in different ways, brought himself face to face with the problems posed by modernization to bourgeois humanist thought, and to the sovereignty of humanist modes of artistic production and reception. The rationalization that accompanied modernization is inseparable from a problematization of the subject defined as self-creating conscience and will, that is to say, of humanism.

In recent theory, modern humanism has usually been subjected to a twofold critique: first, a critique of humanism as bourgeois ideology—the doctrine that valorizes "man" as such and masks differences such as class and historicity—and second, a critique of instrumental or technical reason, which is affiliated with bourgeois ideology and culture. Thus humanism has often been associated with the rise of modern capitalism and the ongoing bourgeois revolution. In architecture, however, this conception of humanism overlaps another that extends from Renaissance theory and the concomitant epistemologies of the human body, perspective and harmony, and visual homologies, and has its corollaries even in present-day architecture. It is an expanded model of humanism including both conceptions that will be intended here.

In humanist thought the role of the subject vis-à-vis the object has been that of an originating agent of meaning, unique, centralized, and authoritative. The individual subject enters the dialectic with the world as its source, as the intending manipulator of the object and the conscious originator of meanings and actions. Modern humanist architecture—Charles Garnier's Opera, say, or Otto Wagner's Postal Savings Bank or Louis Sullivan's commercial buildings—encoded the values and norms of a bourgeoisie still emergent in a market economy, providing a system of representation that exactly sufficed the sense of self, the aesthetic preferences, social habits, and forms of entertainment of that class. But within modernism, and within disparate disciplines, there developed another cultural attitude that shifted away from a dominant humanism. This attitude is evident, for example, in the writings of Samuel Beckett and Bertolt Brecht, the atonal and serial musical compositions of Arnold Schoenberg, the nonnarrative films of Hans Richter and Viking Eggeling, the productivist and constructivist work of the Russian avant-garde, the spatialized history of Rimbaud's poetry, and perhaps even in Kurt Gödel's "incompleteness" paper in mathematical logic. What is important for my argument is that seriality, the renunciation of narrative time, the disprivileging of the purely visual, and the thematization of incompleteness and uncertainty are aesthetic corollaries of the disenfranchisement of autonomous individualism. The subject is no longer viewed as an originating agent of meaning, but as a variable and dispersed entity whose very identity and place are constituted in social practice. Objects and processes are seen as having a material existence independent of, and at times threatening to, the unity of the individual self. In this context, man is what Michel Foucault has called a "discursive function" among complex and already formed systems of signification that he witnesses but does not constitute. Siegfried Kracauer, a contemporary of the architects to be considered here, put the situation of the modernist subject this way:

The world is split into the diversity of what exists and the diversity of the human subject confronting it. This human subject, who was previously incorporated into the dance of forms filled by the world, is now left solitarily confronting the chaos as the sole agent of the mind, confronting the immeasurable realm of reality. [The subject is] thrown into the cold infinity of empty space and empty time.[1]

I shall argue that an analogous perceptual shift, which I shall call posthumanism, can be detected within modern architecture—in particular the architecture of Hannes Meyer and Ludwig Hilberseimer. Posthumanism is the conscious response, whether with applause or regret, to the dissolution of psychological autonomy and individualism brought by technological modernization; it is a mobilization of aesthetic practices to effect a shift away from the humanist concept of subjectivity and its presumptions about originality, universality, and authority. I believe that the experiments of these two architects, generally viewed by the critical-historical establishment as reductive versions of functionalism or *neue Sachlichkeit,* can be more fruitfully examined against the modernist dialectic of subject and object; that these experiments imply positions on how subjects relate to objects in the present world, and how they might relate to them in a possible future one as anticipated in the experiential categories delimited by architecture. I am concerned, then, with analyzing the status of the subject and the ways the subject is variously "constituted," "constructed," or "inscribed" by the different architectures. Of course, it must be recognized that actual individuals, by virtue of their complex and multiple historical and cultural affiliations, always exceed the subjectivities constructed by architecture. Indeed, another sort of study could argue that it is precisely in that excess that concrete critical resistance to dominant ideologies is located.[2] My claim here will be, however, that precise potentials of meaningful action are produced and made available, albeit only in a symbolic mode and at the level of cultural representation, in the architectural objects and their subject-productive force.

The term "subject," meaning both individual consciousness and ideologically produced consciousness in general, is inherently multiple and equivocal. Any reference to an individual self and its relation to ideological, institutional, and disciplinary apparatuses entails a concept of the subject that reaches beyond the particular person. But any completely generalized concept of the subject that suppresses individual differences fails to be adequate to its object in the real world, where those differences are a crucial aspect of social relations.[3] The term's semantic slipperiness is increased still further if we introduce the contradictory meanings of subject as active agent—the source of one's control of one's own destiny—and as passive object of domination—the instrument of an other to whose command one is subjected.[4] Similarly the term "object" comprises a constellation of meanings including the brute facticity of the world, the artifacts of culture, their immanent formal organization, and the forces by which those artifacts are produced, forces that are, in turn, manipulated by subjects. A dialectical understanding of the subject-object framework is thus demanded if our epistemology is to be adequate to our interpretive task. A simple positivism fails to recognize the active, constitutive agency of the subject in creating the world—or at least that part of the world we call history, culture, and society—and thus is complicitous with a passive, contemplative politics that accepts the world as an already finished reality. On the other hand, idealism preserves and develops the active, practical side of subjectivity, but does so only on the abstract level of an absolute, unchanging, transcendental subject. And humanist thought incorporates both passive contemplation and transcendental ideals. A genuine materialist epis-

temology should call into question not only the passive
subject of the positivists but also the autonomous, trans-
individual, constituting subject of the idealists; it should
anticipate ways of mapping possible new structures and new
subjectivities beyond the horizon of the humanist tradition.

To deal with some of the
vicissitudes of architectural practice between the wars, this
study constructs its theoretical basis from a range of disciplines and positions. Perhaps the most significant, sustained
attempt to thematize the changed conceptualization of
objects and the changed relations of subjects in a systematic
aesthetic and critical theory is found in the body of work
generated by Georg Lukács, Walter Benjamin, Theodor
Adorno, Ernst Bloch, and Siegfried Kracauer, which is also
related to the earlier writings of Georg Simmel. Theirs is a
vivid diagnosis of the reification of the subject under industrial capitalism.[5] By dialectically juxtaposing antithetical
concepts and exposing the irreconcilability of subjective
concepts with the objective reality they were supposed to
describe, these authors direct their work to the double task
of piercing through the mere appearances of modernity and
demonstrating the inadequacy of received (empiricist,
humanist, or idealist) concepts used to define it. Later, Louis
Althusser, whose analysis of the subject was made via the
psychoanalytic theory of Jacques Lacan as well as the historical materialism of Marx, reorganized the category of the
subject, defining its constitution in terms of ideology.

Ideology 'acts' or 'functions' in such a way that it 'recruits' subjects
among the individuals (it recruits them all) or 'transforms' the individuals into subjects (it transforms them all) by the very precise
operation which I have called *interpellation* or hailing, and which
can be imagined along the lines of the most commonplace everyday police (or other) hailing: "Hey, you there!"[6]

More recent work in crit-
ical theory has continued (in a certain sense) the project
begun by those authors. Whereas the Frankfurt School analyzes the reified subject and Althusser displaces the subject

into the structure of ideological practices, Roland Barthes, Julia Kristeva, and Jacques Derrida displace the subject into language and textuality, Michel Foucault displaces the subject into history and the genealogies of power, and Gilles Deleuze situates the "schizophrenic" subject in relation to advancing capitalism. While the very real differences between these later, poststructuralist projects of undermining, dismantling, and deconstructing objects and subjects through the endless differing and deferring of signification in textuality, and a materialist project whose economy is articulated on the basis of concepts such as the production of signs and the struggle of specific historical systems of signification, are enough to cast doubt on the possibility of a rapprochement, there are nevertheless significant convergences and mutual challenges between the two.[7] Their common criticisms of idealism, metaphysics, logocentrism (taken as the discourse of a ruling ideology), and the humanist subject suggest that a sharp and serious confrontation between these two systems of thought is precisely what is needed in architectural theory at this moment. With this suggestion one wishes to avoid the reductions both of vulgar Marxism—in particular the reduction of a social formation to some economic base thought to be more solid than signs and relations—and the equally inadequate critical perspective of a domesticated and formalized deconstructionism that talks only about the signs themselves. While the ideas of a number of poststructuralist writers may be glimpsed between the lines of this study, it is the transformations and extensions of the concepts of mediation, reification, and its "utopian vocation" made by Fredric Jameson—who of all recent critics has perhaps most fruitfully merged poststructuralist and Marxist analyses—that especially inform my project.[8]

Both Hannes Meyer and Ludwig Hilberseimer produced bodies of work that delineate precise social agendas as well as aesthetic preferences; each offered an architecture that would be adequate to the social order he envisioned. To explicate the different kinds of affiliations[9] of interest here—between the world of ideas and forms, on the one hand, and the world of politics, power, artistic traditions and institutions, intellectual communities, and ideology, on the other—it will not be enough to speak of disinfected formal objects and how their parts have been equilibrated and integrated into a system that can be understood without external references; nor can we mistake for parts and pieces of the external sociopolitical world those irreducibly artistic categories and concepts. Whatever methods one calls upon to explicate those affiliations will always involve an interpretive leap between two unlike and unequal realms: the one formal, defined by certain conventions of artistic practice, the other some different (and larger) form of social and material reality. Nevertheless, artistic form carries within its own construction a capacity for quite palpable interaction with the world. It is in the different exercises of this capacity that the various positions of our protagonists become manifest, according to the various possible relationships between subject and object.

Hannes Meyer and Ludwig Hilberseimer are most often thought of as second-string architects, if they are not ignored altogether. Within the received view of modernism, Meyer is generally recognized for his involvement with the Bauhaus (he was director from April 1927 to August 1930) and his extraordinary submission (with Hans Wittwer) to the League of Nations building competition, Hilberseimer for his association with Mies van der Rohe (both in Germany and the United States) and his radically rationalized city plans. Among the still spotty expositions of Hilberseimer's work such as those published by the Art Institute of Chicago as *In the Shadow of Mies*—with the notable exception of Richard Pommer's essay in that volume, and perhaps a few of the articles from a group headed by Marco De Michelis and published in a special issue of *Rassegna*—Hilberseimer is related to the modernist canon for better or worse, with few questions asked about the doctrines and dogmas in whose light Mies and other shadow casters stand.[10] In the literature on Hannes Meyer,

Francesco Dal Co's "Hannes Meyer e la 'venerabile scuola di Dessau'" is a provocative essay on Meyer's position in the context of the European avant-gardes and the Bauhaus. This and Claude Schnaidt's *Hannes Meyer*, now more than twenty-five years old, were, until very recently, virtually the only treatments of Meyer's writings and projects other than brief and usually derogatory mentions of him as the "other" director of the Bauhaus.[11] The centennial of Meyer's birth brought new documentations of his work.[12] The question of the intepretation of the work of Meyer and Hilberseimer, however, remains open.

Two characteristics have generally been maintained as definitive of modern architecture. The first is functionalism, the intersection of brute facts of utility with objective design methodologies and standardized means of production. The versions of *neue Sachlichkeit* of Meyer and Hilberseimer have been taken as paradigmatic of functionalism. The second is the avant-garde, in one form or another involving some notion of a self-referential and self-critical formal practice as well as the incorporation of advanced technology. Again, and not without a certain contradiction, the projects and writings of Meyer and Hilberseimer have been seen as participating in avant-garde practice and standing in sharp contrast to the more "traditional," "representational" *Sachlichkeit* of Werkbund members like Hermann Muthesius or Heinrich Tessenow and the *Heimatsschutz*. The concepts of functionalism and the avant-garde have been supposed to describe fundamental demarcations within modern architecture upon which corollaries of utopianism and historical determinism have been based. My analyses of Meyer and Hilberseimer, and my postulate of the posthumanist subject, call into question the interpretive concepts of both functionalism and autotelic formalism as definitive factors of architectural modernism. Insisting on the categories of the subject and reception, as well as the object and production, and emphasizing the ambiguities and contradictions inherent in posthumanist architecture in its various forms, I aim to address both its advances and the internal resistances to its self-declared forward movement.

More recent theorists of the avant-garde have started from some version of its hope of integrating art and life or art and industry.[13] I will attempt to make that integration at once more specific and more complicated, finding the concept more or less explicitly elaborated in the writings and projects of Meyer and Hilberseimer. Indeed, what links the architects chosen for study here is the practice of *Aufhebung* or sublation—the reintegration of art with social practice through either the negation (Meyer) or radical reformulation (Hilberseimer) of traditional concepts of architecture. What distinguishes the two architects is their different positions on the status of the subject thus produced in a collective, mass-cultural, and mass-industrial world. For Meyer, modernity itself, with all its attendant alienating consequences, provides the conceptual grids and categories that modern art and architecture must transform into a positive protopolitical force directed toward the formation of a collective agency. Whereas for Hilberseimer the subject devises architectural representations of the very forces that predicate its demise.

In certain ways my study follows a line struck by Sigfried Giedion, who framed his own problematic in terms of subjective perceptual categories. Giedion attempted to accommodate the threat to the unified subject to a sublimationist model of creation and perception, continuing to claim a power for the ideal of integrated subjectivity over the disintegrating determinants of matter. Nonetheless it will be helpful, by way of introduction, to consider Giedion's account as a paradigm of the received view of modernism and to reinterpret some of its insights.

Giedion specified the subjective character of modernism as a special kind of protracted humanism: an unremitting belief in the individual consciousness as a monadic and autonomous center of activity able to maintain its stability against the plurality of divisive and corrosive effects of modernity. What is of interest in the present context is not the denunciation of Giedion's construction of the centered subject so much as an understanding of the historical emergence of that construction within the discourse of modern architecture. That Giedion's centered subject is a conceptual mirage will be my suggestion here, but more: that the insertion of that centered subject performs a precise ideological function and is itself susceptible to historical causation. Alternative, post-humanist subject positions can be detected within the very formal logic of modern space-time simultaneity and mechanization extolled by Giedion, subject positions that, in their contradiction and disunity, provide concrete challenges to his conception of the self as a homogeneous and consistent whole.

Manfredo Tafuri has used the term "operative criticism" to name certain aspects of the work of twentieth-century modern critics and historians like Nikolaus Pevsner, Bruno Zevi, Reyner Banham, and Giedion, all of whom seem compelled to make of history a guide to actual design practice. "What is normally meant by *operative criticism* is an analysis of architecture (or of the arts in general) that, instead of an abstract survey, has as its objective the planning of a precise poetical tendency, anticipated in its structures and derived from historical analyses programmatically distorted and finalized."[14] Giedion's notion of "constituent facts" specifies his selection and deformation of past codes.

Constituent facts are those tendencies which, when they are suppressed, inevitably reappear. Their recurrence makes us aware that these are elements which, all together, are producing a *new tradition*. Constituent facts in architecture, for example, are the undulating of the wall, the juxtaposition of nature and the human dwelling, the open ground plan. Constituent facts in the nineteenth century are the new potentialities in construction, the use of mass production in industry, the changed organization of society.[15]

What is proposed here, it seems, is an interpretive system in which the particular forms of the period in question are rewritten according to the paradigm of another, overarching history of forms that, through a logic of visual homomorphism, is taken as the former's master text or Ur-form and proposed as its essential meaning. Under this hovering matrix of constituent forms, however, Giedion further insists on a periodization of the modern forms according to a distinctive spatial conception of simultaneity and space-time, his third space conception,[16] which envelopes spheres of cultural production as diverse as cubist painting, Apollinaire's poetry (c. 1911), Einstein's *Elektrodynamik bewegter Körper* (1905), and later verifications of the conception such as Edgerton's stroboscopic photography, as well as the architectural production that Giedion canonized.[17] And so, along with his operative criticism and overarching formalism, Giedion's periodizing practice seems to be covered by what Althusser designated as a model of "expressive causality,"[18] a seamless tissue of entities and events, each of which expresses some isolated and privileged world view, period style, or unified inner truth.

Though Giedion's thesis is now often construed as either naively historicist or rigidly formalist, I would want to grant his interpretive practice at least a local validity on two points. First, as a result of specific historical circumstances, Giedion's theory pertaining to those circumstances arose from a particular and already constituted disciplinary apparatus (he granted a degree of autonomy to the discipline of architecture); and second, it confronted—explicitly, thematically, and in the form of an epistemological and historiographical problem—a difficulty that is, in fact, inherent in all materialist criticism: that of providing mediations between social phenomena, the formal properties of the architectural work, and the psychic economy organized by the latter; or, in different terminology, the problem of the *insertion of the subject.* In Giedion's history, the standard oppositions between the interpreter and the interpreted, private creation and disciplinary conventions, the unconscious and the conscious, the personal or unknowable and the universal and comprehensible, are all displaced and reanchored in a new conception of the historical context and psychic situation, wherein the individual subject can be recentered in its social present by the sheer lucidity of visual form.

The importance of Giedion's conception of visuality, his "optical revolution," can now be considered. His notion of the "Eternal Present" is the subjective corollary of the objective vocation of constituent facts. His main thesis is that (1) the modern movement in architecture was trying to heal a rift in culture and the human psyche that had opened up in the nineteenth century; (2) that rift involved a split in subjective or psychological terms between thought and feeling, and in objective, architectural terms between form and structure, expression and construction, art and industrial production; and (3) the reconciliation of the rift involved an elaboration of a few constituent facts. Such an elaboration would be a means for correlating human experience, space, and knowledge; a means for achieving the necessary oneness of knowledge and feeling.

"We have behind us a period in which thinking and feeling were separated. This schism produced individuals whose inner development was uneven, who lacked inner equilibrium: split personalities. The split personality as a psychopathic case does not concern us here; we are speaking of the inner disharmony which is found in the structure of the normal personality of this period. . . . But behind these disintegrating forces in our period tendencies leading toward unity can be observed."[19] Giedion's characterization of the conditions of modernity, of rationalization and reification in our terms, is not so different from that of philosophers and sociologists such as Georg Simmel, Max Weber, and Georg Lukács, who saw traditional cultural institutions—once unified, genuine, and concrete forms of social relationships—as having long since been dissolved by the corrosive effects of market relations, blasted

into their component fragments, and reorganized by the processes of capitalism with its characteristic tendency toward
greater efficiency according to the instrumental dialectic of
means and ends. When this process finally completes its
structural separation of subject from object and reterritorial-
izes each separately, new hierarchies of functions are produced according to their instrumental use, and the
quantifying, rational modes of thought are overdeveloped
while the more archaic functions, such as Giedion's "feeling," are bracketed off in a kind of psychic marginality.[20]
But at the same time, it seems that for Giedion these now
isolated, fragmented bits and pieces of the older psychological and aesthetic unities acquire a certain coherence and
autonomy of their own, serving in some measure to compensate for the dehumanizing "rift" that rationalization and
reification bring, and rectifying the otherwise intolerable
effects of the new process.[21] So, to return to Giedion's primary example, as vision becomes a mode of reception independent from touch (as the optical and tactile functions are
separated out of the unity of "haptic" reception), it generates new objects of its own, which, though still the products
of fragmentation, abstraction, and rationalization that operate to interdict the experience of the world according to a
more holistic, auratic depth model of "feeling"—of religious
iconography, say, or the experience of "natural" environ-
ments—can, at the same time, be reconfigured and projected
as possible solutions, on an aesthetic level, to that genuinely contradictory situation in the concrete world of everyday life from which they first emerged. The artistic
manipulations of Picasso, Le Corbusier, et al.—which
employ "abstractions" such as monochromy or pure color,
flattened and layered space, and "fragmented," nonperspecti-
val points of view—are individual productions and cultural
manifestations grasped as responses to a determinate situation and having the intelligibility of genuine historical gestures, provided the context is reconstructed with sufficient
complexity. So, in Giedion's words, the cubist "presentation
of objects from several points of view," the "breaking up the

Sigfried Giedion, photomontage of Rocke-feller Center juxtaposed with a stroboscopic study of Harold E. Edgerton, published in *Space, Time and Architecture.* Giedion asserts that in order to perceive modern space "the eye must function as in the high-speed photographs of Edgerton."

introduction

surfaces of the natural forms into angular facets," the "extreme scarcity of colors," the "advancing and retreating planes . . . , interpenetrating, hovering, often transparent, without anything to fix them in realistic position," the "flattening out so that interior and exterior could be seen simultaneously," are "equivalent to psychic responses."[22] Taking on the properly utopian vocation of the newly reified sense of sight, the mission of this heightened and autonomous visual language of space-time can be construed as restorative, at least symbolically, of the experience of psychic gratification and integration to a world drained of it.

The moment around which Giedion's interpretive system turns is, thus, a kind of visual wish fulfillment, posited as the very dynamic of our being as individual subjects. What is necessary to underscore is the dependence of Giedion's "discovery" of the visual logic of space-time on the increasing fragmentation, simultaneity, and abstraction of actual experience in modern everyday life. In such a situation, it is clear that his reassertion of the centered subject, the homologue of the Eternal Present at the level of the individual, is a genuinely historical and practically ideological act. The subject having been split from its object by the logic of social and technical development, the object must now be reconstructed by Giedion in such a way as to bear the place of the subject within itself: "lo spettatore nel centro del quadro" was how Giedion put it.[23] And here, once again, is the conjunction of criticism and design too easily dismissed by Tafuri as "operative." The viewing, interpreting subject must be placed *within* the frame of the object, "not at some isolated point outside. Modern art, like modern science, recognizes the fact that observation and what is observed form one complex situation—to observe something is to act upon and alter it." The process of critical interpretation is transformed by Giedion into one of a hypothetical or imaginary restoration of the historical situation itself, whose reconstitution is at one with visual comprehension. The art work is an object whose interpretation has already commenced but is never complete. As Giedion put it, "There is no static equilibrium between man and his environment, between inner and outer reality. We cannot prove in a direct way how action and reaction operate here. We can no more lay tangible hold on these processes than we can grasp the nucleus of an atom."[24]

Giedion's effort was to chart the commerce between inner and outer reality—especially the impact of mechanization on what he conceived as our unchanging humanity, on the stability of the individual psyche—and to project new means of reconciliation. As such, his interpretive method can precisely and properly be reasserted as *mediation*. Fredric Jameson has defined this concept as

the relationship between the levels or instances [of social practice], and the possibility of adapting analyses and findings from one level to another. Mediation is the classical dialectical term for the establishment of relationships between, say, the formal analysis of a work of art and its social ground, or between the internal dynamics of the political state and its economic base. . . . The concept of mediation has traditionally been the way in which dialectical philosophy and Marxism itself have formulated their vocation to break out of the specialized compartments of the (bourgeois) disciplines and to make connections among the seemingly disparate phenomena of social life generally. If a more modern characterization of mediation is wanted, we will say that this operation is understood as a process of *transcoding:* as the invention of a set of terms, the strategic choice of a particular code or language, such that the same terminology can be used to analyze and articulate two quite distinct types of objects or "texts," or two very different structural levels of reality. Mediations are thus a device of the analyst, whereby the fragmentation and autonomization of social life . . . is at least locally overcome, on the occasion of a particular analysis.[25]

But in the intangible realm between inner and outer reality, between perceptual categories and modes of production, between subject and object, there remains something disturbing about Giedion's specific theory of modern architecture. For precisely at a time when reification was penetrating into the very core of personal experience, leaving no vestiges of a nonalienated reality as its reciprocal or opposing notion, Giedion's theory—which came into being as a protest and a defense against reification—emerged as the perpetuation of a conception of a historical moment, wholly present, in which the individual subject would somehow be fully conscious of his or her determination by such extrinsic structural conditions of modernity, and would somehow be able to reintegrate and resolve these determinations in the visual experience of architectural form. From Marx and Freud to recent poststructuralist theory, we have been shown again and again that such a resolution, such an immanence, is a myth, an ideological mirage. But the reluctance to relinquish the possibility of immanent resolution means more than that Giedion was not able to become, as it were, a poststructuralist. For in the end, his aesthetic ideology is contrary to, and must be evaluated against, the postindividual and posthumanist reversal enacted in the modernism of his own time—the side of modern architecture not considered by him. In practice this architecture aimed beyond the autonomous individualism of the bourgeoisie in its heyday, took on the task of a radical and painful decentering of the consciousness of the subject, which it confronted with a determination necessarily felt as beyond the humanist horizon, and, consciously or not, anticipated an emergent collective process of constructing a new status of the subject after the decay of bourgeois centrism.

In the chapters that follow I analyze different constructions of the subject that employ the very forms of the space-time synthesis and mechanization that Giedion extols, but that enact a critical reversal of his humanist privileging of subject over object. Against Giedion's notion that modern architectural objects provide visual symbols for the integral psychological self, I wish to point to certain modern architectural objects that put into crisis the cognitive status of autonomous vision and the centered self for which that vision is a metaphor, and redirect our attention to those extrinsic processes that lie beyond individual aesthetic mastery. We will see how, in order to displace the unified, centralized subject of bourgeois humanism, certain modernist practices draw upon the effects of reification in the actual experience of such subjects, incorporating into the structure of their works the very effects of social and technical transformations that determine aesthetic representations and pitting what was increasingly felt to be the subjective reality of industrial capitalism against the formal ideologies of humanism. Such work begins from the position that intervention into the very mechanisms of representation and sign construction can be a motivating force of aesthetic production, but then moves in different directions: toward the critical instrumentalization of aesthetic practice and the identification of the transformatory potential of the newly reified materials (Meyer) or toward the reluctant affirmation of posthumanist anomie and distraction within aesthetic practice (Hilberseimer)—all in the name of *Sachlichkeit*. Modern architecture thus dramatizes in its very internal structures the crucial contradiction in the ideology of the subject latent in the writings of Giedion.

hannes meyer and the radicalization of perception

The form of the new means of production, which at first is still dominated by the old (Marx), corresponds to images in the collective consciousness in which the new is intermingled with the old. These images are wish-images, and in them the collective seeks to sublate and transfigure both the incompleteness of the social product and the inadequacies in the social system of production. In addition, these wish-images manifest an emphatic striving for dissociation with the outmoded—which means, however, with the most recent past. These tendencies direct the visual imagination, which has been activated by the new, back to the primeval past. In the dream in which, before the eyes of each epoch, that which is to follow appears in images, the latter appears wedded to elements from prehistory, that is, of a classless society. Intimations of this, deposited in the unconscious of the collective and intermingling with the new, produce the utopia that has left its traces in thousands of configurations of life, from permanent buildings to ephemeral fashions.

Walter Benjamin, "Paris, Capital of the Nineteenth Century"

co-op vitrine and the representation of mass production

Around 1925 Hannes Meyer developed a body of work, including linocuts and other prints, photographs, assemblages, display cases, rooms, and buildings, all designated by the name "cooperative" or "Co-op," a locution that he would use throughout his career to signal a type of form he considered "adequate for our times."[1] Meyer's Co-op work marks a fault line in the development of modern architecture, a cleft in cultural space across which would be played the dialectic of formal paradigms already defined by the avant-garde and the altogether different perceptual conventions of mass technological society.[2] The disparity between these two modes is most apparently registered by what critics of Meyer's work consistently have seen as a tension between an avant-garde "constructivist aesthetic," a visual approach to his work, and a purely "functionalist," utilitarian, and anti-aesthetic organization of building components dedicated to a social program.[3] It is a disparity not of form only, but between two distinct spaces of culture—that of "high" modernist culture with its highly developed formal strategies of self-referentiality and resistance, and that of popular or mass culture and the apparatuses of its production and consumption.

An adequate account of Meyer's modernism must treat this disparity, which is one symptom of the general difficulty of knowing and signifying in modern society, of the difference yet consonance between the values of progressive modernization and those of epistemic and historical continuity within the discipline of architecture. Meyer's position is entirely comprehensible, I think, but only within a framework of changed relationships between design practice, architectural form, and the forces of social production and consumption at large. It can be demonstrated that Meyer reconceives the design process in such a way as to collapse the distinction between the aesthetic, the practical, and the cognitive function of artistic signs. Design for Meyer is a signifying practice—an entry into and unsettling of the conventions of signification[4]—that appropriates physical materials, visual images, and formative principles from industry and the culture of everyday life and seeks to negate the qualitative differences between artistic practice and the production of objects of everyday use. Moreover, the aesthetic response Meyer's work elicits is itself a cognitive-interpretive event, a productive *perform-ative* event that shows the world as emerging through processes that are arbitrarily imposed and changeable rather than natural or universal. Finally, however, Meyer's design practice is an activity that can completely enunciate the desired change of relationships between art and the world only through a radical negation of the very discipline of architecture itself as defined within the received paradigm of modernism.

Walter Benjamin's theorization of the images of modernity motivates my understanding of what I will call the *performativity*[5] of Meyer's architectural work in several ways. First is Benjamin's notion of a wish-landscape, a visual field determined by technologies and class structures wholly present, yet capable of picturing a different mode of production ("the utopia that has left its traces") to be arrived at—as if the surface of history were deployed on a cylinder—by going either backward ("to the primeval past . . . a classless society") or forward (to "that which is to follow"). Second is the imperative of a perceptual reformation demanded by these

Hannes Meyer, Co-op Linocut (horizontal/vertical construction), 1925–1926.

Meyer, Co-op Linocut (graphic construction), 1925–1926.

Hannes Meyer, study: two graphics on glass plates overlayed, 1926.

images, demanded, it seems, because the cultural products cast by the present mode of production no longer fit into its molds ("these wish-images manifest an emphatic striving for dissociation with the outmoded—which means, however, with the most recent past"). Finally is the implication of what Julia Kristeva would later call a "'future anterior' that will never take place, never come about as such, but only as an upheaval of present place and meaning." Such an irruption in the present is not a denial of historicity, of the present as a felt moment in time; on the contrary, it is a historical *refusal* of present inadequacies, a use of historical perspective to defamiliarize the present. "Anteriority and future join together to open that historical axis in relation to which concrete history will always be wrong."[6]

The performativity of Meyer's work, I suggest, is an enabling condition for architecture different from both historical determinism and individual authorial intentionality. When, for example, Meyer expands Marx's dictum that life determines consciousness with the statement that "the revolution in our attitude of mind toward the reorganization of our world calls for a change in our media of expression," he asserts that the transformations of psycho-social structures necessitate the transformation of aesthetic hierarchies and require radically different forms of perception, and further implies that some social structuring force outside individual consciousness activates, conditions, and sets that consciousness in motion.[7] In Meyer's view of artistic production, human agency is not relinquished altogether (as if in some postmodern swoon). Indeed, a crucial point in Meyer's conception of the productivity of architecture is the moment of negativity and resistance registered by the designing agent: "in every creative design appropriate to living, we *reorganize* an organized form of existence."[8] Yet, while still allowing and accounting for the agency of the designing subject, Meyer gives weight to the productive power of the object and the complex interplay between subject and object: "We could call the process of building a conscious patterning or formation [*Gestaltung*] of the socio-economic, the techno-constructive, and the psycho-physiological elements in the social living process."⁹ It is an extraordinary statement, this: the act of building as the mapping of the total situation of subject and object; building as trans-formation—not a transport of an already constituted meaning that exists outside and before architecture but an organization of processes, a set of operations, a production of certain effects not available without the building performance. The performative act carries its referent in its own internal structure; it enacts what it represents. But this does not suppose that the act has effectiveness outside any context. On the contrary, there are only contexts—socio-economic, techno-constructive, psycho-physiological—and the functional destination of the building performance is to effect their unfolding.

Recognizing the partial determination, or overdetermination, of the designing subject by external social forces, as well as the object's productive engagement with the viewing subject, avoids the exclusive appeal to individual artistic agency and purpose by affirming the reciprocity between modes of production and modes of reception. It is the acting out of this reciprocity that I am calling the performativity of perception—understood as the conscious, interpretive engagement of designer, viewer, and object all together plunged into the social dynamic that activates and conditions them. With this, Meyer's radicalization of perception as a collective engagement can be distinguished from other conservative protractions of individual visual gratification, and his conception of antihumanist subjectivity can be launched.

Because modern society does not recognize itself as an ideological construction, it must be represented as such; this is the vocation of any politically engaged art, part of its performance criteria. Hannes Meyer's Co-op Vitrine project of 1925 directs our attention not only to the practical, formal problems of the representation of modern industrial society, but also and more fundamentally to the question of the ideological nature and function of that representation itself.[10] What establishes this connection—for it may not be immediately obvious that the glass display case of consumable products has claims to a representational status at all (even if Amédée Ozenfant would himself include a commodity window display in his canonical *Foundations of Modern Art* in 1931)—is the particular constellation of relationships and perceptual interactions it generates with the viewing subject, as well as the systematic formal procedures by which the perceptual phenomena are constituted. For by the time we are finished here, it will have become impossible in our analysis of Meyer's work to separate production from reception, and both from an enabling ideology.

The Vitrine was designed for the Internationale Ausstellung des Genossenschaftswesens und der sozialen Wohlfahrtspflege, an exhibition of Swiss cooperative products in Ghent and Basel in 1924 and 1925 under the direction of Bernhard Jäggi.[11] With its foregrounding of the object language of thirty-six standard articles of commodity production and trade in a visual display, it seems easy, at first gloss, to stigmatize the project using theories of commodity reification and alienation of subject from object. Such theories describe the way products and productive activities under capitalism are ruthlessly rationalized and reorganized according to the purely instrumental terms of means/ends efficiency: in a world where every product and form of labor has become a commodity, activities of making are stripped of their unique qualitative differentiation and become abstractly comparable through the indifferent medium of capital; and the objects made also shed their intrinsic qualities and use values and come to be arranged under the common denominator of exchange value. In the Co-op Vitrine, articles of everyday use, packaged in various shapes and sizes of cartons, cans, bottles, tubes, bags, and boxes, first appear as the very images of commodity production, distanced even further from their producers and users by the abstract conditions of their display, brack-

Hannes Meyer, Co-op Vitrine with Co-op standard products, exhibited in Basel, 1925.

eted off from the physical space of the consumer, rendered, exactly and merely it seems, as distantiated and fragmented images. Arranged not as individual items but in six compartments as the repetitive components of so many mechanical processes of stacking, extruding, and aligning, they bear no traces of human manufacture, no evidence of an individual producer's control.

Consequently, the Co-op Vitrine threatens the viewer's own sense of unity as an individual. In a section of *The Philosophy of Money* titled "The division of labor as the cause of the divergence of subjective and objective culture," Georg Simmel captures the initial sense of Meyer's presentation precisely:

The unity of an object is realized for us only by projecting our self into the object in order to shape it according to our image so that the diversity of determinations grows into the unity of the "ego."

In the same manner, the unity or lack of unity of the object that we create affects, in a psychological-practical sense, the corresponding formation of our personality. Whenever our energies do not produce something whole as a reflection of the total personality, then the proper relationship between subject and object is missing. . . . Because of its fragmentary character, the product lacks the spiritual determinacy that can be easily perceived in a product of labor that is wholly the work of a *single* person. *The significance of the product is thus to be sought neither in the reflection of a subjectivity nor in the reflex of a creative spirit, but is to be found only in the objective achievement that leads away from the subject.* . . . The broadening of consumption . . . is dependent upon the growth of *objective* culture, since the more objective and impersonal an object is the better it is suited to more people. Such consumable material . . . cannot be designed for subjective differentiation of taste, while on the other hand only the most extreme differentiation of production is able to produce the objects cheaply and abundantly enough in order to satisfy the demand for them. . . . The

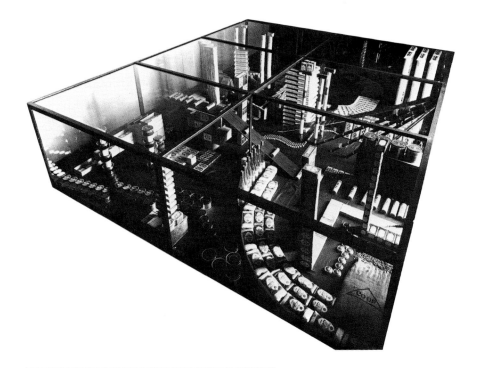

the representation of mass production

Meyer, Co-op Linocut, 1925–1926: diagram of the Co-op Vitrine.

product of labor in the capitalist era is an object with a decidedly autonomous character, with its own laws of motion and a character alien to the producing subject, [and] is most forcefully illustrated where the worker is compelled to buy his own product.[12]

The commodity, now produced independently of individuals, has lost its subjective aura, and even the arrangement of Co-op products as so many fragments in a glass case indicates this disenfranchisement of individual manufacture. The aesthetic structure of the Vitrine is determined by the repetitive and serially structured formation that is the very nature of mass-reproduced commodities and their distribution.

As a straightforward and unreflective display of articles of daily use, Meyer's work may be seen to go no further than this and thus to stand implicated in a purely technocratic, administered, and instrumental logic without a dimension of aesthetic resistance. As an apparatus of visual sign production involving conventions of perception, however, the Co-op Vitrine can be understood in its specific mode of signification only by constructing the *alternative* conditions of perceptual interaction that it proposes relative to the received modernist paradigm. For modernism is notoriously skeptical of the possibility of representing anything, enacting instead various procedures of self-reflexivity in order to cancel the very sorts of referent in the commodity economy that the Vitrine reveals. To construe the Vitrine as producing an alternative to modernist self-reflexivity would clarify its immanent (aesthetic) meanings as well as allow us to account for the production of that quite different thing called ideology, which Althusser defines as "the imaginary representation of the subject's relationship to his or her real conditions of existence."[13]

When we now stipulate the more specific question of representation for our analysis, the ideological coordinates of our problem will come into focus.[14] A powerful instrument given by recent theory is the distinction between the subject of the enunciation and the subject of the statement (*sujet d'énonciation / sujet d'énoncé*).[15] This distinction can be appreciated in the simple act of referring to myself in a sentence. When I write "Today I will purchase that product," the subject, the "I," that I designate seems immediately intelligible; it is a stable point of reference that conceals the more complex depths of the subject that actually produces the statement as well as the ideological mechanisms that enable and constrain that production.[16] The former subject is known to linguistic theory as the *subject of the statement*—the fictive character referred to by my sentence, the subject as it is fixed in discourse; the latter subject, roughly the producer of the sentence, is the *subject of the enunciation*—the subject of the actual act of representing, the subject of the ideological structures that position and control speech, and also, in an expanded sense, the subject of the forces of production and consumption that make the product referred to available for purchase. The subject of the enunciation is lost or concealed the moment it is articulated in discourse; it is, in actuality, never identical with the entity represented. In a linguistics of the *énoncé*, these two subjects seem to achieve a representational unity, but this unity is of an imaginary kind: the convenient, conventionally unified pronoun "I" stands in for the ever-dispersed subject of the enunciation. Whereas in

a linguistics of the *énonciation,* stress is placed on the relational and process-like character of language,[17] which tends
to undermine the conventionalized unities, identities, and
fixities of representational categories, and thereby to decon-
ceal the very apparatuses of signification—the multiple originating operations and codes behind the representation that
issue from "voices" unseen. As Roland Barthes remarks,
"Alongside each utterance, one might say that off-stage
voices can be heard: they are the codes: in their interweav-
ing, these voices (whose origin is 'lost' in the vast perspective of the *already-written*) de-originate the utterance."[18]
There is a radical gap between the subject of the enunciation, a constellation of several cultural apparatuses and
anonymous codes that determine what can be said, and the
representation of that subject, through the work of art or
through ordinary language, as unified in a desired state of
stability and harmony among those faculties.

The level of enunciation
is, in effect then, the level of production itself, broadly cultural and specifically technical—in architecture it includes
the fundamental studio practices of measuring, calculating,
and programming as well as the techniques used to enclose
an area, join parts, mark paths, and distinguish one territory
from another. But the level of enunciation also includes the
economic, technological, and political apparatuses that
enable architectural production. The site of enunciation lies
behind the discourse, behind the signifying practices that
constitute perceptual, visual, architectural form. The level
of representation—the fictional subject of the statement—
lies in front of discourse. The fictions within which we recognize ourselves, within which we imagine our roles as subjects to be played out, are manufactured elsewhere, at the
site of enunciation. Yet we attain our self-apprehension, our
subjectivity, only through the intervention of signification
and ideology, that is, through discursive operations that are
opaque to any independent, ostensive real lying outside or
before their representation. The architectural fiction is the
site of contemplation and consumption, of the commerce

between what Althusser called the ideological state apparatus and the subject it interpellates with the offer of articulate and differentiated positions—fictions with which the subject can positively identify.

Understood in the expanded terms of an act of *énonciation*, rather than as a presentation or mere reflection of already fixed and commodified signs, the Co-op Vitrine qua representation transforms in important ways both the immanent formal structure of the work and the structured perceptual interaction of the pictorial construct with the viewer. It is now the representation itself, the *sujet d'énoncé*, that will take on the task of revealing the origins of its production, the *sujet d'énonciation*. First, rather than the familiar arrangement of isolated individual products in a shop window, the Co-op articles are presented as an image or facsimile of the industrialized manufacturing process itself, each series of products configured as if having issued from the various conveyor belts of an assembly line. Second, this picture of the commodity-producing factory, as it were, is itself framed as the overall scene of collective reception and consumption; the final, finished product to which the consumer of products has the most direct access is, simultaneously, the constituent element of the overall pictorial device that the "pictorial consumer" must apprehend. The work thereby stresses the *process* of commodity *sign* production and reception as well as the reification that that sign must undergo in its transmutation into a pictorial construct, by making the mechanisms of the work's representation and mode of address part of its actual content. So self-reflexivity is there after all, but now in a constellation of other referential procedures, all of which is bound to result in a contradictory aesthetic. The subject of the statement takes on the form and action that are ordinarily the domain of the subject of the enunciation, producing a doubling. The Co-op Vitrine attempts to turn this contradiction, this doubling, to fruitful use, displacing the spectator from his accustomed imaginary possession of the work as a unity but providing instead alternative spaces

Meyer, Co-op Vitrine, details.

the representation of mass production

from which the viewer might appropriate the source of the work's main fiction of mass-industrialized production and consumption.

One of the registers through which the fiction of the Co-op Vitrine is projected is, then, the familiar formal and autotelic production of modernism, but this is quickly interrupted by different, seemingly incompatible modes of address. On the one hand, the Co-op Vitrine incorporates the compositional strategies of seriality, repetition, diagonal and frontal layering, and circumnavigable space, all constituents of a modernist practice already evolved to its most advanced stages in postcubist and elementarist pictorial and sculptural practices such as suprematism and constructivism. At the same time, without sacrificing the formal rigor and self-referentiality of a thoroughly modern art form, Meyer introduces into this work an *iconic* potential—in the sense that the Model "T" Ford, Havana cigarettes, and the Gilette razor are icons—that seeks to engage a wholly different audience in wholly different terms than those routinely associated with modernism, terms closer to the instrumentalized factographic and cinematographic researches of productivism and even dadaism than to the valorization of autonomy, abstraction, and hermetic withdrawal of high modernism.[19]

For example, when in 1921 Raoul Hausmann declares, "Our art is already today film! At once event, sculpture, and image!"[20] he defines a collective, mass-technologically structured form of object perception as well as a strategy of formal articulation. And when, in the same year, A. V. Babichev declares, "Art is an informed analysis of the concrete tasks which social life poses. . . . If art becomes public property it will organize the consciousness and psyche of the masses by organizing objects and ideas,"[21] he invokes themes of organized production, consumption, and subjective engagement that are continuous with Meyer's concerns in the Co-op Vitrine. Such statements and the sorts of work to which they are attached point to a more general crisis of representational systems within the modernist paradigm than has been acknowledged in the standard architectural historical literature, a crisis involving nothing less than a changed psychic and cognitve relationship to objects.

In the mid-1920s the most politically committed artists recognized that those artistic forms, procedures, and conditions of reception received from bourgeois society and its aesthetic institutions would have to be systematically dismantled and redefined in an effort to establish the new conditions of what Walter Benjamin called "simultaneous collective reception," and that those latter conditions would involve changed perceptual conventions for objects of everyday use as well as objects of art, eroding the boundary between the two. An illuminating comparison with Meyer's Co-op Vitrine comes in a remarkable essay by the painter Johannes Molzahn, "Economics of the Advertising Mechanism," published in *Die Form* in 1925–1926. For the light it sheds on the psychic and cognitive nature of the perceived interrelations of systems of production, commodity products, and aesthetic reception, it is worth quoting the article at some length.

Just as the natural forces of water, wind and fire can only be harnessed to industrial use by interposing some form of resistance to them (turbines, windmills and so on), to convert the forces into mechanical energy, in the same way the productive forces that we find in industrial production become expressive only when similar conditions are fulfilled and the production-psyche is successfully converted into acceptance by the consumer. The comparisons of the functions can be illustrated in parallel tables:

Industry		Advertising
Natural forces: water, fire etc.	=	production, materials
Converter: turbine, windmill	=	propaganda machinery
Effective power: mechanical		
energy	=	consumption, sales

LAJOS KASSAK
Warenprospekt 1926

O. BAUMBERGER, ZÜRICH
PKZ-Plakat

the representation of mass production

As we have now set out the production-psyche of the natural forces, that which drives the production-machinery through a process of conversion and keeps it going, and appears in the Table as effective power, similarly we have found the converter in the propaganda-machinery, which drives the consumption mechanism and keeps that moving. We now have to find out the means employed in the propaganda-machinery, to find a converter serving the same purpose in our field as the turbine does in the field of industrial production. Our first problem will be to recognize the psyche of consumption, or acceptance, with its organs and functions, and to deduce from that the means of affecting them. It is not difficult to perceive this acceptance-mechanism in the spirit of the people or its expression in the spirit of the age, which takes material form through an optical-acoustic appeal to the senses. . . . The propaganda of production must therefore rely primarily on optical functions. But propaganda is in essence information in graphic presentation; the question is, then, to determine which elements of graphic presentation have the greatest optical capacity to make a lasting impression on the psyche . . . We can demonstrate the conversion effect of the symbol presentation in yet another example. Let us take a magnifying glass and hold it between the sun and a piece of paper so that the paper is at the focal point of the lens, and catches fire. In thus creating fire we have converted the sun's energy into active energy. The conception of a symbol-effect is convincing if we show this same experiment to a primitive tribe; the impact would be absolutely shattering and express itself in wild flight from this "magic," which has so taken and impressed the whole psyche of the primitive man. The lens has become a symbol of the sun, the unknown function of the lens has engraved itself on the subconscious, a mystery. In this example we have established the principle that the industrial symbol has to construct if it is to produce its effect. The trade-mark has the function of the lens, it stands for the lens as the lens stood for the sun to the primitive people. At the focal point, which corresponds to the concentration-point of the industrial symbol, the same process of conversion has taken: the production-force becomes effective in the psyche of the consumer, perhaps in the manner indicated schematically [in the "Fire-Psyche" diagram accompanying the text]. Thus the trademark is always the most elementary means, the link between *production* and *consumption*.[22]

The emblematic product as the lens through which to see production: it is a suitable metaphor within which to read the Co-op Vitrine, and its appropriateness is confirmed by Meyer's reproduction of the Vitrine as an illustration (along with "Kinoplat" and "Zeitungsprospekt") to his essay "Die neue Welt," in a section significantly entitled "Die Propaganda." Meyer writes,

The modern poster presents lettering and product or trademark conspicuously arranged. It is not a poster work of art but a piece of visual sensationalism. In the display window of today psychological capital is made of the tensions between modern materials with the aid of lighting. It is display window organization rather than window dressing. It appeals to the finely distinguishing sense of materials found in modern man and covers the gamut of its expressive power: fortissimo = tennis shoes to Havana cigarettes to scouring soap to nut chocolate! Mezzoforte = glass (as a bottle) to wood (as a packing case) to pasteboard (as a packing) to tin (as a can)! Pianissimo = silk pyjamas to cambric shirts to Valenciennes lace to "L'Origan de Coty"![23]

Thus situated, the project not only operates to repudiate that more traditional and conventional view of representation—which is able to see such a work as the Co-op Vitrine only as sheer communication of a fixed external social condition or idea, as a crystallized isomorph of a world already finished—and to install an alternative signifying practice that foregrounds the procedures of interpretive framing and modes of address, but also vehiculates a new conception of subject-object relations, a neutralization or obversion of Simmel's conception introduced earlier. This must now be articulated more fully.

Implicit in Simmel's conception of modernity is the absence of concrete and integrated experience (*Erfahrung*) and its displacement by a kind of psychologism—the absorption of the contradictory fragments of the world into the monadic armature of our indi-

DIE PROPAGANDA

HANNES MEYER, BASEL
Die Vitrine Co-op. 1925 / Phot. Th. Hoffmann, Basel

M. BURCHARTZ & J. CANIS, BOCHUM
Zeitungsprospekt, 1926

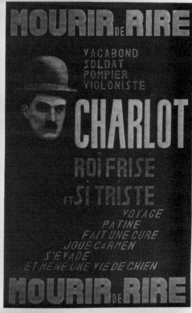

KINOPLAKAT

Page entitled "Die Propaganda," from
Meyer, "Die neue Welt," showing the Co-op Vitrine, a
newspaper classified advertisement, and a cinema
poster.

vidual inner experience (*Erlebnis*). "The unity or lack of unity of the object that we create affects, in a psychological-practical sense, the corresponding formation of our personality."[24] The persuasiveness of Meyer's Co-op work will best be felt not so much as a reversal of this theme as the identification of an alternative condition in which subjective interiority itself is defeated. As consumers we are dispersed outward across the exteriority of the fields of signs or aesthetic surfaces (what Walter Benjamin called wish-images) that are the immediate result of collective modes of production, of which the individual subject, like the individual article of consumption, is a *decentered effect,* and to which bourgeois individualism, illusionism, and interiority cannot lay claim. Nor is it a matter of eliminating subject positions altogether; rather a new space must be generated for the emancipation of a different kind of subject out of the punctual experience of objectification. Meyer provides his own summary of the transformative potential of mass industrial and cultural techniques and channels of communication:

The standardization of our requirements is shown by: the bowler hat, bobbed hair, the tango, jazz, the Co-op product,the DIN standard size and Liebig's meat extract. The standardization of mental fare is illustrated by the crowds going to see Harold Lloyd, Douglas Fairbanks and Jackie Coogan. Grock and the three Fratellini weld the masses—irrespective of class and racial differences—into a community with a common fate. Trade union, co-operative, Ltd., Inc., cartel, trust and the League of Nations are the forms in which today's social conglomerations find expression, and the radio and the rotary press are their media of communication. Co-operation rules the world. *The community rules the individual.*[25]

        The Co-op Vitrine adheres to and refunctions the formal strategies of the modernist avant-garde even as it folds into itself those enunciative formations of industrialized production and mass consumption on which its representation is born. This doubled circuit of signs is an aesthetic resolution and imaginary projection of an as yet unattained condition of collective modes of production and reception, and should be seen as part of a general attempt by Meyer in his Co-op work to devise such aesthetic apparatuses as quasi-material transmission or commutation systems that will help produce, even force, a new, corresponding collective subjectivity. As Benjamin writes, "These images are wish-images, and in them the collective seeks both to sublate and transfigure the incompleteness of the social product and the inadequacies in the social system of production."

And so now to the compass of significations in the Vitrine developed so far must be added another register: the sign system organized by the Co-op Vitrine is class-directed; a viewer's affiliation with a workers' collective consciousness, as opposed to bourgeois individualism, confers the capacity to apprehend its signification. This apprehension is not merely a matter of finding class signals added to the work (Meyer referred to the color of the Vitrine as "signal red"), but rather of understanding how its structure, processes, and rules of formation inevitably delimit a domain of ideological effectivity and give visual form to certain cognitive and emotive materials of everyday life in much the same way as the propagandist forms of rhetoric under which Meyer himself categorized it.

Consider, as a preliminary example of the latter, the short play *Der Traum* by Hannes Meyer and Jean Bard, staged simply with a phonograph recording, life-sized puppets, and actors in Ghent, Belgium, in 1924, as part of the same exhibition of cooperative production as the Vitrine. In the play a poor family appears in a "dreamlike apparition of the actual community." A scene of misery is described, with a mother and two children sleeping as a black spider descends, horrifying the mother and upsetting the children. Enter the father who pulls a sandwich from its wrapper. "Stillness and anticipation." The wrapper is a Co-op poster, which the father then places on the wall to the excitment of the family. The family returns to their sleep and the dream commences: Co-op packages descend, containing food and products of daily use.

"The picture of the future advances, gigantic [*riesengross*]."
An apparition of a hand with refund and reimbursement
(*Rückvergütung*), laden with money, advances then dis-
solves. The dream ends.[26]

Behind this example of
class-specific theatrical propaganda, and behind all of Meyer's Co-op work, lie the sedimented experiences of Siedlung
Freidorf, the community facility built by Meyer between
1919 and 1924 for the Swiss Co-operative Union, under the
direction of Bernhard Jäggi and Henry Faucherre, professor
of political economy at the University of Zurich, along with
Karl Mundig, who coined the name Freidorf, and Rudolf
Kündig.[27] The promoters of Freidorf found the inspiration
for their patronage in two figures directly related to the
international and Helvetic cooperative movements, Heinrich Pestalozzi and Heinrich Zschokke. Faucherre cited the
eighteenth-century educational reformer Pestalozzi as the
veritable source of the Freidorf "adventure."[28] In his novel
Leonard and Gertrude (1781), Pestalozzi pays particular
attention to collective self-help and self-determination, as
well as to family education and the key role of the mother,
whose common sense, sound judgment, and liberating sup-
pleness contrast to patriarchal, authoritarian strength, influ-
encing first her family, then her village, and finally the
state. Faucherre credited Pestalozzi as the initiator of the

**Scene from the play *Der Traum*, staged by
Hannes Meyer and Jean Bard, illustrated in "Das
Theater Co-op," *Das Werk* 11, no. 12 (1924).**

the representation of mass production

modern cooperative movements and the principle influence on later planners like Robert Owen, who had visited Pestalozzi in Switzerland. On the other hand, Zschokke's didactic novel *The Goldminer's Village* (1817)—which narrated the systematic transformation of a village toward collectivity and described in detail the benefits for all, emphasizing that different forms of behavior are reflections of tensions between a humanizing possibility and specific social situations—was, for its founders, nothing less than a prototype of Meyer's Siedlung.

In the general sociopolitical climate around the year 1919, the Freidorf experiment was understood to have a certain revolutionary and transformative dimension that was not lost on Meyer.[29] Meyer himself was a member of the cooperative and a resident of Freidorf from 1921 to 1926, as well as the chief of its building commission. In the latter capacity he designed not only the buildings but also the graphic logo for the cooperative—which appears, for example, on the coupons used in place of Swiss marks for exchange of everyday goods—as well as the packages and window displays of the standard products of the *magasin d'alimentation*, at which all members of the cooperative were obliged to shop. It is from these early experiences in the specific economic situation and way of life in the workers' cooperative that the Co-op Vitrine derives.

His Co-op theater and Freidorf experience may point to Meyer's concern for worker's lives, but how can we theorize the claim that the very structures of aesthetic reception in the Co-op Vitrine are made possible by class considerations? In *History and Class Consciousness*, Georg Lukács develops a theory of reification (*Verdinglichung*) as a negative and critical account of rationalization and commodity fetishism structurally related to class, which provides a potential framework for an understanding of Meyer's project.[30] For Lukács, with the progressive alienation of the activity of workers from their labor, their products, their fellow workers, and ultimately from their entire life experience, human relations in modernity had become, exactly, thinglike (*sachliche*); reification, then, has a fundamental *cognitive* dimension as a process of mapping human relationships within society, structuring our engagement with objects, and delimiting the categories through which we conceive all other people and things. The distortions of reified bourgeois society consist of the separations and "antinomies" of subjective experience and objective history, private self and public life, isolated empirical details and overarching abstract principles, and so forth; and its cognitive limits are signaled by its incapacity to come to terms with the category of *totality*, with the unity of subject and object. Consequently, the tendency of the middle class is to understand external objects in a static mode of contemplation—not in terms of production or use, origin or purpose, but rather through a myopic and motionless gaze in a suspended moment of time. For the bourgeois, an object is above all a commodity—a fixed, given, immediate thing whose cause is wholly secondary to its consumption—and this static relationship to objects is, of course, but a "reflection" of the life experience of the bourgeois in the socioeconomic realm. And though he may gaze at the apparent elements of his environment and social relations within capitalism, the bourgeois is not aware of this reality as a product of historical forces, and therefore as open to change. Bourgeois ideology, then, is for Lukács a kind of inertness, a veil, a set of strategic lapses and omissions of parts of the raw material that preclude the possibility that certain questions can even arise.

Though the proleteriat lifeworld is also structured by reification, and the vestiges of bourgeois ideology still woven into the modern proletariat's psychological formation, the worker's perception of reality was significantly different from that of the bourgeois. The worker still knew the finished product as a node in the process of production and use—a process involving the interrelationship of tools and procedures, situation and purpose, acts and consequences—and it is this knowledge that produces in proleterian thought the capacity for dissolving the antinomies and inertness inherent in bourgeois epistemology. For inasmuch as reality is thought as a construction and a process, it is thought historically and as containing within its present moment the possibility of radical transformation. It is thus proletarian thought that, for Lukács, penetrates the fetishized immediacy of bourgeois reality to become the privileged mode of knowledge through which the world is comprehended as a "totality," as a process open to change through that union of consciousness and activity that is praxis.

In what could be construed as nearly a staging of productivist aesthetics, Lukács articulates a collective, class-specific, process-based knowledge of reified reality:

The individual can never become the measure of all things. For when the individual confronts objective reality he is faced by a complex of ready-made and unalterable objects which allow him only the subjective responses of recognition or rejection. Only the class can relate to the whole of reality in a practical revolutionary way. (The "species" cannot do this as it is no more than an individual that has been mythologised and stylised in a spirit of contemplation.) And the class, too, can only manage it when it can see through the reified objectivity of the given world to the process that is also its own fate. For the individual, reification and hence determinism (determinism being the idea that things are necessarily connected) are irremovable. Every attempt to achieve "freedom" from such premises must fail, for "inner freedom" presupposes that the world cannot be changed.[31]

What is important for us here is the notion that it is precisely the self-consciousness of a certain subject position within a certain mode of production—which is a consciousness of oneself as a member of a class in a society that is a historical construction—that produces in proleterian thought the capability of rethinking subject/object relations from a vantage point of concrete totality. Fredric Jameson, following Lukács, has put the point succinctly: "The outside world, as the result of human labor, considered now not as nature but as history, is of the same substance as the subjectivity of the worker himself: the subjectivity of men can now be seen as the product of the same social forces that create commodities and ultimately the entire reality of the world in which men live."[32] From this perspective, representation itself is tied to the concept of totality: without a structure of the kind that maps its elements from various levels and spheres as sheer *relationships* and crossings of subject and object rather than as substantive packets of *content*, representation is inconceivable in any way save the most trivial and linear reflection of a fixed real by a more or less accurate copy. Lukács finds in the artistic production of realism—or more specifically the realist novel, where the characters and their interactions emerge as concrete particulars within the articulated relations of a changing social whole—a narration of the social totality with an epistemic and aesthetic moment that modernist self-reflexive art, in its autonomy, abstraction, and antirepresentational insistence, cannot achieve. Realism makes the connections between the actual workings of a society and its appearances. And so, even though the achievement of a realized totality may remain absent from modern life, it can nevertheless be reasserted on the representational plane of artistic form.

I invoke Lukács's theory of class, reification, and realism so specifically here not because I believe that it is entirely adequate or unproblematic. Indeed, translated into the context of architecture Lukács's endorsement of realism would privilege the workers' life experience, craft labor, and the continuity of traditional form in a way that is explicitly at odds with the sort of description I have been making of Meyer's work inasmuch as the latter conflates strategies of realism *and* self-reflexivity and emphasizes the positive potential of the very depersonalized machinery of modernity that Lukács in his humanism rejected. I invoke Lukács's thought rather because it yields a general way to relate artistic form to the structure of the psychic subject as the latter is differently constructed according to its position in specific modes of production. It is this interactive relation of form, subjectivity, and mode of production, in an openly political art, that is operative in the Co-op Vitrine. And I would suggest that Co-op form has as much content, albeit more rudimentary and limited in its articulation, as the older (and now justifiably discredited) realisms with which Lukács is concerned. In its investigations of commodity sign production and reception, its stress on the analogous process-like character of artistic signifying practice, both as production and as reception, and its positing of a continuum in the life of the commodity product from the factory to the shop window, Meyer's Co-op form attempts to articulate mechanisms by which to obliterate the most fundamental antinomies of modern existence: those between public and private, action and thought, the political and the artistic, the collective and the individual, between my being-for-others and my being-for-myself, in short, between object and subject. And if Meyer's is now an aesthetic that avails itself of the formative principles of mechanized reproduction as a privileged, if fragmentary, form of modern reality rather than of the strategies of realist narrative, as in Lukács, and if it is repetition, seriality, banality, and the like that become the valid conceptualization of the totality of our experience of modern society, it is not because Co-op form betrays a legitimation of the existing order, but rather because it identifies the *transformatory potential* of that order out of which an authentic collective life and a single international culture of the future might be developed. We are reminded again of Benjamin's citation: "In the dream in which, before the eyes of each epoch, that which is to follow appears in images, the latter appears wedded to elements from prehistory, that is, of a classless society."

A crucial reversal of standard Marxist aesthetics thus takes place: it is henceforth precisely the mechanization, commodification, and rationalization of everyday life—the very forces of reification recognized by Simmel and Lukács—and their psychological consequences, that are *recommended* as the raw material of a critical aesthetic practice for producing new subjectivities. According to Meyer, aesthetic practice must submit to reification, making commodity form tangible and perceptible in order to refunction the commodity status. And likewise the socialist state would arise from the dynamic of capitalism, synthesizing mass technology and mass consumption. While Simmel and Lukács correctly identify reification as the precondition for the emergence of modernism, they overlook the possibility of the different resolution achieved by Meyer: what Jameson has called the utopian vocation of the reified material, ideologically reconfigured or re-presented, to promote at least a symbolic experience of collective life. Reification and modernism are structurally related, but their conjunction must now be thought not in terms of narrating the redeemed humanist subject or its threatened psychological precincts, but by means of the very different representational categories of propaganda, dispersion, and reproduction, organized around the collective subject of the posthumanist future.

contra the bourgeois interior:
co-op zimmer

In his essays "Fashion" and "The Problem of Style," as well
as in *The Philosophy of Money*, Georg Simmel analyzes the
phenomena of fashion and style as the manifest effects of a
never-resolved tension between attempts at individual differentiation and the overwhelming absorption of individuals
into a homogenizing social structure.[1] On the one hand,
the adherence to the homogeneity of a dominant fashion
bestows upon the individual a certain stability and suprain-
dividuality that counters the fragmentation and abstraction
of commodity fetishism. On the other hand, fashion is a
means of expressing and preserving some semblance of
inner freedom, of reasserting one's absent individuality in
the face of "the superiority, autonomy, and indifference of
the cosmos."[2]

The consecutive shifts of
fashion over time and the plurality of styles at the present
are related respectively as diachronic and synchronic structures of differentiation. The rate of changes in fashion is an
indication of the languishing of cultural energies: "Changes
in fashion indicate the amount of deadening of nervous
excitement; the more nervous an epoch is, the more rapidly
will its fashions change, because the need for the attraction
of differentiation, one of the essential agents of fashion, goes
hand in hand with the languishing of nervous energies."[3]
Similarly, the proliferation of styles, the "disloyalty" to any
one style, is a consequence of the individual's overstimulation, indifference, and restlessness:

The lack of something definite at the center of the soul impels us
to search for momentary satisfaction in ever-new stimulations, sensations and external activities. Thus it is that we become entangled
in the instability and helplessness that manifests itself as the
tumult of the metropolis, as the mania for travelling, as the wild
pursuit of competition and as the typically modern disloyalty with
regard to taste, style, opinions and personal relationships.[4]

Given the objective autonomy of fashion and style, we as
individuals are now confronted with "these forms on the
one side, and our subjectivity on the other."

Modern man is so surrounded by nothing but impersonal objects that he becomes more and more conditioned into accepting the idea of an anti-individualistic social order—though, of course, he may also oppose it. Cultural objects increasingly evolve into an interconnected enclosed world that has increasingly fewer points at which the subjective soul can interpose its will and feelings. And this trend is supported by a certain autonomous mobility on the part of objects. . . . Both material and intellectual objects today move independently, without personal representatives or transport. Objects and people have become separated from one another.[5]

Style thus emerges for Simmel as a paradoxical form of protective distance between subject and object. Style is a sublimation of subjective contradictions—the tension between individualism and an overarching socialism—and of the oppressive externalities of modern life that threatens the subject's constitution. Style is a veil, however illusory, behind which the fragmented subject can escape the nervous intensity (Nervenleben) of modernity.

It is no surprise, then, that stylization is most intensified in the specialized spatial realm of the bourgeois interior and its household objects, the realm where an autonomous individualism is clung to most desperately and symbolized most completely. "The Problem of Style" was written after the time when artists and architects had devised the notion of Gesamtkunstwerk— a total stylization and imaginary projection of authorial integrity, whose very conceptualization is possible only when the apparatus of style has first been isolated and developed into an independent sign system. This autonomization of style then enables its various constitutive forms (from tableware and chairs to construction details to entire city scenes) to carry more elaborate symbolic meanings. Gottfried Semper, Alois Riegl, and others had already argued that utilitarian objects and the handling of their different materials and labors give us an insight into the culture of a period. But as long as the notion of style is seen as the simple product or epiphenomenon of a particular social life, its

symbolic extension is limited by our description of that
social life. Only the autonomization and specialization of
style as enunciated by Simmel makes possible the *desire* for
a modern style *yet to be invented,* and the projection of that
desire onto objects in the world.

The libidinal energy of
the *Jugendstil* stylizations is striking. And it is in this context of desire and the increasingly rarefied researches into
style that the figure of Adolf Loos appears. The Loosian
"solution" to the desperate desire to find a modern style,
his answer to all the overly anxious, overly eroticized
Jugendstil fantasies of inventing a total architectural language adequate to the emergent differentiations of bourgeois
society, is a kind of negation of the negation of that desire—
a critical procedure whereby the desired language of differentiation, the style, is magically revealed by way of its very
renunciation.

Do we need "artists of applied arts"? No. All the industries that
have succeeded to the present in staving off this superfluous element from their work have reached their highest level. Only the
products of those industries really represent the style of our time.
They so fully express the style of our time that we—and this is the
only valid criterion of judgment—do not in fact even notice that
we have a style. . . . What we need is a *civilization of carpenters.* If
the artist of the applied arts would only go back to painting pictures or take to sweeping the streets, we would have it.[6]

For Loos, as concerns
buildings and objects of everyday use, the dreams and fantasies of design must confront the reality principle of the division of labor—the superego of capitalist society, and the
differentiated cultural field of the present which it sponsors.
Indeed, it seems that Loos's entire ideology of a *Sachlichkeit* imposed through social utility—his Anglo-Saxon empiricism and fascination with American engineering, his
attention to everyday concerns such as plumbing, under-
wear, and shoes, the famous effacements and renunciations
of formal pretensions—is aimed at providing something like

a censoring device for the desiring, designing subject. It is this reality principle that is the means of canceling the superfluous decoration and ornamental excesses that do actual cultural harm. As Theodor Adorno writes,

Pleasure appears, according to the bourgeois work ethic, as wasted energy. Loos's formulation makes clear how much as an early cultural critic he was fundamentally attached to that order whose manifestations he chastised wherever they failed to follow their own principles: "Ornament is wasted work energy and thereby wasted health. It has always been so. But today it also means wasted material, and both mean wasted captial." Two irreconcilable motifs coincide in this statement: economy, for where else, if not in the norms of profitability, is it stated that nothing should be wasted; and the dream of the totally technological world, free from the shame of work. The second motif points beyond the commercial world. For Loos it takes the form of the realization that the widely lamented impotency to create ornament and the so-called extinction of stylizing energy . . . imply an advance in the arts.[7]

At the same time, the desired differentiations sought superfluously by "artists of applied arts" are already given by the various labors associated with different uses and held separate within an articulate cultural field.

The work of art is brought into the world without there being any need for it. The house on the other hand satisfies a need. . . . The work of art is revolutionary, the house is conservative. . . . So the house should have nothing to do with art, and architecture should not be numbered among the arts? Exactly so. Only a very small part of architecture belongs to art: the tomb and the monument. The rest, everything which serves an end, should be excluded from the realm of art.[8]

A certain unpleasure must be accepted in order to comply with cultural and social needs, and moreover, this demands the maintenance of certain boundaries. As Karl Kraus put it, "Adolf Loos and I, he in facts and I in words, have done nothing but show that there is a difference between the urn and the chamber-pot and that culture plays itself out on this difference. The others, however, the defenders of positive knowledge, can be divided into two groups: those who take the urn for a chamber-pot and those who mistake a chamber-pot for an urn."[9] And then, too, there is a differentiation and autonomy at the level of languages of material; as Loos put it, "Every material possesses a formal language that belongs to it alone and no other material can take on the forms proper to another. . . . No material permits any intrusion on its own repertoire of forms."[10] This principle of *Materialgerechtigkeit* is also based on the division of labor. It is the insistence on divisions, boundaries, and plays of difference based on wholly *present* distinctions of labor, use, and materials that produces the radical formal discontinuities in the commercial building on the Michaelerplatz, holds the life of the interior of the private houses separate from the public sphere of the metropolis, and further differentiates the private space of the bourgeois family into distinct zones of habitation and correlated furnishings. Loos's *Raumplan* is a continuous spatial sequence, but the rooms it comprises are discretely related to the specific life habits of their occupants: the men's smoking room and the leather sofa, the *Zimmer der Dame* with its raised seating occupying the center of the house,[11] the dining room where the drama of the family's social life is staged, Lina Loos's bedroom,[12] Josephine Baker's swimming pool. Similarly, the labors involved in the production of the coexisting Egyptian stool, modern bench with its Liberty fabric, ceiling beams and fireplace sitting nook, and Kokoschka paintings on the mantel with nineteenth-century clocks and lamps, are all radically different, but their value is equal in the thoroughgoing relativity of a *Sachlichkeit* based on what Adorno called "a utopia of concretely fulfilled presence, no longer in need of symbols."[13] They attest to what Stanford Anderson has termed Loos's "critical presentism"[14] and constitute a critique of the pompous bourgeois interior and, simulta-

neously, an acceptance of what adequately functions, physically and psychologically, regardless of its style.

It is in Loos's "critical presentism"—what I take to be his reconciliation of bourgeois commercial activity, aristocratic formal traditions, and present technology, his formalization of bourgeois schizophrenia, his acceptance of the destiny of the capitalist mode of production, and his radical defense of individual private life—that we detect the same "strange interplay between reactionary theory and revolutionary practice" that Walter Benjaminin identified in Karl Kraus.

Indeed, to secure private life against morality and concepts in a society that perpetrates the political radioscopy of sexuality and family, of economic and physical existence, in a society that is in the process of building houses with glass walls, and patios extending far into the drawing rooms that are no longer drawing rooms—such a watchword would be the most reactionary of all were not the private life that Kraus had made it his business to defend precisely that which, unlike the bourgeois form, is in strict accordance with this social upheaval; in other words, *the private life that is dismantling itself.*[15]

Adolf Loos, Müller house, Prague, 1929–1930, men's study.

Loos, Müller house, ladies' room.

Adolf Loos, Steiner house, Vienna, 1910, living room.

And if Loos's practice, with its stress on the use value of objects as a criterion of their modernity, may be read as a critique of the autonomization and specialization of style mentioned above—that is, the conceptualization of style or formal language as a thing-in-itself—nevertheless, his insistence on the insuperable partitions between languages of form is continuous with the contemporaneous structural processes of reification, by which human relations and social forms are systematically broken up into their individual components and abstracted from concrcte experience. As with the Co-op work of Meyer, reification becomes the historical concept by which the emergence of Loos's different version of the posthumanist subject can be understood. The dissolution of the older organic and seamless social fabric, its displacement by the well-nigh universally commodified labor power of highly differentiated individuals (from plumbers to shoemakers to Kokoschkas and Schoenbergs), and the confrontation of these individual labors within the matrix of equivalencies of metropolitan life, allow Loos to hypothesize a highly differentiated subjectivity. Yet, unlike with Meyer, this securing of subjective differentiations is achieved only within boundaries of the existing antagonisms identified by Simmel, between public and private, society and the individual, all of which Loos's schizophrenic subject replicates or reproduces at the level of architectural theory.

Simmel's account of style and Loos's denunciation of the same thus share a referent in the *Nervenleben* of the monadic metropolitan protagonist. However, what Simmel theorized in historical anxiety as the hypersensitivity and fetishization of the mind, Loos cynically asserts as the ideal consciousness of the modern individual. For Simmel, as we have seen, style is the buffer between the subject, its raw nerves exposed, and the world.

Here, the distance that art already places between ourselves and the objects is extended yet a stage further, in that the notions that form the content of the ultimately stimulating psychic experience no longer have a visible counterpart in the work of art itself, but are only provoked by perceptions of quite a different kind. In all this we discover an emotional trait whose pathological deformation is the so-called "agoraphobia": the fear of coming into too close a contact with objects, a consequence of hyperaesthesia, for which every direct and energetic disturbance causes pain.[16]

In contrast, Loos's subject was to "have modern nerves, the nerves that the Americans possess today,"[17] and style could therefore be renounced. And where Simmel saw the barriers between individuals and their social environment as the extreme consequences of the money economy, understood as the very motor of the accelerating opposition between subjective and objective culture, Loos saw the countervalue of silent walls that separated the protected private interior from the public exterior as the only possible interventionary mark of an architectural culture for the present.

Meanwhile, in other registers of representation, "the modern" has a related but quite different ideological function to play, serving as an ideal antithetical to that of private life in either its reactive or critical versions, lending up its forms, reification and all, to visions of individuality dissolved into an effect of collective life. It is here that Meyer's Co-op Zimmer, contra the bourgeois interior, makes its conceptual presence felt.

"Co-op Zimmer" is something of a misnomer, for the project is, in fact, a photograph. Of course, a historical interpretation of any no longer existing interior must be based primarily on photographs. (It is perhaps of some interest to recall Loos's assertion that his interiors could *not* be perceived in photographs.) But Meyer's Co-op interior has been *always only* a photograph. The "room" is mocked up of white fabric, two folding wood and canvas chairs, a cot raised on conical feet to allow air to flow underneath, and a phonograph on a collapsible stool; the uncropped version also shows shelves of food products. The circles of the gramophone, the double square of the chair hanging on the wall, the triangles of the stool legs, and the rectangle and conical feet of the cot are combined in what could be taken as an elementarist geometrical construction virtually collapsed onto its canvas background.

The Co-op Zimmer is an assemblage, a circuit or pattern of preliminary and interrelated signs, a "conspicuous arrangement" (Meyer), not of reified, isolated objects of contemplation but of quasi-independent signs that still function within some larger cultural machinery that includes a conceptualization of the nomadic mobility enabled by the portable furniture, the alimentary products, and the invasion of the bedroom by the jazz band whose sound is now severed from its instruments and flattened onto a reproducible disk.[18] Meyer's interior is a text, if you will, provided that term can be metonymically extended to such things as life habits and daily routines, means of knowing, belonging, and practicing, all fixed through chains of signification. And if we have recently learned the impropriety of asking the "meaning" of such arrangements, we can nevertheless ask of the connection of Meyer's text to, and function within, other arrangements. In particular, it is inseperable from the article in which, along with the Co-op Vitrine, the Co-op interior first appeared, Meyer's "Die neue Welt." The Co-op interior appears as the example of "Die Wohnung" on a

spread entitled "Der Standard," illustrating the essay's aesthetic of standardization, repetition, mechanized media, advertisement, nomadism, impersonality, and collectivity, and its polemical folding of one set of signs into the terms of another. Meyer introduces the Co-op Zimmer as follows:

The demands we make on life today are all of the same nature regardless of our social sector or stratum. The surest sign of true community is the satisfaction of the same needs by the same means. The upshot of such a collective demand is the *standard product.* The folding chair, roll-top desk, light bulb, bath tub and portable gramophone are typical standard products manufactured internationally and showing a uniform design. They are apparatuses in the mechanization of our daily life. Their standardized form is impersonal. They are manufactured in quantity, serially, as a serialized article, as a serialized device, as a serialized structural element, as a serialized house. The standard mental product is called a "hit." Because of the standardization of his needs as regards housing, food and mental sustenance, the semi-nomad of our modern productive system has the benefit of freedom of movement, economies, simplification and relaxation, all of which are vitally important for him. *The degree of our standardization is an index of our communal productive system.*

The essay itself is an urgent and intense description of the "psychological precon-

Hannes Meyer, Co-op Zimmer, 1926.

Hannes Meyer, Co-op Linocut (self-portrait), 1924.

contra the bourgeois interior

DER STANDARD

**DIESELMASCHINENFABRIK DER SCHIFFSWERFT
HARLAND & WOLFF LTD., GLASGOW**
*Eisenkonstruktion, Wellblechwände, Glasdächer
Phot. H. Wittwer*

**MUNITIONSARBEITER-SIEDELUNG WELL HALL
ZU ELTHAM, KENT**
*Building Departement Woolwich Arsenal / Grundriss siehe
Seite 225 / Holzkonstruktion, Eternitwände, Teerpappedach*

H. DE FRIES, BERLIN / MODELLENTWURF ZUR EXPORTMESSE IN HAMBURG 1925
*Grundriss siehe Seite 225 / Gebäudelänge 360 m / Breit aufgespaltene Baukörper sichern grösstmögliche Lichtzufuhr / Keine
geschlossenen Höfe / Ausstellungs- und Büroräume im Doppelstocksystem / Grosse Längsstrasse im Gebäudeinnern / Drei-
geschossige Auslegervorbauten über der Strassenbahnlinie / Treppenhäuser mit direktem Zugang von vorhandener Baumallee*

Spread entitled "Der Standard," from
Hannes Meyer, "Die neue Welt," *Das Werk* 13, no. 7
(1926), showing the Co-op Zimmer with other serialized productions and industrialized landscapes.

DER STANDARD

DIE LANDSCHAFT
Schlachtfeld St. Jakob bei Basel anno 1926

DIE SIEDELUNG
Gartenfräse System v. Meyenburg

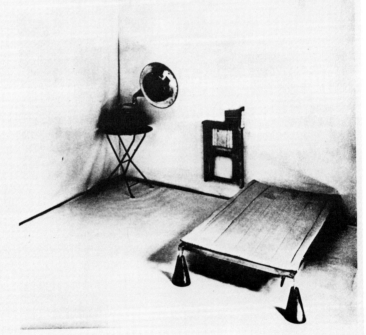

DIE WOHNUNG
Co-op. Interieur 1926

contra the bourgeois interior

ditions" of a subjectivity already identified by Simmel as paradigmatic of modernity: a nervous personality that "originates in the bustle and excitement of modern life," and in "that increasing distance from nature and that particularly abstract existence that urban life, based on the money economy, has forced upon us," a personality that is produced by the experience of the metropolis itself, "with every crossing of the street, with the speed and diversity of economic, professional, social life." Meyer's opening lines rewrite Simmel's description of the "leveling tendencies" and "fragmenting images" of "the clamorous splendor of the scientific technological age."[19]

The flight of the "Norge" to the North Pole, the Zeiss planetarium at Jena and Flettner's rotor ship represent the latest stages to be reported in the mechanization of our planet. Being the outcome of extreme precision in thought, they all provide striking evidence of the way in which science continues to permeate our environment. Thus in the diagram of the present age we find everywhere amidst the sinuous lines of its social and economic fields of force straight lines which are mechanical and scientific in origin. They are cogent evidence of the victory of man the thinker over amorphous nature. . . . Motor cars dash along our streets. On a traffic island in the Champs Elysées from 6 to 8 p.m. there rages round one metropolitan dynamicism at its most strident. "Ford" and "Rolls Royce" have burst open the core of the town, obliterating distance and effacing the boundaries between town and country. . . . Illuminated signs twinkle, loud-speakers screech, posters advertise, display windows shine forth.

But Meyer reverses the valence of the subjective consequences of such overstimulation, seeing its effects as rather expanding and sharpening our consciousness.

The simultaneity of events enormously extends our concept of "space and time," it enriches our life. We live faster and therefore longer. We have a keener sense of speed than ever before, and speed records are a direct gain for all. Gliding, parachute descents and music hall acrobatics refine our desire for balance. The precise division into hours of the time we spend working in office and factory and the split-minute timing of railway timetables make us live more consciously.

Co-op Zimmer produces a concept of a smoothly traversable, nomadic space, a *"diagram* of the present age," which is continuous with a new collectivism and objectively determined by the imposition of new products and external "fields of force" that operate to dissolve established boundaries within various forms of experience and cognition.

Borrough's calculating machine sets free our brain, the dictaphone our hand, Ford's motor our placebound senses and Handley Page our earthbound spirits. Radio, marconigram and phototelegraphy liberate us from our national seclusion and make us part of a world community. The gramophone, microphone, orchestrion and pianola accustom our ears to the sound of impersonal-mechanized rhythms: "His Master's Voice," "Vox," and "Brunswick" see to the musical needs of millions. Psychoanalysis has burst open the all too narrow dwelling of the soul and graphology has laid bare the character of the individual. . . . National costume is giving way to fashion and the external masculinization of woman shows that inwardly the two sexes have equal rights. Biology, psychoanalysis, relativity and entomology are common intellectual property: Francé, Einstein, Freud and Fabre are the saints of this latterday. Our homes are more mobile than ever. Large blocks of flats, sleeping cars, house yachts and transatlantic liners undermine the local concept of the "homeland." The fatherland goes into a decline. We learn Esperanto. We become cosmopolitan.

By extending and prolonging the sense of each singular verbal image in the passage above, and producing a kind of transverse communication between verbal and visual images, Meyer weaves a network of externalities that map the reality of "the new world." In the chains of diverse references organized serially as facts in declarative sentences, the reader cannot help feeling a kind of dispersion, as of tracers sent out in scattered

Meyer, Co-op Fotos, c. 1926: photographs of high tension wires, building crane, and turbine hall, all near Basel.

directions registering functions of instruments, disciplines, modes of thought, habitats, and habits, all of which are constituent parts of the transformed lifeworld configured by the Co-op Zimmer.

The next passage of Meyer's essay begins with those new "factographic," reportorial, and advertising methods of visual sign production that the most advanced artists in Europe and Russia were beginning to develop, and quickly moves to the psychovisual effects of those methods.

The steadily increasing perfection attained in printing, photographic and cinematographic processes enables the real world to be reproduced with an ever greater degreee of accuracy. The picture the landscape presents to the eye today is more diversified than ever before; hangars and power houses are the cathedrals of the spirit of the age. This picture has the power to influence through the specific shapes, colors and lights of its modern elements: the wireless aerials, the dams, the lattice girders; through the parabola

of the airship, the triangle of the traffic signs, the circle of the railway signal, the rectangle of the billboard; through the linear element of transmission lines: telephone wires, overhead tram wires, high-tension cables; through radio towers, concrete posts, flashing lights and filling stations.

It does not simplify Meyer's enterprise to insist that the images conjured up attempt to represent modernity, for what we understand by the significance of Meyer's pictorial reportage of the mass industrial and mass cultural landscape has less to do with the latter as a source of sheer aesthetic experimentation than it does with this picture's claim to cognitive and practical as well as visual and aesthetic status. The appropriation and presentation of the multiplicity of diverse images testify to Meyer's preoccupation not only with the industrialization process but also with the forms of experience that are the subjective consequences of such a process. This play of images—whose emblematic value is reasserted by the presence in Meyer's article of exemplary photographs including scenes of industry, its use objects, and its repetitive morphology—seeks to satisfy not only the appetite for form, but

Hannes Meyer, "Photographing: camera sees camera, " c. 1928.

also the appetite for *matter*. The pictures stand as facts of seeing, as the actual forms of our knowledge of things. And their richness may therefore be recognized in terms of their ability to assimilate material and productive values to visual and psychological effects, to convert the qualities of one into the forms of the other, and thereby to reunite the two levels of subjective mental labor and the objective realities of production. Co-op form attests to the possibility that forms of simultaneous collective reception, by linking the structure of subjectivity directly to the inexorable movement of mass production, can afford a kind of protopolitical and practical apprenticeship for the collective society to come. The concrete experience of the visual products of mechanization—which, understood in terms of received theories of alienation and reification, would have to stand condemned—when understood as affording epistemic access to, or a symbolic and psychological mapping of, the now vivid and tractable consequences of modernity, may be reconceived as a functional diagram for cognitive retooling.

In the work of Loos the presence of the real is signaled not only by the isolation of the interior from the city, but also by the spatial and material discontinuities in the very fabric of the building and the heterogeneity of kinds of labor given form in the furnishings, all of which constantly threaten to fragment the Loosian interior into a disjunctive series of *vertical* indicators of present actualities and the life habits developed to manage them—the elements of the *Raumplan* expressing the contents of metropolitan life. The Co-op interior, on the other hand, understood as one point of ramification in the surface of a multiplicity of texts, maps its real on a *horizontal* plane, on what Gilles Deleuze calls a single "plane of consistency" that does not distinguish between contents and their expressions even though it organizes and distributes (plans) their effects.[20] Which is not to deny that the entities, events, and actualities Meyer recounts indeed exist, but rather to return to the repudiation of that traditional view of representation that sees the real as something preexisting somewhere remote from the art work, to which the latter, through subjectively reflected and conventionalized illusion, refers. In contrast, the constellation that is Meyer's new world absorbs the present actualities to which it makes such obsessive reference, reorganizes and extends their lines of connectivity, creates new potential subject/object relations, and thereby constitutes the very raw material of which it can then claim to be the description or representation; the constellation yielded by the work just *is* the real. Reality is not something that, in its plenitude, shines through the ideally transparent work; rather the real is won within the work itself,[21] but is no less real for that. Which is precisely what we are able to grasp, once we understand representation as an act of enunciating—as process, productivity, and performativity.

What is more, the recasting of artistic practice within the categories of technical labor entails a repudiation of the traditional base/superstructure model of reality and art, installing artistic production as a co-force of material production generally. In 1923 Boris Arvatov had characterized this new status of artistic work as analogous to the products of craft labor: "The artist began to relate to the picture, not as a field for the illusionistic depiction of objects, but as a real object. He began to work on the picture as a worker in wood works on a piece of wood. . . . He became in his own way a specialist and the only difference was that for him the construction was an aim in itself."[22] But the artistic process here compared to craft production, and the connotations carried by the terminology of "worker" and "specialist," Meyer transferred to a more advanced level where the rapprochement of art and production is achieved with the formative principles of mass technology—montage, repetition, seriality, dispersion.

Fredric Jameson has argued that what I have construed as a particular sort of representational procedure operative in Meyer's 1926 constructions is characteristic of utopian thought generally:

It is possible to understand the Utopian text as a determinate type of *praxis*, rather than as a specific mode of representation, a praxis that has less to do with the construction and perfection of someone's "idea" of a "perfect society" than it does with a concrete set of mental operations to be performed on a determinate type of raw material given in advance, which is contemporary society itself— or, what amounts to the same thing, on those collective representations of contemporary society that inform our ideologies just as they order our experience of daily life.[23]

The utopian label seems right for Meyer. It is not an unfamiliar one. But I want to suggest more than the hopeful naiveté that is usually meant by the designation and to relate his utopian stance, together with the corollaries of collectivism and nomadism, to a conception of the subject as it is constructed within and by distinct modes of production that are historically conceived but not entirely constrained by the present.

A comparison with Loos's presentism is again helpful. As we have seen, Loos's interior architecture is a particularly vivid demonstration, over and against the *Gesamtkunstwerk* of *Jugendstil* with its optical illusion of individual existence, of subject positions still available to architectural representation in the early 1920s. What we must now observe, however, is that that demonstration traces its norms, however accommodating or liberating, on a background of an economy still not fully industrialized and rationalized. The characteristic, typal objects and motives of Loosian *Sachlichkeit*—the leather goods and umbrellas, wood and marble paneling, oriental carpets, Kokoschkas, and all—still show traces of production by artisanal labor and distribution by an organization of merchants over the small shop counters designed by Loos; the individual human origins of the typal objects of this period have not yet been completely erased. Moreover, Loos's subject positions as described by his architecture retain the ideal of individualism and are based on a present in which the bourgeoisie was still a rising and progressive class, the nuclear family still a viable structure, and the monadic subject still in possession of some degree of resistance to the complete penetration of commodification into the innermost depths of the psyche.

We need only juxtapose Meyer's own description of the economies of "Trade union, co-operative, Ltd., Inc., cartel, trust and the League of Nations" as the forms of social expression of *his* present to feel the difference.

Yesterday is dead; Bohemia is dead. Dead are atmosphere, color values, burr, mellow tones and random brush-strokes. Dead the novel: we have neither the suspension of disbelief nor the time to read. Dead picture and sculpture as images of the real world: in the age of films and photos they are a dissipation of effort and the endless "beautification" of our real world through the interpretations of "artists" is presumptuous. Dead is the work of art as a "thing in itself," as "art for art's sake": our communal consciousness will

"Magazines and books adequate to our time" selected by Meyer from his library, published with "Die neue Welt."

contra the bourgeois interior

not tolerate any individualist excesses. . . . Co-operation rules the world. The community rules the individual.

Henceforth the products of mass culture are completely without depth, horizontal connectivities replace vertical representations, and signs of individualism are precluded from the outset. While Loos's thinking maintains a continuity between the bourgeois order and what is to develop out of it, Meyer's demands an absolute break with the past and a taking hold of the ineluctable progress of history toward the socialist future. "Our knowledge of the past is a burden that weighs upon us, and inherent in our advanced education are impediments tragically barring our new paths. The unqualified affirmation of the present age presupposes the ruthless denial of the past." The Co-op form stands as a sign of the kind of mental retooling the human subject must undergo to divest itself of its historically conditioned defects and failures of development and begin its journey toward the classless future.

To be sure, then, Meyer's Co-op Zimmer has its preconditions in capitalist modes of production even more advanced than those Loos could perhaps conceive across the watershed of World War I. Meyer's interior, however, is distinguished from those of Loos by the anticipatory representation of an altogether different international culture of the future that seeks to emerge from the dominant modes of production of the present. And this same partisan commitment to that utopian mode of production also distinguishes the two in terms of subjectivity. For while the subjects constructed by Loos and Meyer are both born of their historical present and, as such, are historically decentered, Co-op form differs not only in its more complete flattening and dispersion of the subject, but also in being predicated on a conception of the subject at the other end of historical time, indeed on the possibility that some transformation of society will have put behind it that class organization, alienated labor, and the market economy from which it emerged. It is only from *this* utopian vantage ground that Meyer's antihumanist subjectivity has any purchase.

This said, and with Jameson's thesis in mind that utopian thought can be understood essentially as a process of mediation or *neutralization*[24]—a resolution, by way of figural thinking, of a real social contradiction between infrastructure and superstructure—Co-op form can be construed as the structural resolution of one of the most persistent dilemmas of historical materialist thought: the insertion of the subject into an as yet unachieved but presently emergent mode of production. As such, Co-op form is, moreover, the structural obversion of Simmel's theory of style, which is itself presented as the resolution or mediation of monadic subjectivity and the capitalist mode of production. All of which can now be represented diagrammatically as a structure of signification with what A. J. Greimas calls his "semiotic rectangle."[25] This rudimentary structure is capable of generating an entire field of mediatory combinations out of an initial binary opposition. First, a complex term C mediates between two primary "contraries" or terms of opposition, S and $-S$. Two secondary terms of opposition, *not S* and *not -S*, are expressed as "contradictories" or involutions of the first. This second opposition, shown in diagonal relation to the first, produces as its resolution what is effectively a double cancellation of the initial mediation, the latter's neutralization, the so-called neutral term, N. In our present case, Simmel's concept of style is the complex term, and Loos's antistyle can be situated coincidentally with Simmel's style as a mediation of the intolerable contradictions between the monadic subject and capitalism, except with a negative valence. The term of contradiction or negation of capitalism— the "not-capitalism," so to speak, of the semiotic rectangle—then comprises not only the sense of the anticipated mode of production of achieved postcapitalist socialism according to a classical historical materialist interpretation, but also the forms of *reception* and other consequences of such a process, which Meyer described in "Die neue Welt."

The involution of the centered, monadic subject—the "not-subject" of the semiotic rectangle—can analogously be thought of in negative terms as the loss, dissolution, and cancellation of the subject, or in positive terms as the displacement of the monadic, centered subject by a different kind of emancipated *Unmensch,* emptied of interiority to become a decentered subject-*effect:* what I have called the nomadic, collective, antihumanist subject. Finally, Co-op form, which organizes both the objects of a future mode of production and antihumanist subjectivity as a mode of reception, can be understood as the neutral, utopian term of the structure, what I have earlier called the obversion of Simmel's complex term of style.

	C ▎**style (Simmel)**		
	▎**antistyle (Loos)**		} inversion
S		−S	

centered humanist subject	capitalist mode of production
"not-capitalism," or anticipated new mode of simultaneous collective reception	"not-subject," or decentered, nomadic, collective, antihumanist subject
−S̄	S̄

N ▎**Meyer's Co-op form**

The scheme suggests, in general as Jameson argues, that the vocation of the new, neutral term, here Co-op form, is "to permit a desperate (and impossible) final attempt to eradicate the contradictions of the system by some extreme gesture."[26] It also repudiates the conventional understanding of Meyer's utopia as a mere invocation or image of some ideal society, and substitutes a notion of utopia as a process whereby something *is done to the real,* and whereby the operations performed and actualized are initiated and carried by a *reading* of the Co-op projects themselves.

Now, recognizing that the signifying object, the Co-op form, in some sense ade-

quately names that which propels this process, this activity
of reading, we have also finally circled back to the notion,
invoked earlier, of performativity, now understood in the
properly utopian sense in which critical engagement
between subject and object performs and constitutes that
which in the present world always escapes us. Concretely,
this emphasis on performativity implies that the potential
for conceptualizing change, the potential even of meaningful
protopolitical action, is produced and made available, albeit
only in a symbolic mode, in the analyses of the aesthetic
construct and the ideological-material conditions that determine its formation.

But further, by focusing
his efforts on the status of the subject as constructed and
situated by those same conditions, Meyer invites us to conceive of the function of the centered subject of bourgeois
humanism as a kind of imposition of blindness or obstruc-
tion of inquiry into the hidden institutional frameworks and
ideological factors that determine the work and the conditions under which it is apprehended. This is the case most
obviously in the work of architects where the objects themselves operate to discourage if not preclude considerations of
the necessary constitutive preconditions of their formation;
but it is also the case, it should be added, in those critical-
interpretive principles that confine a "correct" reading of an
architectural object to an acceptance of the position from
which the immanent characteristics of the architectural
object have exclusive importance over its external historical
and ideological determinants: the position of a transcendental subject. In contrast, Meyer will seek, within the terms
provided by Co-op form, to develop a more full-blown architecture—a project for constructing, for acting, for *building*—
that problematizes architecture *as such*, as a discipline, an
ideology, a cultural institution, and that dismantles our routine, institutionalized business of design and our habitual,
institutionalized modes of perception, all in order to show
just how deeply questionable are the architectural, interpretive,
and cultural values bourgeois humanism has taken for granted.

co-op building between avant-garde and instrumentalization: the petersschule

In the section of *Das Prinzip Hoffnung* titled "Building in Empty Spaces," Ernst Bloch characterized the *neue Sachlichkeit* in architecture: "Today, in many places, houses look as if they were ready to travel [*reisefertig*]. Although they are unadorned, or precisely because of that, they express their farewell. Their interior is bright and sterile like hospital rooms, the exterior looks like boxes on top of mobile poles, but also like ships. They have flat decks, portholes, gangways, railings; they shine white and to the south, and as ships they like to disappear." Writing in America during 1938–1949, Bloch found little hope expressed in such architecture, product as it was of "the late capitalist hollow space" and abstract technology. "Rather this hollow space penetrates the so-called art of engineering [*Ingenieurkunst*] as much as the latter increases the hollowness by its own emptiness." Nevertheless,

recently there is a particularly alienating motive, which is basically the *only original* one. It is *engineering as architecture,* which has a significant utopian effect. Now it is engineering into which architecture as the real art has been incorporated and from which it has to reemerge on the threshold of a concrete society. What it means here is the new combination of the old utopia of crystallization [of C.-N. Ledoux and others] with the *desire to disorganize.* This kind of combination is precisely related to the abstract technology itself with which the new architecture is so closely linked and provides also disorganization *sui generis* for the crystalline urban utopia. . . . Thus the house without aura . . . corresponds to the machine that no longer resembles the human being. Functional architecture reflects and doubles anyway the icy realm of commodity world automation, its alienation, its labor-divided human beings, its abstract technology.

Only a new classless society would make a "true" architecture possible. Thus for Bloch, "the only significant thing in all this is the direction of the departure of these phenomena generated by themselves, i.e., the house as a ship."[1]

It is on the whole a negative judgment of the architecture of the *neue Sachlichkeit*

and in its formal description could just as well apply specifically to the building projects designed by Hannes Meyer.
Yet one aspect of the architecture described by Bloch hangs
in our minds with disturbingly ambiguous resonance: *the
architecture likes to disappear.* It is this antisocial quality
of this sharp, stark, "hollow" architecture, its "desire to disorganize," but also and not inconsistently its utopian effect,
that must concern us now as we verify the interpretations I
have made thus far against Meyer's "Co-op building," the
Petersschule project for Basel of 1926–1927.[2] That this
architectural machine "no longer resembles the human
being" we will agree. But it is precisely in defining the
nature of the Petersschule's dislocation of the spectator
from his accustomed imaginary possession of an internally
unified work of architecture resembling his desired unified,
centralized self that we will gain a description of the architectural object such that its protopolitical, utopian character
comes into view. For in the case of the Petersschule it is not
a matter of the architect's inventing representational images
adequate to the content of "the new world," but rather of
producing the content of that world through an *Umfunk-
tionierung,* or refunctionalization, of existing forms and a
reorganization of the perceptual conventions by which the

**Hannes Meyer, Petersschule project, Basel,
1927, perspective.**

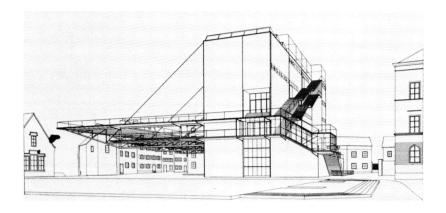

object is apprehended. In readying itself for travel the Petersschule must take on certain seemingly negative and reified characteristics of the very condition it seeks to transform, as well as of the ideologies and institutions that, incompletely liquidated, still survive from older modes of production it seeks to leave behind. The building turns to the existing social and physical context for its raw material but chooses forms of interruption. Its dissonance is to that extent mimetic. What this will mean in the Petersschule, not unlike in the Co-op Vitrine, is a paradoxical and disjunctive imbrication of different architectural modes. First are modernist autotelic formal strategies, previously worked out as critical negations of traditional, institutionalized perceptual conventions. Second are techniques of a different functionalist or utilitarian kind that involve an assault on the modernist notion of aesthetic autonomy, even as a strategy of resistance, and imply an instrumentalization of the architectural object now indistinguishable from an industrial tool.

As we have seen, Meyer's Freidorf experience should be understood to stand behind his Co-op work, and so for the Petersschule as well. After 1900 a number of progressive architects turned to a rationalized, mensurable, artless, and practical architecture that attempted to synthesize and maintain the best of English and German domestic building traditions. For Meyer it was this same architecture, conjoined with the reformist planning of the garden city movement, that seemed to best accommodate and represent the cooperative life at Freidorf. Within this mode, the buildings of the Siedlung are configured as *Zellenbauten,* their monumentality dissolved by a celluar structure repeated throughout. Meyer's own description of the project is sufficient. As well as the garden city model of planning, Freidorf was based on Palladian proportional systems. In 1916 Meyer had

used my free time to draw all Palladio's plans on thirty standard sheets of paper (size 420/594) in common scale. This work on Pal-

Hannes Meyer, Siedlung Freidorf, near Basel, 1919–1921, aerial view from the northwest.

ladio prompted me to design my first housing scheme, the Freidorf estate, on the modular system of an architectural order. By means of this system all the external spaces . . . and all public internal spaces . . . were laid out in an artistic pattern *which would be perceived by those living there as the spatial harmony of proportion.*[3]

The conception of form here as "applied psychology"[4] reconfirms the beginning of Meyer's trajectory toward the radicalization of perception. Proportional harmony for Meyer is the architecturalization of the harmony of socialism (a compositional harmony to be replaced in his subsequent work with a "constructed" asymmetry and modularity which "symbolizes nothing").[5] Likewise the Siedlung's red color, what Adolf Behne called a "symphony in red,"[6] stands as a symbol of Freidorf's leftward-leaning social commitments. Already in this early project the architecture is perceived as an instrument of collective perceptual change. The standardization and serialization of the Palladian system evacuates the traditional, *Heimat* denotations of the buildings and attempts to reinstall a different sort of collectivity. Meyer continues his description:

All the building elements used at Freidorf were standardized and these standard elements conferred a certain unity upon each type of house. At the start there were no Swiss standards for building with standardized elements and in this important field of house building we had to start from scratch. It was in this way that Freidorf standards came into being: dimensions, shapes and materials for framing timbers, mouldings and balusters, for four types of window and three types of door, the house entrance, staircase and verandah, central stove and animal hutches. Although the co-operators no doubt appreciated the economic aspects of this standardization, it mostly ran counter to their sense of beauty. In regard to architectural simplification, the Freidorf standards go to the utmost limits of what the individualistic Swiss will tolerate in matters of taste and any further paring away of "architecture" will be branded as "prison and barrack" building and meet with an almost unbroken front of public resistance. . . . Both inside and outside [the cooperative hall] has yielded to the law of uniformity governing the estate and only the double scale on which everything is built marks the public building. Man looks small once he enters the temple of the community. Even the layman, faced with the interplay of wall surfaces and window apertures, becomes dimly aware of the influence of an all-dominating module.[7]

The function of Meyer's repetitive module is to inscribe across the architecture the reiterative, serial building system of a collective society, to unfold architecture into the exteriority of mass technology and standardization that would be more aggressively presented in the Petersschule and the League of Nations projects.

But the homogeneous "spatial harmony" of Freidorf was inadequate for Meyer's subsequent tasks. As Adorno has taught us, in issues of modernity,

aesthetic harmony is never fully attained; it is either superficial polish or temporary balance. Inside everything that can justly be

called harmonious in art there are vestiges of despair and antagonism. Art works are said to dissolve all that is heterogeneous to
form; in fact, however, they are form only in relation to what they
seek to eliminate. . . . Without this reminder, without contradiction and non-identity, harmony would be irrelevant aesthetically. . . . Dissonance is the truth about harmony.[8]

By 1926 Meyer had questioned and inverted the tradition on
which his Siedlung was based as a viable mode of revolutionary and transformatory signification, renouncing Freidorf as the "product of an incomprehensible time."[9] In the
Petersschule, the fundamental harmonizing principles of
the Siedlung Freidorf are exploded by modernity and the
machine, its nonidentity with its physical and social sur-
roundings asserted, with dissonance as the result. Again
Adorno is helpful: "the immanent dynamic of autonomous
works of art and the growing power of external reality over
the subject converge in dissonance."[10]

Meyer's studies and trav-
els during 1921–1925 in Germany, France, Belgium, Hol-

**Hannes Meyer, Co-op Linocut (abstract
architecture), 1925: diagram of the entrance hall of
the communal building at Freidorf.**

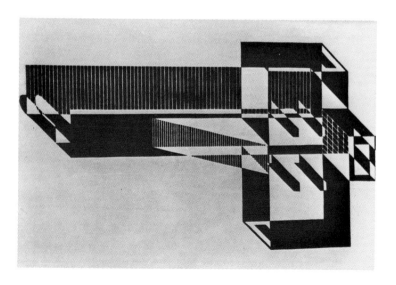

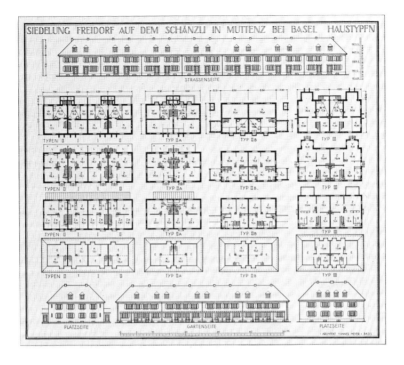

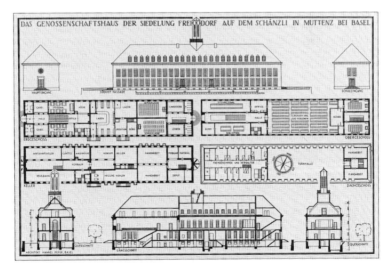

Meyer, Siedlung Freidorf, house types: plans and elevations.

Meyer, Siedlung Freidorf, communal building: plans, elevations, and sections.

between avant-garde and instrumentalization

land, Scandinavia, and Finland[11] acquainted him with various avant-garde movements and the most progressive elementarist, constructivist, and productivist theories in Europe and the Soviet Union, which, in their attempt to link artistic activity directly to material-social production, also voiced an optimism concerning the revolutionary powers of mechanization, Taylorism, and the Americanization of culture. By the time Meyer began the Petersschule project, the standardization and machine production of buildings and building components and the correspondingly changed role of art was a well-rehearsed topic, but still one of intense ambiguity and irresolution. Indeed, within the Soviet context, theorists like Boris Arvatov and Sergei Tretyakov strove for a materialist definition of art practice that challenged the premises of bourgeois aesthetics, but also implicitly those of Leninist aesthetics as well. What links bourgeois and Leninist conceptions of art is the emphasis on an ontological and epistemological independence of artistic values, an artistic consciousness that is a subjectively reflected and passive repository for finished products of thought. When Arvatov denounced "easel art"—art as a supplementation and sublimation of a disharmonized reality—and when he called for art not as something autonomous and self-contained but rather as a desublimated destruction of the division between artistic technique and social technology in order to help build an international workers' state—"the possibility of using a mighty and all-enveloping technology consciously to create and build [society's] life"[12]—he directly challenged bourgeois avant-gardism *and* socialist realism. For socialist realism, rather than a project for an emergent new life, amounts to a communicable duplicate or replica of preestablished modes of knowing and being through preestablished modes of representation, a reflection of the myth of harmony between the state and the proletariat at a moment when their interests were, in fact, divergent.

Herein, too, lies the ambiguity of the work of the two figures who were most influential in Meyer's development, El Lissitzky and Le Corbusier, and their attitudes toward machine technology and the immanent principles of artistic construction. Between 1921 and 1926 Lissitzky, presumed to be doing aboveground work for an international constructivism, was at the same time adjusting his position in adequation of emergent Leninist directives for art and its audience after the New Economic Policy[13] in ways that were parallel (though certainly not equivalent) to ongoing socialist realist experiments. Lissitzky's 1924 declaration—"We have had *enough* of perpetually hearing MACHINE, MACHINE, MACHINE, when it comes to modern art production. The machine is no more than a brush, and a very primitive one at that, which portrays a view of life on the canvas"[14]—places the emblematic brush in the inverse position of Arvatov's productivist equation of the same year between artistic method and the general industrial processes—"The specific instrument of aesthetic painting, the brush, plays an increasingly small role in art; it is supplanted by planes, files, emery paper, drills, etc."[15] In 1926 Lissitzky theorized contemporary art explicitly in terms of the historically specific needs of audience and patron and methods of distribution (through posters and books) rather than mechanical production: "It is shortsighted to suppose that machines, i.e., the displacement of manual by mechanical processes, are basic to the development of the form and the figure of the artifact. In the first place it is the consumers' demand that determines the development, i.e., the demand of the social strata that provide 'commissions.' Today this is not a narrow circle anymore, a thin cream, but everybody, the masses."[16] But already in 1922, without sacrificing the autonomy and self-referentiality of a thoroughly modern art form, Lissitzky employed the methods of photomontage to reintroduce into his Veshchist work new sources and strategies for iconic representation consistent with the desire to reach a new mass audience whom strictly modernist abstract art had failed to engage.[17] And by 1927, as Benjamin Buchloh has articulated, he had shifted from photomontage to the factographic practices in which "homogeneity in the single print is favored over fragmentation, iconic representation of an absent referent is favored over the indexical materiality of the trace of a verifiable process, tactility of the construction of incoherent surfaces and spatial references is exchanged for the monumentality of the camera-angle's awesome visions and the technological media optimism that it conveys,"[18] in order to further his engagement of the needs of a particular social group.

It is in the effort to shift the address of their aesthetic constructions toward the demands of mass consumers that the work of Lissitzky and Meyer converges. But the particular spatial strategies of their constructions differ rather precisely according to their different contextual intentions: to align with a period of reconstruction and affirmational representation after the New Economic Policy in the Soviet Union, in the case of Lissitzky, or to generate anticipatory forms of socialized visual consumption in the absence of a realized western socialism, in the case of Meyer.[19]

Lissitzky's depiction of a reconciled art and life in his Proun paintings of the 1920s— his "half-way station between architecture in painting"—is accomplished through a rather rarefied mode of sublation: his pieces of the world have been transfigured into thoroughly special, uncommon, abstracted meanings, saturated with the mystical, transcendental aspirations of suprematism. The remoteness of his practice is captured by Ernst Kallai: "The man of the future, liberated from social anarchy and the dark ferment of psychosis . . . is today still a beginning, a single cell, simple, elementary, but with definite possibilities of future heroic realization. For this very reason, however, *in no case must he become entangled in the net of contradictory, impure relationships of the present, with its tattered and mediocre reality.*"[20] In the transcendental space of the Prouns, the last contingencies of raw materiality and circumstantiality are absorbed into forms built up stereometrically from dematerialized planes intersecting along an imaginary, generative armature. In other works, with the insertion of figures and iconic elements into this preestablished spatial structure—as in his 1922 illustrations for Ilya Ehrenburg's *Six Tales with Easy Endings*—the surface tension of the Proun is relaxed in favor of a kind of pictorial space into which we can enter: a space apart from life, a space in which the mind is free to make its own connections, to dream of the new world to emerge fom the final denouement of the revolution, to escape from the "contradictory and impure" present, to be suspended between the contaminated real and the disinfected unreal.[21] This shift in Lissitzky's work was legitimate in the context of Lenin's New Economic Policy, which called for a more reconstructive, affirmative representation of cultural continuity and psychological gratification. Though he could agree with Lissitzky's dictum that the mission of art "is not, after all, to embellish life but to organize it,"[22] Meyer, at this point in the trajectory of his own Co-op work, still sought to conjoin aesthetic and technical logics and *force* new logics of mass perception by restricting and selecting his tools and materials—linocuts, photographs, "mechanized paintings,"[23] and simple assemblages—in order to maintain a causal or indexical relationship between sign and procedure, to have the aesthetic signs be understood as traces of production procedures, to enact the eventuality of socialized production. And so, whatever lessons he may have learned from Lissitzky were redirected toward constructions that still manifest the tactility of construction, mechanical quality, and indexical materiality that Lissitzky by 1927 had abandoned.

Consider, for example, Meyer's Co-op Construction of 1926, itself a kind of station on the way to architecture, the only example of Meyer's own work published in *ABC* 2, which he edited.[24] With its striated space, rectangular planes, diagonal placement within its frame, geometrical purity, and emphasis on visual layering and transparency as indexical potentials of photography, it resembles in its formal organization nothing so much as one of Lissitzky's Prouns or Moholy-Nagy's photograms. But in the context of Meyer's Co-op work (the title "Co-op Construction" is not unimportant), the piece takes on another signification. The glass fragments are unworked, they are palpably glass, they do not consent to a purely visual apprehension but, in their unmediated juxtaposition of material fragment to fragment, tend toward factural and technical construction. More important, the white ovoid is, after all, an *egg* that, beyond its geometrical purity, tends toward an identification with the alimentary products of cooperative societies like Freidorf and the utopian modes of production, distribution, and consumption they anticipate. As Jacques Gubler has written, "the co-op egg of 1926 is consumable, not by way of the oneiric, not in the sense of surrealism, but rather by way of the oral."[25] And, indeed, the work does send out such tracers into metaphor even though that single metaphorical frame cannot contain it. For the alimentary aspect, the metaphor, of the egg is just as surely canceled by the fact that the construction is *made out of* an egg and then photographed; it is assembled from selected pieces, not painted or carved, which links the activity of sign production to the activity of work,[26] and it is distributed in a journal, which links it to available techniques of simultaneous collective reception. A mechanically

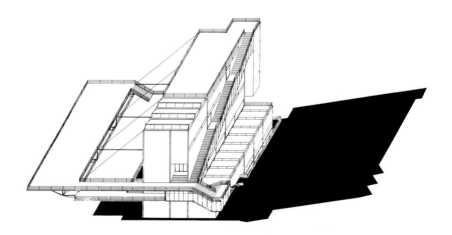

W. BAUMEISTER, Mauerbild, 1924.

CO-OP. Construction 1926/I.

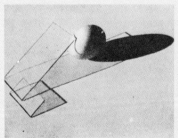

Meyer, Petersschule project, 1927, axonometric.

Title page of *ABC* series 2, no. 2, showing (lower left) Meyer's Co-op Construction I, 1926.

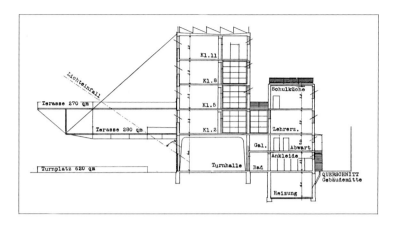

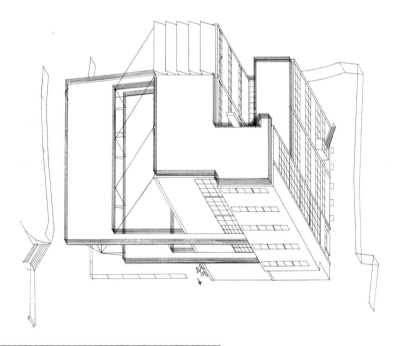

**Hannes Meyer, Petersschule, competition
project, 1926, section, axonometric.**

reproduced image of a biologically reproduced product, its object quality intensified by the juxtaposition with glass in light: what we as viewers do with this piece must, then, inevitably oscillate between our metaphor-making habits and the blockage of metaphor by the sheer perceptual facts. The construction and distribution of the object begins to enter the process of collective-cooperative organization directed toward the socialization of all objects of consumption and use—a kind of visual Esperanto—but to enter through the door of the aesthetic. In this doubled signficance, formal and constructive, visual and factural, the Co-op Construction stands between the experiments of the avant-garde and an altogether different instrument of social-perceptual change. To locate Meyer's work in this space in between is to grasp the structure of Meyer's sign system as a ceaseless self-production: not as a form that "embodies" a content, an essence, somehow poured into it, but form as constitutive of a content not otherwise available.

Meanwhile, between 1920 and 1922 within the discourse of *L'Esprit Nouveau,* Le Corbusier had developed the Maison Citrohan, a standardized house constructed of a monolithic concrete frame, comprising a simple volumetric unit with a single major light source, a roof terrace, an exterior stair, and, in a version raised on pilotis, a balcony wrapping around its volume. As the name indicates, the Maison Citrohan was emblematic of an entire ethos of building now standardized and mass-produced like a car. And it can stand along with Lissitzky's 1925 "Wolkenbügelhochhaus" ("cloudhanger high rise") for Moscow and a 1922 Vkhutemas project from N. A. Ladovsky's studio for a restaurant suspended from a cliff over the sea (published in *ABC* in 1925)[27] as a primary predecessor of the Petersschule, in terms of both its volumetric typology and its emblematic status as a reproducible unit.[28] The first competition project for the Petersschule is structured on an "undressed, standardized concrete" framework with eight columns and roof terraces, possibly a transformation of the Maison Citrohan's structure. And the

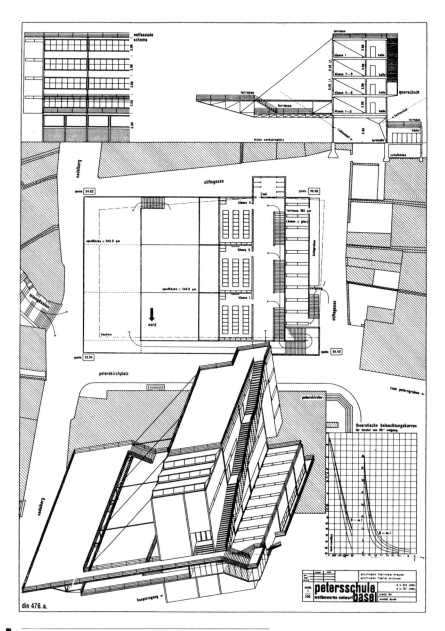

Meyer, Petersschule project, 1927, montage of elevation, section, plan, and axonometric.

balcony of Maison Citrohan, wrapping around the basic volumetric unit, is exaggerated in the Petersschule to become the suspended platforms for the play area. Alternatively, the volumetric unit of the Petersschule can be seen as an analogue to the reiterative volumes of the restaurant suspended from a cliff or of Lissitzky's "cloud hanger," and the various attachments of suspended platforms, walkways, and stairs as techno-psychological expedients—appropriated industrial components organized in terms of utility and intensified visual effect, increasing the building's use value and accommodating it to the particulars of its site.

Concerning hierarchies of production among art, architecture, and other technical and cultural practices, however, Meyer departs from Le Corbusier's research. While Le Corbusier maintained a distinction between the practical-technical role of the engineer and the artistic-poetic role of the architect in order to preserve the humanist autonomy of the latter, Meyer sought to eliminate traditionally conceived art altogether in favor of pure technique and the technical organization of a building in a collaborative enterprise. Thus to Le Corbusier's "engineering on the one hand, architecture on the other,"[29] Meyer would reply, "The new building is a prefabricated unit for site assembly and, as such, an industrial product and a work of specialists: economists, statisticians, hygienists, climatologists, industrial engineers, standards experts, heat engineers . . . and the architect? He was an artist and has become a specialist in organization!"[30] As in similar pronouncements by Soviet productivists, the term "specialist" here carries a paradoxical repudiation of the individuation of the artist separate from other kinds of workers, and thereby articulates a sense of sublation of art and life divergent from that of both Le Corbusier and Lissitzky.

In a rudimentary sense, Meyer's conception of the mechanization of building, already enunciated in the Co-op work considered earlier, is summarized in the manifesto "ABC fordert die Diktatur der Maschine," published by Mart Stam and Hans Schmidt in

ABC. It will be helpful in advancing the present argument to compare this summary to Le Corbusier's position.

The machine is neither the coming paradise in which technology will fulfill all our wishes—nor the approaching hell in which all human development will be destroyed

                      The machine is nothing more than the inexorable dictator of the possibilities and tasks common to all our lives. But we are still in a state of becoming, of transition. The machine has become the servant of bourgeois individualist culture born of the Renaissance. Just as the servant is paid and despised by the same master, so the machine is simultaneously used by the citizen and damned by his intellectual court, his artists, scholars and philosophers. The machine is not a servant, however, but a dictator—it dictates how we are to think and what we have to understand. As leader of the masses, who are inescapably bound up with it, it demands more insistently every year the transformation of our economy, our culture. . . .

                      We have taken the first step: the transition from an individualistically producing society held together *ideally* by the concepts of the national State and a racially delimited religious outlook, to a capitalistically producing

Vkhutemas (N. A. Ladovsky's studio), project for a restaurant suspended from a cliff over the sea, 1922–1923.

El Lissitzky, Wolkenbügelhochhaus project for Moscow, 1925.

Le Corbusier, Maison Citrohan, 1922.

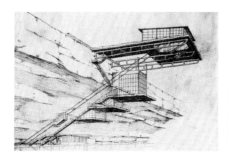

society *materially* organized in response to the need for industrialization and the international exchange of goods. . . .

*We have to take the second
step:* the transition from a society that is *compelled* to produce
collectively but is still individualistically oriented to a society that
consciously thinks and works collectively. Empty phrases? Empty
phrases to the ears of bourgeois armchair sceptics—implacable
necessity to the masses who have today been thrust out to to the
edge of survival.[31]

In contrast to this link-
ing of machine technology to the capitalist mode of production in terms of *how* the technology is used and to whose
advantage, foregrounding capitalism's emancipatory possibilities from the vantage of their fuller realization in the posthumanist future and thereby demanding a corresponding
and historically inevitable transformation of artistic institutions, Le Corbusier saw the consequences of mechanization
primarily in received humanist terms of hierarchy, affect,
and the maintenance of distinctions. For instance, in his
L'Art décoratif d'aujourd'hui of 1925, he offered a selection
of photographs of a turbine, ship propellers, and a light
house beacon[32] as an "apology for what is simply banal,
indifferent, or void of artistic intention." Yet at the same
time he could compare the evocations of these modern
machines to the most primitive and powerful of emotions.

He was thunderstruck by a turbine of which he could see no more
than the envelope, though he could hear its fearsome roar, because

he knew that as a result of this noise, something would now run along those wires, those cables, and bring light and energy to the furthest corners of the country, and death to those who touched them. This light-house beacon by Sauter-Harlé, standing as pure as a negro god, sent out a beam of intense light over fabulous distances on stormy nights at sea. . . . Everything overwhelmed him, even the astonishing taste shown in the colors used by engineers to finish off their products.[33]

Le Corbusier's is a poignant struggle to reconcile the fact of machine technology, the signs of industry, their representation and rearrangement in photographs, advertisements, paintings, and buildings, with the inexorable desire for contemporary objects with all the auratic power of a primitive totem. A theme throughout *L'Esprit Nouveau* is the tension between the values of industrialization and those required to practice his classically conceived art, between standardized mass culture and the traditional conception of the auratic object, or to put it another way, between the lighthouse beacon and the "negro god." Moreover, Le Corbusier's is an effort to distinguish and uphold the continuity of the cult of genius with respect to a humanistically conceived tradition of art. "We have to pass judgment: The Sistine Chapel first, then chairs and file cabinets—to tell the truth, problems of a second order, as the cut of a man's suit is a second-order problem in his life. Hierarchy. First the Sistine Chapel, that is, works where passion is inscribed. Then, machines for sitting, for classifying, for illuminating, *machine-types*, problems of purification, of cleanliness."[34]

It is precisely Meyer's refusal of such a reconciliation, his reversal of the hierarchy of "art" and techniques of mass production, that has routinely offended his critics. "Die neue Welt" announces:

Art has an undisputed right to exist provided the speculative spirit of mankind has need of it after the graphic-colored, plastic-constructive, musical-kinetic overthrow of its philosophy of life. . . . The artist's studio has become a scientific and technical laboratory. . . . The new work of art is for all, not a collector's piece or the privilege of a single individual. . . . Dead is the work of art as a "thing in itself," as "art for art's sake.". . . And personality? The heart?? The soul??? Our plea is for absolute segregation.[35]

Meyer's ruthless denunciation of art has been seen by critics as a naive empirico-critical positivism, an instrumentalization of architecture that implicates his work in a purely technocratic and administrative economy. But accusations based on his subordination of aesthetic autonomy to positivist instrumentality ignore, for one thing, that authorial autonomy and artistic purity was being progressively dismantled by dadaism after 1913 and by Soviet constructivism and productivism right up until the time of Meyer's own work. The technological, social, and political changes that conditioned that dismantling, and the blocking of certain kinds of aesthetic apprehension that resulted, constitute a historically irreversible reality to which Meyer was sensitive. What Meyer called his "first research into the meaning of the 'scientification' (*Verwissenschaftlichung*) of architecture,"[36] the design of the Petersschule, should not be understood as a matter of autonomous technology overtaking design but rather the contrary, of design piloting technology and deciding how architectural practice must correspondingly be transformed. Meyer recognized that industrial production is not wedded to the social relations that engendered it; it could be brought into service for other forms of society. And indeed, design could precipitate them.

Meyer would later elaborate his conception of a changed design practice in an essay, "Wie ich arbeite," published in *Architektura CCCP* in 1933.[37] In the essay Meyer stresses design as collaborative work and emphasizes how objectivity and rigid standardization—of building components, of functional spaces, of drawing formats (in the "tersely standardized form" of DIN or OCT standards, or in axonometrics showing the elements of the building in measurable relationships and "mercilessly" exposing errors of judgment)—inexorably evacuate the individual authorial subject. And in his "Über marxistische

Raoul Hausmann, *Les Ingénieurs*, 1920.

Architektur" of 1931, he further asserts thirteen points of socialist architecture, including the following:

5. The ABCs of socialist architecture in a planned economy are composed of norms, types and standards. We normalize dimensional requirements to typical space and typical equipment. We organize these typical elements as standard organic building entities for the socialist praxis of life [*socialistische Lebenpraxis*].

6. As the socialist planned economy materializes in the sphere of building, the steady diminution of the multiplicity of standard elements (equipment, building parts, spaces) is an indication of the steady socialization of mass life [*Massenlebens*]. . . .

11. In line with the Marxist maxim that "being determines consciousness" the socialist building is a factor in mass psychology. Hence cities and their building components must be organized psychologically in keeping with the findings of a science in which psychology is kept constantly in the foreground. The individual pretensions to perceptions [*Empfindungsansprüche*] of the artist-architect must not be allowed to determine the psychological effect of the building. The elements in a building that have a telling psy-

chological effect (poster area, loudspeaker, light dispenser, staircase, color, etc.) must be organically integrated so as to accord with our most profound insights into the laws of perception. . . .

13. For [the Marxist architect] architecture is not an aesthetic stimulus but a keen edged weapon in the class struggle.[38]

So the point of the technical reproducibility and standardization in the Petersschule, and the foregrounding of their effects, is not only a technical one. The insistence on design as technique rather than inspired creation, the conception of architecture as an industrial product, in short, the disenfranchisement of the humanist demiurge to which both Lissitzky and Le Corbusier still clung, hollows out the imaginary plenitude of artistic creation and deconstructs the work of architecture into its material determinants and the social conditions of its making. The building *just is* these determinants and conditions. It is in this sense that the architecture tries to disappear, to become an aleatory effect.

Much depends, therefore, on technique. In the statement accompanying the 1926 competition project, Meyer asserts that "the classroom, the decked and undecked play areas, and the toilets are the inseparable constructive units (cells) of the school building."[39] And, indeed, a vertical block of toilets together with the stairways, a block of classrooms, the suspended play decks, and a lower block of ancillary functions constitute the basic configuration of the building. The toilet block, emblem of hygiene, is attached to the classrooms. Each classroom floor has direct access to its own play deck—the first and second floors (above ground) are connected by gangways to the suspended decks; the third floor opens directly onto a lower roof terrace; the fourth floor is connected by an outdoor stair to the upper roof terrace. The gymnasium opens onto a ground-level recreational space. The suspended decks are held away from the classroom block by a dimension determined by the angle of light penetrating into the gymnasium and onto the playground. The entire arrangement of the basic units in this competition project can be

explained in terms of the maximization of the area for outdoor recreation and the amount of light penetrating into the
building, these coupled with the methods of its technical
construction.

Technique normally
functions in architectural design as a way of gathering up
utilitarian and material demands into a significant order of
individual intention, into a style. Perhaps this is especially
so in modernism (Le Corbusier is an obvious example),
where a particular technique gives formal consistency and
unity to industrialized building processes, allowing us to see
the content or intention behind the built work or drawn
project. But technique in the case of the Petersschule is
more a matter of diagramming potentials for occupation
(spaces of learning and play) than embodying individual will
to form. *Scientification.* Desired conditions are stated in the
work and the signs of making are present to be sure, but the
technique itself disqualifies certain architectural skills of
composition, expressivity, and transfiguration that are the
marks of a single maker. The desired conditions are, first,
Pestalozzian sociocorporal ones: "The goal: No commanded
study but rather experienced knowledge! No deformity of
the spine but rather hygiene! No school cripples but rather
vital youth!" The architectural inscription of light and
movement in the configuration of the decks and terraces for
outdoor recreation is the sign of these desires. Second is a
related urbanistic desire. The competition project was
submitted under the "motto: compromise," the signal of
Meyer's belief that the constrained building site assigned by
the competition was "absolutely unfit for a contemporary
school."[40] And the revised version of the Petersschule for
publication in the journal *Bauhaus* has the effect of refunctioning the sectional workings of the city, designating automobile parking on the street level and cellular rooms with
corresponding *Freiflächen* or open decks above. In a sarcas-
tic, boldfaced conclusion to his explanation of the project—
"HOCH DIE DENKMALPFLEGE!" ("Cheers to the preserva-

tionists!")—Meyer implied that it would not be an unhappy consequence of the adventitious insertion of the new Petersschule if the surrounding old environment were allowed to wither away.

This is nothing less, I would suggest, than Bloch's utopian desire to disorganize. Like a prosthetic apparatus for a crippled and crippling city unable to function adequately on its own, the Petersschule organizes its elements in such a way as to reveal the present order as unsatisfactory, physically and socially, and to propose an antisocial response as a possible way out: the Petersschule would like to disappear, to leave the old city behind. Short of that, it *produces the concrete effects* of what the city lacks. Like a prosthetic device that is both the mark of and compromised solution to a debilitation, the Petersschule produces a *significant absence,* that is to say an absence that it at the same time *represents.* In contrast to the hermetic "silence" of the architectural sign, purified and reduced to its presumed "essence"—from Lissitzky's Prouns, to Le Corbusier's purism, to de Stijl or Mies's wall-as-an-independent-principle, all produced in an effort to salvage a degree of artistic resistance and independent value over against an ever-encroaching commodified and instrumentalized world—the Petersschule presents the building as a reorganization of the very "thingified," *sachlich* components and materials of the everyday world. *An architecture of non-consent,* the effect of which is estrangement, and absences of different sorts—absence of finish or refinement or closure, absence of the self-identity and independent value of the visual sign, absence of the subjective interiority of creator or viewer, absence of determinate meaning, absence of emotive depth and the myth of plenitude. Out of these absences comes the recognition that what had seemed, within conceptions of "architecture-as-such," essentially natural and given is in fact historically and socially produced, and therefore open to radical transformation. As Terry Eagleton has written,

The socialist revolution will take its poetry from the future, and since the future, much more palpably than the past, does not exist, this is as much as to say that it takes its poetry from absence. For it seems to me that the "future" of which Marx's text speaks here is not to be grasped as a utopian model to which the present must be conformed—not, in short, as a positivity—but is rather nothing less than the space into which the thrust of socialist transformation ceaselessly projects itself, the space created by that thrust.[41]

With the Petersschule the word *materialism*—understood as a productivist relation to the mode of production as well as a mere obsession with the stuff of building—imposes more than suggests itself. But we must extract the term from its primarily positivist and deterministic associations and continue to insist on its constitutive dimension, its projective force. Meyer's materialism is, for one thing, an attempt conceptually to overcome the division of labor.

The nine muses were long ago abducted by practical men and have stepped down again into life from their high pedestals, more humdrum and more reasonable. Their fields have been expropriated, confused and blurred. The boundaries between painting, mathematics and music can no longer be defined; and between sound and color there is only the gradual difference of oscillatory frequency. The depreciation of all works of art is indisputable, and there can be no question that the continued utilization of new and exact knowledge in their place is merely a matter of time.[42]

As we have seen, within Meyer's epistemology, knowing and acting are both practices and both forms of production; how we can know the world is thought together with how we can change the world. And the denunciation of art is itself a means of erasing boundaries between sociocultural fields, annulling the separation between physical and mental activity, negating the distinction between worker and intellectual, and refusing the division of labor that is fundamental to bourgeois society.

But materialism is also, as I have suggested, aesthetic pleasure in its own right. In his essay "bauen" of 1928, Meyer would repeat and expand a list of materials, first announced in "Die neue Welt," now spaced out on the page so that even the graphic materiality of the words themselves could not be missed.

ferroconcrete	wire glass	aluminum
synthetic rubber	cork composition	euböolith
synthetic leather	synthetic resin	plywood
foam concrete	synthetic horn	gum elastic
wood's metal	synthetic wood	torfoleum
silicon steel	ripolin	asbestos
cold glue	viscose	acetone
cellular concrete	eternit	casein
rolled glass	goudron	trolit
xelotekt	canvas	tombak

we organize these building materials on economic principles into a constructive whole. thus the individual shape, the body of the structure, the color of the material and the texture of the surface come automatically into being and are determined by life.[43]

The Petersschule is an assemblage of just such materials whose qualities, tough and impersonal, "come automatically into being."

The building is built on a steel framework resting on only 8 columns and with outside walls of this section: facing of chequered aluminum sheet—pumice concrete slabs—air space—kieselguhr slabs—air space—polished Eternit sheets. Fitting out [bautechnische Ausstattung]: steel framed hopper-type windows, aluminum sheet doors, steel furniture, halls and stairs covered with rubber flooring.[44]

By conferring specific forms on its materials—by purging materials of all mythical, auratic, transcendental meaning—the Petersschule uses them as a rhetorical form analogous to propaganda. Whereas one ordinarily would expect some overarching, unifying spatial or formal system that would give a fullness and presence to the various building components and materials, the Petersschule disenfranchises the compositional and the visual as dominant categories of architectural constitution. Previous hierarchies governed by the distinction of art from objects of everday use are now dissolved by the formative principles and categories of machine production. Volumetric components are conceived in functional terms—simple adjacencies grouped according to use—which, if not completely independent of visual affect, at the very least complicate the effect. And "elements that have a telling psychological effect," according to Meyer, such as the stairs, walkways, and suspended platforms, are standardized or confiscated like so many found elements, and affixed or grafted onto the basic unit of the building. All of which operates to negate the relational compositional strategies identified with traditional art of human facture, and to substitute things untouched by personality. Each material is experienced *as such* and as infiltrating our everyday lives with the new concrete effects of the industrial image landscape and social field; *no distinction can be made between the content and its expression.* A provocative way of describing the Petersschule is suggested by Gilles Deleuze's "abstract machine," which he defines as "the aspect or moment at which nothing but functions and matters remain."

A true abstract machine has no way of making a distinction within itself between a plane of expression and a plane of content because it draws a single plane of consistency, which in turn formalizes contents and expressions according to strata and deterritorializations. The abstract machine in itself is destratified, deterritorialized; it has no form of its own (much less substance) and makes no distinction within itself between content and expression, even though outside itself it presides over that distinction and distributes it in strata, domains, and territories. An abstract machine in itself is not physical or corporeal, any more than it is semiotic; it is *diagrammatic.* . . . It operates by *matter,* not by substance; by *function,* not by form. Substances and forms are of expression "or" of content. But functions are not yet "semiotically" formed, and matters are not yet "physically" formed. The abstract machine is pure Matter-Function—a diagram independent of the forms and substances, expressions and contents it will distribute.[45]

The format of Meyer's presentation of the Petersschule project as published in *Bauhaus* should be taken for what it is: almost three-quarters of the single-page layout is devoted to diagrams and calculations; the "building itself"—its form, its substance—is only one component of the total architectural apparatus that includes these diagrams. Taking the format seriously means not only seeing it as propaganda but understanding the building itself as an instrument, a concrete instance of the diagram, part of a larger machine for the production of the desired effects of light, occupation, and sensuous experience. "The diagram acts as a non-unifying immanent cause that is coextensive with the whole social field: the abstract machine is like the cause of the concrete assemblages that execute its relations; and these relations between forces take place 'not above' but within the very tissue of the assemblages they produce."[46]

Space itself in the Petersschule is made material and temporal: we apprehend it only as we traverse it; the space is a product of the disjunctive building parts and materials, the way in which they are used, and the time in which we encounter them. Whereas humanism, in its ceaseless effort to fill the void between ourselves and the world, forever finds ways to convert things into their forms, into names, into totems, Meyer intensifies the raw materiality of the thing—the glaring brightness, the hardness, the smell, the taste—and thrusts the experience of that thing, previously indifferent and unimaginably external, toward the subject with unpadded harshness. His materialism emphasizes the heterogeneous properties of things and their effects in real space and real time, and induces a play of sensuous energies in the viewer, a compulsive pleasure taken in the quiddity of the building

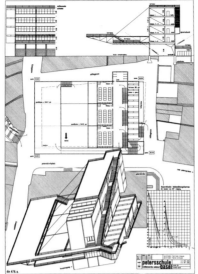

die 476. k.

architekt hannes meyer basel/bauhaus-dessau
architekt hans wittwer basel

die petersschule basel
(wettbewerbsentwurf **1926**)

die aufgabe:

neubau einer 11 klassigen mädchen-volksschule mit turnhalle, zeichensaal, schulbad und suppenküche etc., 528 schülerinnen. sinnwidriger traditioneller schulhaus-bauplatz im altstadtgebiet von basel, im schatten hoher randbebauung, schlecht belüftet und im hinblick auf das umfangreiche bauprogramm mit 1240.0 qm gesamtfläche erheblich zu klein. übliche überbauung ergäbe max. 500 qm schulhof, mithin 1.0 qm turnmehfläche pro schulkind.

das ziel:

keine schulkrüppel! anzustreben wäre ausschließliche oberlichtbeleuchtung aller schulräume (vergleiche die resultate von fall 1 und 2 der beleuchtungsberechnung) und die bestimmung eines neuen baugeländes nach maßgabe planvoller stadtentwicklung. gegenwärtig erscheint die verwirklichung solcher forderungen aussichtslos, und es ergibt die auseinandersetzung mit dem alten schulhaus den umstehenden kompromiß.

der vorschlag:

größtmögliche entfernung des schulbetriebes von der erdoberfläche in die besonnte, durchlüftete und belichtete höhenlage.

im erdgeschoß nur schulbad und turnbetrieb im geschlossenen raum. die verbleibende höffläche wird dem öffentlichen verkehr und dem „parking" freigegeben.

an stelle eines hofes sind 2 hängende freiflächen und alle oberflächen des gebäudekörpers der jugend als tummelplatz zugewiesen, im ganzen 1250 qm sonnige spielfläche, der altstadt entrückt.

freitreppe und verglaste treppe verbinden, parallel geführt, spielflächen und innenräume.

das eigengewicht des hauskörpers ist nutzbar verwendet und trägt an 4 drahtseilen der stützenlose eisenkonstruktion der 2 schwebenden freiflächen.

die gebäudekonstruktion als eisenfachwerkbau auf nur 8 stützen und mit diesem außenwand-querschnitt: aluminiumriffelblechverkleidung — bimsbetonplatten — luftlamelle — kieselgurplatten — luftlamelle — glanzeternitplatten.

bautechnische ausstattung: eiserne kippfenster, aluminiumblechtüren, stahlmöbel, flure und treppen mit gummibodenbelag.

rechnerischer nachweis der beleuchtungsstärke aller schulräume

fall **1**) östliches seitenlicht aller klassenzimmer.
fall **2**) shed-oberlicht des zeichensaales.
fall **3**) zweiseitiges seitenlicht der turnhalle.

berechnung der beleuchtungsstärke auf tischhöhe

fall **1**) klassenzimmer mit senkrechter fensterwand. (östliches seitenlicht.)

berechnet wird nur die beleuchtungsstärke für den ungünstigsten arbeitsplatz (P), dieser befindet sich in der vom fenster entferntesten reihe an der rückwand.

berechnungsverfahren nach higbie:

daten für die formel:
abstand des punktes P vom fenster .... $a = 5,1$ „
länge des fensters .... $m = 10,2$ „
abstand des oberen fensterrandes von der tischfläche .... $f = 2,4$ „
„ „ unteren „ „ „ „ .... $f' = -$ „
beleuchtungsstärke des fensters .... $b = 100,0$ ftcdl.

$$E_P = 50 \left[tg^{-1}\frac{(10,2)}{5,1} \cdot \frac{5,1}{\sqrt{5,1^2+2,4^2}} \cdot tg^{-1}\left(\frac{10,2}{5,1^2+2,4^2}\right) \right] = 486,0 \text{ lx.}$$

$$E_P' = 50 \left[tg^{-1}\frac{(10,2)}{5,1} - tg^{-1}\frac{(10,2)}{5,1^2} \right] = 435,0 \text{ lx.}$$

beleuchtungsstärke im punkte $P = E_P - E_P' = 41,0$ lx
(12 hefner-lux $^{-1}$ lx $^{-1}$ = 1 footcandle).

lichtverlust durch gegenüberliegende gebäude etc. wird auf grund empirischer werte festgestellt, hier beträgt er für alle stockwerke etwa 5 v. h.

die beleuchtungsstärke im punkte P an ort und stelle erreicht einen um etwa 40 v. h. höheren wert (zufolge der rückwürfe des lichtes an decke und wänden).

die leitsätze der D. B. G. verlangen für les- und schreibräume eine mittlere beleuchtung von 50—60 lx. die vorgesehene fensteröffnung gewährt also auch dem dunkelsten arbeitsplatz eine ausreichende beleuchtung. nahe der fensterwand ist die beleuchtung 10 mal stärker und in zimmermitte 4 mal stärker als im punkt P. die durchschnittliche beleuchtung beträgt etwa 180 lx, bei einer fensterfläche von etwas mehr als $^1/_3$ der bodenfläche.

fall **2**) shed-oberlicht des zeichensaales.

berechnet wird die beleuchtung in jeder shed-axe.

berechnungsverfahren nach higbie und levin.

daten für die formeln:
abstand des punktes P_1 von der fensterfläche .... $a_1 = 2,5$ m
„ „ „ P_2 „ „ „ .... $a_2 = 5,5$ „
„ „ „ P_3 „ „ „ .... $a_3 = 8,5$ „
(diese abstände horizontal gemessen) „
länge des fensters .... $m = 11,0$ m
abstand des oberen fensterrandes von der tischfläche .... $f = 3,3$ m
„ „ unteren „ „ „ .... $f' = 2,6$ „
(diese abstände in der fensterebene gemessen) „
beleuchtungsstärke des fensters .... $b = 100,0$ ftcdl.

$A_1 = \frac{a_1}{f} = 0,75,$ $A_1' = \frac{a_1}{f'} = 0,96,$ $A_1 = \frac{a_1}{f} = 1,70,$
„ $A_2 = \frac{a_2}{f} = 2,15,$ $A_3 = \frac{a_3}{f} = 2,60,$ $A_3 = \frac{a_3}{f} = 3,30,$

$B = \frac{m}{f} = 3,30,$ $B' = \frac{m}{f'} = 4,20.$

die beleuchtungsstärke in jeder shed-axe, erzeugt durch das zugehörige fenster, ist gleich dem unterschied zwischen den beleuchtungswerten von tenstern der höhe f und f'.

aus dem diagramm ergibt sich

beleuchtungsstärke in $P_1 = 56 - 39 = 17 \times 12 = 204$ lx. = E_1
„ „ $P_2 = 13 - 9 = 4 \times 12 = 58$ „ = E_2
„ „ $P_3 = 5 - 3 = 2 \times 12 = 24$ „ = E_3
die gesamtbeleuchtungsstärke in $P_1 = E_1$ .... = 204 lx
„ „ „ $P_2 = E_1 + E_2$ .... = 262 „
„ „ „ $P_3 = E_1 + E_2 + E_3$ .... = 286 „

diese werte sind um weniger als $^1/_3$ voneinander verschieden, gegenüber dem vielfachen beim seitenlicht. die durchschnittliche beleuchtung beträgt etwa 250 lx bei einer fensterfläche von etwa $^1/_3$ der bodenfläche.

fall **3**) zweiseitiges seitenlicht der turnhalle.

berechnet wird die beleuchtung an den beiden längswänden und in der saalmitte.

beide längswände mit 2 m hohem fensterfries auf die ganze länge und unmittelbar unter der decke.

berechnungsverfahren nach higbie: (wie bei klassenzimmer mit seitenlicht).

daten für die formel: (P nahe längswand ost)
abstand des punktes P vom fenster (ost) .... $a_1 = 2,0$ m
„ „ „ P „ „ (west) .... $a_2 = 9,0$ „
länge des fensters .... $m = 23,0$ „
abstand des oberen fensterrandes von der tischfläche .... $f = 4,5$ „
„ „ unteren „ „ „ .... $f' = 2,5$ „
beleuchtungsstärke des fensters .... $b = 100,0$ ftcdl.
beleuchtungsstärke durch fenster (ost) .... = 249 lx
„ „ „ (west) .... = 29 lx

lichtverlust durch gegenüberliegende gebäude, ostseite .... = 5 v. H.
„ „ „ westseite .... = 12 v. H.

gesamtbeleuchtung in P = 253 lx.
daten für die formel: (P nahe längswand west).
abstand des punktes P vom fenster (ost) .... $a_1 = 9,0$ „
„ „ „ P „ „ (west) .... $a_2 = 2,0$ „
(die anderen werte wie oben).

beleuchtung durch fenster (ost) .... = 29 lx
„ „ „ (west) .... = 249 lx
lichtverlust: ostseite = 5 v. h., westseite 27 v. h.
gesamtbeleuchtung in P = 212 lx.
daten für die formel: (P in saalmitte).
abstand des punktes P vom fenster (ost und west gleichviel) $a = 5,5$ m
(die anderen werte wie oben).

beleuchtung durch fenster (ost und west gleichviel) = 110 lx.
lichtverlust: ostseite = 5 v. h., westseite 18 v. h.
gesamtbeleuchtung in P = 195 lx.

Meyer, Petersschule project as published in *Bauhaus* 2 (1927), with "mathematical proof" of the lighting system's effects.

parts, but also in the contradictions, the disruptions, the gaps and silences, all of which explodes the received social meanings of those things. "The diagrammatic or abstract machine . . . constructs a real that is yet to come, a new type of reality. Thus when it constitutes points of creation or potentiality it does not stand outside history but is instead always prior to history."[47] The canceling of fixed meanings, the shattering of the illusion of individual centrality, in short, the production of absence, all organize a political metaphor: *things can be made different.* Bloch's empty space becomes *productively* empty.

So, then, there is no materiality without *excess,* without a flow of contradictory and disruptive signification, and no absence, of whatever sort, without a structure of presence that reciprocally links space and time. In the Petersschule's materialist opposition to all transcendental stabilizers of signification, which induces an experience of the world increasingly as a succession of completed material substances seemingly operating through automatic mechanisms (the diagrams and calculations), the viewer becomes disoriented and dislodged from conventionally secure spaces of aesthetic apprehension and tends toward the merely factual understanding and description of objective reality from which he feels estranged. But the practice of estrangement, or the production of a *Verfremdungseffekt,* if we may now use, correctly I think, that concept from Brechtian theater—the staging of action in such a way that what had seemed natural and unquestionable is now revealed as historical and thus open to revolutionary change—such production is plausible for the viewer only if a certain verisimilitude is posited. So the Petersschule can do its work of canceling, disrupting, and decentering only if certain identities are maintained.

Traditionally, one of the devices that has insured a sense of palpable presence in a building is the understanding of the building as a transcription of the human body. Geoffrey Scott, sustaining observations derived from Heinrich Wölfflin, identifies two complementary principles of an architecture of humanism. One is founded on our response to the appearance of stability or instability and our corporeal identification with the building itself: *"We have transcribed ourselves into terms of architecture."* Another is founded on our unconscious investment of the building with human movement and human moods: *"We transcribe architecture into terms of ourselves."* Thus Scott concludes that "architecture, to communicate the vital values of the spirit must appear organic, like the body" and declares:

The scientific perception of the world is forced upon us; the humanist perception of it is ours by right. The scientific method [of criticism] is intellectually and practically useful, but the naïve, the anthropomorphic way which humanizes the world and interprets it by analogy with our own bodies and our own wills, is still the aesthetic way; it is the basis of poetry, and it is the foundation of architecture.[48]

But such inscription of the body is, of course, never innocent. For example, in the monumentalized modernism of at least some of the Italian rationalists, syntactical and typological invention within a classicizing, anthropomorphizing conceptual frame becomes the basis for reconnecting the architectural sign with its affirmative cultural and disciplinary conventions, now in service of the fascist State. Giuseppe Pagano, Marcello Piacentini, Ludovico Quaroni, and others assimilate the critical analytical and negational tendencies of modernism, reconnect the architectural sign to a preestablished referential realm, and demonstrate the availability of seemingly autonomous or critical formal manipulations for institutionalized and domesticated ends. A synthesis of formal abstraction with a conception of spatial order and harmony derived from classical proportional systems serves in the buildings of these architects merely to prop up the myth of cultural continuity and progress, to hypostatize a past culture and glory and drag them into the present.[49]

From another front, expressionist architecture renovates the body and the phenomenology of its representation as orientation points that might prove resistant to the uncritical, potentially instrumentalizing tendencies of industrialized architecture. (One thinks of Hans Poelzig, in particular, as architecturalizing the threat to the humanist body.) And yet, in a society where objects appear as alienated and cut off from human purposes, this, too, is a consoling doctrine: the world is grasped in relation to *me*, as a correlate of *my* body and *my* consciousness; this restores the individual subject, which the technological avant-garde sought to liquidate, to its rightful throne, seen as the source and origin of all meaning.

Jacques Lacan's so-called "mirror stage" of development serves as an exemplary situation of how the subject is structured with respect to the body.[50] The mirror stage denotes that moment when the child acquires a sense of its own bodily unity through a process of identification with an external object, the image in the mirror. The apprehension of bodily unity is the support of the division between a coherent self and that "other" against which the self is perceived. For the very exteriority of the mirror image anticipates what will become in Lacan's account the fundamental characteristic of the ego: a narcissistic mirage of coherence and centrality seducing the subject to misrecognize its actual alienation and fragmentation. In the mirror the child finds reflected back to itself a gratifyingly unified and responsive image of itself. (The child moves its arm, the mirror obliges in kind.) The identification with an image of one's self is constitutive of that self, and this constitution is the structural precondition for any ideological manipulation or massage of the subject.

Architecture based on the human body is, too, a kind of mirroring object and similarly lures the ego by offering an image of its mirror self. Scott's is only the most direct declaration of this architecto-somaticism, and Italian rationalism and German expressionism only the most obviously ideological uses of its effects.

Whatever the strengths or weaknesses of these positions, all
imply an attempt to restore the symbolic authenticity of
traditional content or individual authorship, to recolonize
architecture within humanist conceptions of cultural institutions, functionality, and individuality. The Petersschule
does not leave the body behind, and even less does it posit
the body as an ideologically neutral referent, but rather
inverts the signs of the body in ways that extend similar
inversions in Le Corbusier's Maison Citrohan—the base of
the building is nullified, the roof of the building is occupi-
able, the elevational and volumetric organizations interdict
visual frontality and the search for human countenance. But
what is more important is that the threat of corporeal dissolution already conceptualized by expressionism is converted
by the Petersschule into a threat of dissolution of that different entity whose construction on the model of the body
image is designated by Lacan's mirror stage: the centralized
subject, the personality, the individual itself.[51] And it is not
difficult to associate this threat of dissolution, which stuns
the psychological subject into a recognition of ideological-
material mechanisms as its causes, with the mixture of
anguish and exhilaration, of pain and compulsion, that I
have described as Meyer's materialist pleasure.

        The structure of presence
in the Petersschule also involves, as I have said, considerations of the advancement of technology and the links
between the transformations of technology and the transformations of artistic practice and social forms. Further, it
involves the city, the physical and social context into which
the Petersschule irrupts. The site of the Petersschule lies on
the eastern periphery of the inner city wall of Basel, a former Roman fortification, adjacent to the Peterskirche.[52]
Meyer's project isolates itself on the site, holding the street
line to the west and leaving over half of the eastern part of
the site free on the ground plane. The entry, which is an
extended spatial and temporal sequence through the system
of open and glazed stairs, begins at the western street, visible from the square in front of the church, and wraps

Paul Klee, *Hero with the Wing,* 1905.

between avant-garde and instrumentalization

around the north side of the building. The passageway formed by the *Freiflächen* or suspended platforms on the north of the building operates like an upper-level loggia; in concert with the deep entry door to the first level and the large window of the ground level, it describes a zone of circulation at the northern edge of the site extending the space of the narrow passage that enters the site from the east and continues parallel to the south facade of Peterskirche. All of this furthers the preeminence of the diagonality so apparent in the perspective and axonometric drawings. The sectional organization of the building is also determined by the *Freiflächen* (which Meyer proposed in substitution for the playground required by the building program): the ground level is left open for public circulation and parking; only the gymnasium, swimming pool, and kitchen are located at ground level or below. The building engages the specificities of its site but implies an entire sectional reorganization of the traditional city.

Meyer writes, "The school itself is raised as far as possible above ground to a level where there is sunlight and fresh air . . . and all the flat roofs of the building are assigned to the children for recreation, providing a total area of 1250 sq. meters of sunny space away from the old town." The emphasis of these last lines on the salutary vocation of architecture, conjoined with and enabled by its technical advancement, is standard modernist fare, but I wish to draw attention, one last time, to the unexpected fit between the Petersschule and Bloch's description of "building in empty spaces": "Today, in many places, houses look as if they were ready to travel. . . . Their interior is bright and sterile like hospital rooms, the exterior looks like boxes on top of mobile poles, but also like ships. They have flat decks, portholes, gangways, railings . . . , and as ships they like to disappear." On the one hand, Meyer's materialism seeks to dissolve the Petersschule as a purely visual object. On the other hand, the flying decks of the Petersschule—perhaps even more intensely than the earlier projects of Ladovsky's studio, or Lissitzky's project for a

"Horizontal Skyscraper" of 1923–1925—organize a constructional metaphor that struggles to distance and extract the building from its context, to enunciate a conception of space that is *other* than the one we have. The building is "ready to travel," provided we understand by that statement not only that the building is a visual metaphor but also that it is the *actual* production of a *concept* of an alternative space. We should link the metaphor of the platforms and the group of children engaged in Pestalozzian learning with other images like those that appeared in the pages of *ABC*—the planetarium construction, Lyubov Popova and Aleksandr Vesnin's propaganda apparatus, and Lissitzky's Lenin Tribune project in *ABC 1*; the circus tent and amusement park ride in *ABC 4*—all of which attempt to *figure* the various city-machines conjoined with mass society in signs of collective participation within the spectacle of modernization.

Looking at the asymmetry of the *Freiflächen* grafted onto the functional volume of the school, one is also reminded of the poignant image of Paul Klee's "Hero with the Wing," and of Klee's diary entry,

Today is the great transition from past to present. In the huge pit of forms there lies rubble to which one still clings in part. It furnishes the stuff for abstraction.
A rubble field of spurious elements, for the formation of impure crystals.
That is how it is today . . .
In order to work myself out of my rubble, I had to fly.
And I did fly. In that shattered world I remain only in memory, as one thinks back sometimes.
Thus I am "abstract with memories."[53]

Meyer's abstraction similarly derives from the effort to fly, so to speak, to commute the present into the future.

the bauhaus and the radicalization of building

the dessau bauhaus is not an artistic,
but a social phenomenon.

as *gestalter*
our activities are determined by society,
and the scope of our tasks is set by society.
does not our present society in germany call for
thousands of people's schools, people's parks, people's houses?
millions of pieces of people's furniture???
(what are the connoisseur's gibberings worth when set against
    these)
(after the cubistic cubes of bauhaus *sachlichkeit?*). . . .

the new bauhaus school
as a center of education in shaping life
makes no selection of the gifted.
it despises
the imitative intellectual mobility of talent,
it is alive to the danger of intellectual schism:
inbreeding, egocentrism, unworldlines, aloofness.
the new *building* school.[1]

With this tough and exact rhetoric Hannes Meyer addressed
the representatives of the Bauhaus student body on the
occasion of his appointment to the post of director in February 1928. It is the sort of rhetoric that has prompted critics
and historians to label him functionalist, naive radical, petit
bourgeois, and "gravedigger" of the Bauhaus.[2] In the context
of the analysis here, however, the rhetoric can be understood to be indicative of Meyer's effort to bring into the
Bauhaus the related propositions of aesthetic practice as
social production and the aesthetic object as an image of the
productive cycle, now with the concomitant hope of
actually intervening in the organizational structure of that
cycle. At the Bauhaus Meyer attempts to carry his previous
research in what I have called the performativity of architectural perception through to the processes of architectural
design themselves, the latter now expanded to include factors such as studio organization, advertising, production

decisions, and drawing. He thereby pushes the hypothesis of an engaged architecture to a limit unknown at the Bauhaus during Walter Gropius's administration. As most commentators have recognized, such a radicalization seeks its pedagogical manifestation in the search for a more concrete and interventionary role for the school in the actual production and distribution of its designs, a diminution of the importance of studies of form and exercises in self-expression, and a substantial accentuation of social, technical, and practical aspects of building, the effect of which is to overturn some of the most ingrained and cherished educational principles of the Bauhaus tradition. What critics have not seemed willing to admit is that the insertion of Meyer's radical hypotheses into the tradition of the Bauhaus resulted in anything other than futility and waste.[3]

Since Peter Bürger's *Theory of the Avant-Garde,* a few accounts have emerged that rediscover or reinterpret the general problematic of the social engagement of architecture.[4] Bürger argues that, rather than merely to change received representational conventions, the major goal of the historical avant-garde was to undermine and transform the very institution of art and its ideology of autonomy. In Bürger's account the avant-garde was primarily an attack on the "highness" of high art and its separateness from everyday life as these had evolved under the precepts of nineteenth-century aestheticism. The avant-garde attempted to incorporate and thematize the relationship between art and its institutional framework of production, distribution, and reception, then to dismantle "institution art" and reintegrate art with social practice as a whole, or, to use his formulation, to *sublate* art into life.[5] Such a distinction surely goes some way toward breaking apart that vexatious notion of a monolithic "modern movement" in architecture, permitting a preliminary articulation of some of the different programs within modernist practice and encouraging a revaluation of the routine equation of modernism with the avant-garde, but it is still not fine enough to aid us here. For by arguing for a definition of the

Hannes Meyer, Co-op Foto (self-portrait):
photocollage of building crane and portrait of Meyer,
from *9 Jahre Bauhaus* (1928).

avant-garde that embraces social and political themes and practical, utilitarian concerns, Bürger can set such a practice against nineteenth-century bourgeois aestheticism and its ongoing transformations in the twentieth century, but he cannot then adequately differentiate an altogether different "avant-garde" that indeed began with a renunciation of "*l'art pour l'art*"[6] but then encompassed and absorbed *other* movements, sought to normalize relations with existing institutions and authorities, and came to dominate the discourse: the one perhaps best exemplified by Gropius's lifelong concern with a policy of reconciliation among the common formal languages of the avant-gardes, the social and technological research of production art, and the consistent endeavor to preserve the traditional, institutional autonomy of the artist. It is against this latter conciliatory position (the "cubistic cubes" and stylized constructivism Meyer referred to) that Meyer's attack was directed.

Shifting from the earlier position of the Arbeitsrat für Kunst, which in 1919 in Berlin had affirmed that "the political revolution must be used to liberate art from decades of regimentation," and that "art and people must form a unity,"[7] Gropius at the Bauhaus increasingly demonstrated an equivocation about the role of intellectual labor and a synthesizing, conciliatory tendency summarized in the new slogan of 1923, "Art and Technology—a New Unity," all of which ultimately amounted to little more than a proposition for an industro-elementarist style organized and operated by artists from above.[8] As Francesco Dal Co has argued, in what is still the principal critical comparison between the Bauhaus of Gropius and that of Meyer,

The fundamental contradiction hidden in the work of Gropius becomes clear when we underline the evident mystification into which those fall who want to credit Gropius with having conducted a "heroic battle" for the unification of the work of intellectual design [*progettazione*], for the overcoming of the division between art and the world, between art and work, between art and society, definitively, that is, for overcoming the principle of the division of labor as the fundamental structure of bourgeois society.[9]

The development of Gropius's Bauhaus can be understood as a confirmation and verification—a molecular epitome—of the larger evolution of the modernist paradigm as the latter has been constructed by Dal Co, Manfredo Tafuri, and the Venice School. According to their interpretation, the ongoing depletion of traditional artistic values is the signal inside art of a wider cultural decomposition and loss of consistent and repeatable meanings. Avant-garde experiments between 1919 and 1930 were an attempt to seize upon that very loss, to register it, and to make it over into form. The endeavors to produce out of present conditions pictures of various alternative realities—the alternative spaces of practice that the "isms" of the modern intend to name—specify the historical aim of the avant-garde formulations to have been to accept the contradictions of modern culture, to make contradiction the very object of art—through the registration and intensification of given experiences, through chance and irrationality, through irony or disgust, even through the annulment of art itself. This process of continually activating the contradictions of the real—presenting art as the dialectical negation of what is given in the present—is, for the Venice School, the historical factor that unites all the experiments of progressive and radical art of the twentieth century.[10] The historical destiny of the Bauhaus can then be seen within this paradigm as an ideological necessity to convert avant-garde negativity into a positive force by discovering "the Plan for the Real"—a program for social development and artistic reintegration, an overarching order for modernity—and attempting to realize that plan, to *produce* that form of reality that the pictorial avant-gardes had been able only to envision.

But Gropius, and with him the Bauhaus up to 1928, will never resolve this contradiction intrinsic to intellectual work; the demand and the ideological prefiguration of the program and of the plan on a general social level, is also, on the one hand, the ultimate aspiration of bourgeois art; it is, on the other hand, also its extreme ideological product; *it is*, therefore, the last possibility of the survival of art; art now becomes a *directly* social function and as such annuls its own intrinsic values to become annexed itself, as value and function of society. In the practice of [Gropius's] Bauhaus, however, all this remains largely unrealized. It is a present but constantly refused destiny.[11]

For Gropius the condition for the new "unification" of art and life remains a construction wherein the process of design is a process of creating an eidetic image—a mental image of a new art, vivid and detailed, but in fact disengaged—which is to say, design remains intellectual work as such and only. Reading Gropius's early writings, in particular the Bauhaus program of 1919, and looking at the work of the Bauhäuslers after 1923, it seems right to affirm a relationship to, and the notable influence of, the radical artistic movements in the organization and subsequent development of the school. The Bauhaus was, in Tafuri's words, "the decantation chamber, the refinery, of the European avant-gardes . . . and the ideological symbol of the unity of the modern movement as a whole."[12] Accepting the weight of this tradition, Gropius nevertheless shows his willingness to endorse the formal experiments of the avant-gardes but to change their social role and meaning at the same time, transferring the critical negational strategies of the immediate postwar period to an affirmative, operative level. This transference signaled a break not only with the anti-art and often destructive activities of the dadaists, but also with the proposals of the Novembergruppe, the constructivists, and the productivists for a more concretely engaged architecture. Gropius sought to defuse the protopolitical mechanisms of radical art, demonstrate their availability for use in mediating between crafts and industry, and raise artisanal work to a new level through the application of the formal research of the pictorial avant-gardes, thereby reestablishing contacts with the

tenets of the Werkbund and weaving emergent artistic
experiments into the fabric of the bourgeois aesthetic tradition. The "refused destiny" of his Bauhaus, therefore,
appears as the projection back over the avant-garde, whose
experiments would seem to have demonstrated definitively
the irreversibly changed historical conditions of aesthetic
production and reception, of an earlier episteme of the master craftsman and the *Gesamtkunstwerk*, with the result
that the forms and signs produced by the one were reconceived in terms of the practice and structural hierarchies of
the other, as if in an attempt to recoup aesthetic invest-
ments already liquidated.

It is symptomatic in
these terms that Gropius is so impressed with the example
of László Moholy-Nagy, who in 1924 showed at Der Sturm
gallery in Berlin a series of "enamel pictures executed by
industrial methods," produced by dictating instructions for
the making of the pictures over the telephone "to a head of
a coat-of-arms shop." Moholy writes: "In 1922 I ordered by
telephone from a sign factory five paintings in porcelain
enamel. I had the factory's color chart before me and I
sketched my paintings on graph paper. At the other end of
the telephone the factory supervisor had the same kind of
paper, divided into squares. He took down the dictated
shapes in the correct position."[13] As a simple metaphor for a
supposed interventionary procedure and negation of the distance between art and life, which Gropius hoped to realize
practically in the Bauhaus, this anecdote shows how remote
design in fact could remain, and how far the Bauhaus ideology was from a real overcoming of the division of labor,
from a real sublation of institutional art (in Bürger's sense).
The sense of Moholy's anecdote is subtly different from a
seemingly similar text of 1924, published by Hans Arp and
El Lissitzky in *Kunstismen*: "With the increasing frequency
of the square in painting, the art institutions have offered
everybody the means to make art. Now the production of
art has been simplified to such an extent that one can do no
better than order one's paintings by telephone from a house

painter while one is lying in bed."[14] In contrast to the latter
text, which implies a renunciation of the traditional role of
the individual artist and his specialized vision, in Moholy's
example art is still transcendental and mystified; resisting
the clutter of externalities, art tries to control, in its own
institutional terms, what Walter Benjamin called the presence of the "technological accident," to which we will
return later.[15]

Upon Meyer's appoint-
ment as director of the Bauhaus, Oskar Schlemmer wrote to
Otto Meyer, "The Bauhaus will reorient itself in the direction of architecture, industrial production, and the intellectual aspect of technology. The painters are merely tolerated
as a necessary evil now."[16] Perhaps in anticipation of immi-
ment marginalization under the new regime, or perhaps on
principle, Marcel Breuer, Herbert Bayer, and Moholy-Nagy
had already resigned before Gropius's decision to leave the
school was officially announced. Moholy made his intentions clear in a letter to the *Meisterrat* in January 1928.

As soon as creating an object becomes a specialty, and work
becomes trade, the process of education loses all vitality. There
must be room for teaching the basic ideas which keep human content alert and vital. For this we fought and for this we exhausted
ourselves. I can no longer keep up with the stronger and stronger
tendency toward trade specialization in the workshops. . . . The
spirit of construction for which I and others gave all we had—and
gave it gladly—has been replaced by a tendency towards application. My realm was the construction of school and man.[17]

The criticism of speciali-
zation and the counteremphasis on the construction of man
are directed, no doubt, at Meyer's negation of traditional
artistic practice and the subjectivities it engenders. One
might think that Meyer and Moholy would be close in their
conceptualization of design. Both claimed to be more concerned with social issues of design than with form alone;
Meyer had published Moholy's essay "Ismus oder Kunst"
along with a *Bildconstruktion* and a *Metalconstruktion* in

ABC 2; their positions would seem to be commensurable. But the terms of their disagreement are instructive for a fuller understanding of Meyer's thinking.[18] Moholy's stress on man rather than the social-material product, his preoccupation with forms that bore no real relationship to either the actual techniques of production or the actual demands of mass consumption, and his pseudoscientific teaching methods of a "master" all entailed a sublimationist, humanist conception of art that Meyer could not countenance. And Meyer's stress on the collectivity of the "design brigade," and his recasting of design practice within the categories of labor and material production, implied an undermining of artistic institutions that Moholy could not tolerate.

Walter Peterhans, "Hollow Concrete Blocks," 1929. The photograph was taken on the construction site of the ADGB school.

the radicalization of building

Meyer's transformation of the Bauhaus *was* destructive; but it was not destructive only. It is enough only to recall a few positive achievements here. Within the new educational program, for the first time in the school's history, building became a program on its own, with Ludwig Hilberseimer appointed its director. Other appointments made by Meyer included Anton Brenner, who had studied with Peter Behrens and worked with Ernst May in Frankfurt; Edvard Heiberg, a Norwegian architect and theorist; Alcar Rudelk, a construction engineer; Walter Peterhans, whose conception of photography as a science Meyer had hoped would contribute to the "training [of] camera reporters and advertising photographers";[19] and Mart Stam, a Dutch architect and co-editor of *ABC*, and Hans Wittwer, who both contributed to the program as guest lecturers on mechanical engineering and town planning. Theoretical discussions were fueled by guests that included the Viennese logical positivists Rudolph Carnap, Otto Neurath, and Herbert Feigl, as well as Karel Teige, Hermann Finsterlin, Ernst Toller, Piet Zwart, and Dziga Vertov. "I never design alone," wrote Meyer. "That is why I consider the choosing of suitable associates to be the most important act in preparing for a creative work in architecture. The more contrasted the abilities of the designing brigade, the greater its capabilities and creative power."[20]

With new and previously appointed faculty, four departments were established within the school: building, headed by Hilberseimer; interior design, which incorporated the previous workshops in metal, wall painting, and furniture, and was headed by Alfred Arndt, a former student whom Meyer appointed; advertising and publicity (*Reklame*), headed by Joost Schmidt, which incorporated the graphic and printing workshops as well as a new photography program under Peterhans; and textiles. Meyer had also intended to introduce courses on Gestalt psychology, sociology, and social economics. The school would now address the needs of the proletariat, designing standard, mass-produced products to be anonymously absorbed into everyday life.

The focal point of the school were three eight-hour workshops per week, now organized to work as collective, collaborative "vertical brigades" and "cooperative cells." It was Meyer's intention to take the Bauhaus away from being "a 'university of design' which made the shape of every tea-glass a problem in constructivist aesthetics,"[21] and to make the workshops self-supporting by marketing their designs through a commercial organization, the Bauhaus G.m.b.H. Wallpapers designed at the Bauhaus were made and marketed by Rasch and Co., Hanover, and brought in significant royalities for the school. Meyer wrote, "In 1929 alone (the year they were introduced) more than 20,000 rooms in Germany and neighboring countries were papered with them. From the educational point of view, they provided an opportunity of dealing with the problem of 'color in the interior' as a general principle and also of making 'hygiene in the worker's house' a reality, by producing cheap washable wallpapers."[22] The advertising and textile departments were also commercially successful and each achieved its aim of a working liaison with industry to mass-produce goods at low cost. Meyer wrote,

The annual production, amounting to about RM 128 000 (1928) has been almost doubled. . . . In the last business year, RM 32 000 was paid out to students in the way of wages and this enabled those who were less well-off to study there. A Bauhaus travelling exhibition publicized our ideas in Basle, Breslau, Dessau, Essen, Mannheim and Zurich. . . . Industrial firms came along with urgent requests, engaged Bauhaus students on their staffs, and concluded licence agreements for Bauhaus fabrics, lamps, standard furniture and wallpapers. Thus there was every prospect of our finances being improved in future in the only really sound way, namely through self-help.[23]

As Meyer wrote, "The imposing exterior of the early Bauhaus was increasingly replaced by an internal strengthening in the collective sense. The Bauhaus today reflects an undeniable degree of proletarianization."[24] It is an ironic fact that the close cooperation with the workers' movement and the trade unions, and the involvement of Meyer and a few students in the miners' strike, would eventually result in his dismissal from the Bauhaus.

Walter Benjamin's comparison of the painter and the cameraman through the analogy of the magician and the surgeon provides the terms for a comparison of Gropius and Meyer:

> The magician maintains the natural distance between the patient and himself; though he reduces it very slightly by the laying on of hands, he greatly increases it by virtue of his authority. The surgeon does exactly the reverse; he greatly diminishes the distance between himself and the patient by penetrating into the patient's body, and increases it but little by the caution with which his hand moves among the organs. . . . Magician and surgeon compare to painter and cameraman. The painter maintains in his work a natural distance from reality, the cameraman penetrates deeply into its web. There is a tremendous difference between the pictures they obtain. That of the painter is a total one, that of the cameraman consists of multiple fragments which are assembled under a new law.[25]

Benjamin's characterization of the technological fact through the synecdoche of the camera—a figure that I understand to include all "extraneous accessories" such as mechanical equipment, production procedures, and the multiple producers behind the work of film—and its penetration into the lifeworld not only helps to distinguish between the different positions of Gropius or Moholy and Meyer, but also helps to specify the makeup of that realm between art and life that we have been interested in crossing. In this characterization, the ultimate service of an insertion of the technological fact into architectural production is the demystification of the work of architecture and the process of its design. If by mystification we mean not only the privileging of aesthetic intuition and the mysterious genesis of the creative idea but also a kind of commodity fetishism or

reification of the art object, now redefined as "the efface-
ment of the traces of production from the object" (Marx),
then the demystification of the object, its dereification or
aesthetic refunctioning, might be understood initially to be
the aesthetic reinscription of those same traces (which is
precisely what we have already seen at work in the Petersschule's configuring of various externalities), in the same
way that the aesthetic consequences of the camera's surgi-
cal movement among the organs might initially be posited
as the foregrounding within the medium of film of the camera's own mobility and scale of view.

By closeups of the thing around us, by focusing on hidden details of
familiar objects, by exploring commonplace milieus under the
ingenious guidance of the camera, the film, on the one hand,
extends our comprehension of the necessities which rule our lives;
on the other, it manages to *assure us of an immense and unexpected field of action.* . . . Here the camera intervenes with the
resources of its lowerings and liftings, its interruptions and isola-
tions, its extensions and accelerations, its enlargements and
reductions.[26]

The advantage of this formulation here is that through it we
are led back to the questions of representation, subject positions, and a possible field of action for architecture, as the
thematization of the technological fact comes to include
issues of our reception and manipulation of the production
process, that is, considerations on the side of the subject as
well as on the side of the object. And the distance between
art and life becomes traversable via just those lines and
webs that lead laterally out from the architectural object
and its immanent characteristics to its outside, to the technical determinants and limits—including studio practices,
client relations, and production decisions—in short, to the
greater totality of the real whose perceptibility is opened up
by the object itself. It is to an example of this organization
of experience by built form that I now turn.

            The most important
building project of Meyer and the Bauhaus brigades was the

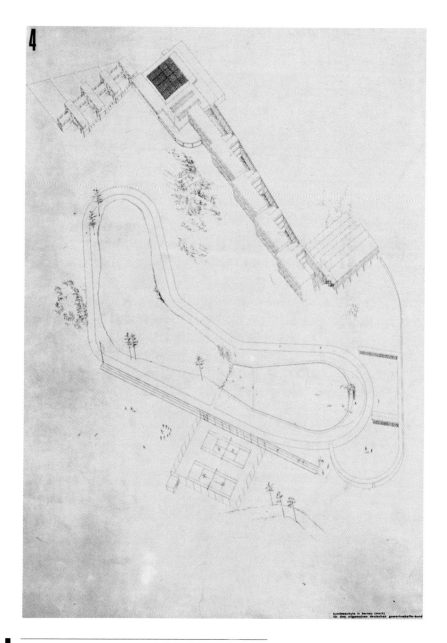

**Hannes Meyer, Federal School of the
General German Trade Unions Federation (ADGB),
Bernau, 1928–1930, aerial perspective.**

Meyer, ADGB school, aerial view.

Federal School of the General German Trade Unions Federation (ADGB) of 1928–1930 at Bernau near Berlin.[27] Financed
by the ADGB, the school was to house members and offi-
cials attending short courses (one to two months) and comprised residential blocks and teachers' dormitories as well as
classrooms, a lecture theater, dining hall, and gymnasium.
According to Meyer, he won the competition for the project
because "he not only designed a striking set of buildings but
also put forward a new form of socio-educational organization for this educational center."[28] One hundred twenty
male and female students were organized in cells of ten
members distributed in four building blocks of three floors
each, thus establishing a spatial diagram of social relations.
In the design, Meyer revised the basic building proposition
announced in the Petersschule of a simple volume of framed
construction (here concrete rather than steel), now with five
structural bays (corresponding to the five pairs of students
per floor) treated as a functional-constructional integer
repeated in a series across the site. "The purpose of this
rigid grouping was to give the individual worker, during his
comparatively short stay, the opportunity to identify himself with the communal life of the school as quickly and
closely as possible through comradeship with his roommate
and through the life of the cells." Modulations of that integer correspond exactly to sociofunctional differentiations:
the constructional bays change in the one dormitory block
with single rooms; the teacher's apartments constitute a
separate wing; the gymnasium and other public spaces are
distinguished and elaborated out of the basic building sys-

the radicalization of building

tem. As in the Petersschule, the circulation is contained and denoted by glazed passageways looking out to the site, grafted, almost as if retrofitted, onto the series of building units. Construction procedures and sequences are everywhere revealed (in contrast, for example, to the Bauhaus school building itself in Dessau, whose constructional disjunctures were famously rendered whole by aesthetic fiat). In general, "the building organization is merely a plastic translation [*plastische Übersetzung*] of the socio-pedagogic functions . . . a direct transcription [*Übertragung*] of the functional diagram."

Architecture as diagrammatic act: the building is conceived as a translation machine for sociofunctional construction and differentiation, both diagram of and intervention into the manifold forces and processes of the social field, a circuit of material signifiers, as if of preexisting elements assembled together, each a diagram of its own activities and inhabitations and a transcription of previous forces. Architecture demystified: details in which one would normally seek to read meaning of a more properly aesthetic and intentional kind are obdurately shown to be "merely" what was demanded technically of the building as a servomechanism.[29] All of which must not be confused with the different modified autoreferentiality in which the designed object—through a laying on of hands as it were—comes "to be about" its newfound technical potentials, in the way, for example, that Marcel Breuer's tubular steel furniture of 1925, or Georg Muche and Richard Paulick's steel house in Dessau of 1926, or the Dessau Bauhaus itself internalize their technological contingencies, drawing technology into the aesthetic text and endowing it with subjective intention.

Moreover, the reconceptualization of architecture not as an aesthetic object—the fictive organization of an organic whole that we normally mean by "good design"—but as a commutation system—a program, a set of procedures, an apparatus for the production of events, of what Meyer called "psychological

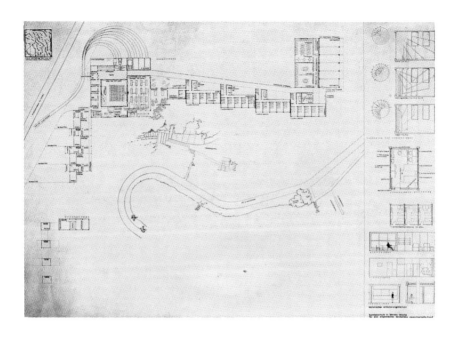

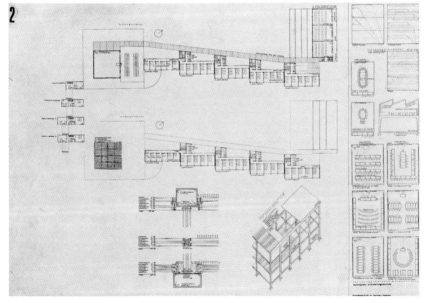

Meyer, ADGB school, plans and diagrams.

29

Meyer, ADGB school, housing blocks during construction.

Meyer, ADGB school, housing blocks after completion.

Meyer, ADGB school, view from student room.

Meyer, ADGB school, corridor of residential block.

the radicalization of building

effects"—leads to an expansion of this diagrammatic vocation of architecture into other scales and categories, as Meyer's own descriptions of the experiences of the ADGB
convey. Architecture's corporal-temporal dimension, for
example (I have already broached the issue in the Petersschule) is intensified: "The visitor knew he was approaching
the school by a change in the road surface; in the middle of
the wood a concrete road branched off from the main over-
land highway and the jolting of the wheels was replaced by
a smooth glide." On the verandah "the motor actuating the
sun blind followed the movement of the sun from east to
west, running like a toy locomotive on the ceiling rail, and
drew the shadegiving cloth along behind it." And then
graphic systems and equipment become—as diagrams, orga-
nizers, and producers of effects—architectural devices in
their own right:

A color system helped the visitor to find his way. In this concourse
were light signals (reminiscent of railway signals) which shone
green, yellow, blue, and red, and inside the three-storey residential
wings the basic reddish color changed, as one mounted, from scar-
let to vermillion, to pink, and to the three "cell" colors on the wall
of the entrance to each corridor. . . . At the touch of a button the
lecturer could increase or decrease the size of the 45-ft. wide hall
window like a camera shutter. Another button set in motion the
three elements of the end wall so that maps, diagrams, pictures,
etc. slipped noiselessly into position. Another button controlled the
lighting system and could produce any degree of illumination from
the dim light of the diffusers to the dazzling glare of the stage
lights. The flooring was red, the furniture black, and the cellophane
material of the walls silver. The lecturer himself appeared as a silhouette against a white square of rear wall.

This should be understood as more than a description of
equipment. By organizing new spaces and new events, the
ADGB participates in the construction of "the new world"
by reprogramming its inhabitants, training them in new perceptual habits (bodies as railroad cars!), producing new categories of experience, delineating new subject positions that

are ultimately the ideological markers by which we negotiate the real itself.

Nor is this demystification only a matter of revealing the traces of functional and constructional contingencies and of organizing new effects within the (still relatively closed) economy of material signifiers. For as the object thus unravels itself, it must inevitably disperse even further into its outside and a range of factors now intrude into the conceptual space where once an architectural "language" was held distinct. Studio practice and the entire structure of production decisions are brought into play (recall Meyer's insistence on working with associates in a designing brigade rather than alone). For Meyer, drawing itself is a site for reprogramming ideologies and causalities. Progressing in definite stages of "diagrammatic representation" and "standardization," the drawing "embodies the results of bringing spaces into conformity with a type and shows in graphic form the requirements of a techno-economic, politico-economic, and psycho-economic nature . . . in tersely standardized form [that] makes rational use of paper, drawing material, and labor."[30] In a drawing for the Workers' Bank, Berlin, a 1929 project for the ADGB, Meyer employs montaged photographic elements to mark specific affective moments punctuated in the architecural field: the view of Berlin across the Spree through oblique windows, the direct connection to the extended transportation network, the "work apparatus," all part of the multiple relations among bodies, equipment, movements, procedures, technologies programmed by this spatiotemporal regime.

If the plan form of the ADGB school attests to Meyer's continued fascination with the dynamic graphic experiments of the elementarist and constructivist avant-gardes—and has thus led critics to posit a contradiction between Meyer's stylist affiliations and his aformal, positivist-functionalist techniques[31]—we must now see that that aesthetic paradigm itself is only one of many texts superimposed by Meyer in an active securing of new

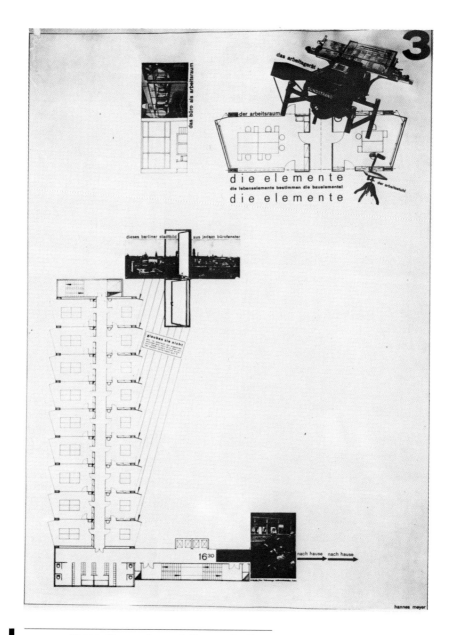

Hannes Meyer, plans and diagrams for the Workers' Bank, Berlin, 1929, project for the ADGB.

perceptual conventions in the project, part of the raw material out of which the work is constructed, along with both the more conventional considerations of site and program and the reprogramming apparatuses already noted. In what might be thought of as a scaled-down version of Ernst Bloch's synchronicity of the nonsychronous (*Gleichzeitigkeit des Ungleichzeitigen*),[32] Meyer interrelates forms and processes of radically different modalities and imbricates specific moments—stylistic, functional, technical, social, psychological—into the larger project in process. Extending through different scales of form and experience, to the smallest details of the building or the smallest psychological effect produced, this procedure attempts to envelope the totality of perceptions and actions and thus to approximate the ideal of the collective project, or praxis as such. And with that characterization we can return to the distinction between the avant-gardisms of Meyer and Gropius, now seen in terms of the different forms of their desired mediation between technology and aesthetic practice.[33]

Gropius
"Art and Technology: a new unity"

autonomous art
traditional practice of fine
    art or master craft
	facts of technology and
	    production (realm of the
	    object)
	industrial processes

representation, reception,
    and ideology of technology
    (subject positions)
techno-, politico-, and
    psychoeconomies
	anti-art
	demystification
	transcription of
	    sociofunctional diagram

Meyer
architecture as interventionary
production of effects

As a mapping of the ideological closure generated out of the initial attempt to unify art and technology, this semiotic rectangle now demonstrates the full difficulty and paradoxical force of Meyer's work as I have presented it. For the involution or double negation of the initial binary opposition, art and technology—emerging as it does out of the compulsion to expunge all illusions of an autonomous aesthetic realm, yet still requiring some aesthetic dimension in order to construct out of the objective and punctually felt fact of technology its desired forms of simultaneous collective reception—entails nothing less than *a different sort of practice,* which I have described as the diagrammatic, interventionary production of various functional, social, and psychological effects. Rather than modifying an already established practice to a given end—"applying" design to the technological fact, with all the inherited relations involved in "artistic" production left in place—Meyer's shift at the Bauhaus amounts to the abandonment of the notion of the resistant avant-garde artist in favor of some other role that we might call, following Benjamin's model, "the artist as producer," a role that addresses "the far-reaching demand that [intellectuals] should not supply the production apparatus without, at the same time, within the limits of the possible, changing that apparatus in the direction of socialism."[34] For, indeed, Meyer's revision of the terms of architectural practice is made in an effort to anticipate the classic Marxist movement toward workers' control of production as part of the transition from the dynamic capitalist state to socialism. And yet, Meyer's work by 1927 had already anticipated within the logic of formal investigation an ideological program that remained central to his work at the Bauhaus. Thus, even though Meyer moves some distance from standard notions of the avant-garde artist, his position is never entirely severed from its avant-garde heritage. There is rather a constant oscillation in the trajectory of his practice: a dialectic of internal formal and external sociocultural determinations. ("Is our work to be determined from inside or outside?"

Meyer asked, and his own answer seems to have been: "Both.") The significant factor for us is less Meyer's adroitness as a theorist of social revolution than his artistic understanding of what that practically and ideologically would entail: a canceling of architecture's own history and a conversion of its very forms and techniques of innovation into commutation devices for a subjectivity whose full appointment could only remain in the distant future.

All of which returns to the question of representation. The received interpretation of the successive historical and ideological shifts from traditional representational form, to abstract and autotelic "modern" form, and then to "utilitarian" or "functionalist" work—such as that of the Soviet productivists, the *neues bauen* of Martin Wagner or Ernst May, or of Marxists like Mart Stam, Hans Schmidt, and Meyer—is something like this: The ornamental, representational qualities of, say, neo-classicism or academicism are historically contingent and rhetorical accretions on an essential architecture that consists fundamentally of abstract tectonic and spatial organizations (or what used to be called typologies). To renounce traditional symbolic or representational form—that is, to abdicate the possibility of "speaking" about something else outside of architecture—as the avant-garde artists and architects (including Meyer in at least some aspects of his work) were supposed to have done, is to produce an altogether different kind of object, a nonrepresentational, nonrhetorical, self-identical form. A utilitarian turn, such as Meyer's at the Bauhaus and the ADGB, for example, is then seen as substituting for that essentially cognitive, aesthetic object a nonaesthetic, functional, and social purpose.[35] Thus how we understand the ideology of the utilitarian turn, or of functionalism generally, rests upon a very particular interpretation of the previously developed avant-garde formal strategies.

But the notion of the avant-garde work as an abstract and nonrepresentational architecture has been based on a reading of its forms and its

modes of reception that is too narrow; and the concomitant
interpretation of Meyer's "avant-gardism" as opposed to his
"functionalism" stands at the end of a chain of wrong infer-
ences. For within even the most inwardly turned instances
of modernism, things do manage to get represented. Architecture can construct a physical world, or present commentaries about the nature of the architectural discipline and
institution, or narrate a vision of how we should live; in
any case one is dealing with representation. It is just that
now what used to be called the sociohistorical context of
architectural production must be understood as existing at
the same level as the object produced, in the sense that we
cannot approach either separately and directly, as distinct
things-in-themselves waiting to be "discovered" in their
respective essences, but only through their prior differentiation, interpretation, translation, and transmutation. This
realization—that the various so-called contexts of an object
are not mere surrounds but are embedded in the very form
and medium of architecture—is perhaps the most important
materialist contribution of Meyer's work that connoisseurs
of interiority have continued to suppress: the imperative
induced in viewers to critically produce or (re)invent relationships among the architectural fact and the social, historical, and ideological subtexts from which it was never really
separate to begin with.

        In particular, if my
attempt to remap the trajectory of Meyer's work according
to a double movement of "internal" formal investigations
derived from avant-garde research *and* a direct confrontation
of those "external" determinations of psychic life under capitalism is correct, then no part of Meyer's work can be said
to be nonrepresentational in any but a reductive sense.
Meyer's work seeks to fulfill the aesthetic, ideological, and
protopolitical mission to recode the reified content of the
objective, material world and to make it available for simultaneous collective reception on a subjective, aesthetic level.
The vestiges of the raw material of mechanical reproduction
and reification remain visible within Meyer's projects, con-

Adolf Hofmeister, caricature of Hannes Meyer, 1930: "From Bauhaus to Moscow. Watch out architecture!"

stituting the materials out of which the historical subtext of capitalist commodification can be constructed. At the same time, however, the transmutation of the world and its data, thought in terms of perception as a semiautonomous, performative activity, can be understood as an anticipatory representation of a future, nomadic society and a future or utopian mode of production and reception that seek to emerge from the hegemonic mode of production of the present. The possibility of the concrete aesthetic representation of progressive social development is the precondition for Meyer's formal research having any moment at all.

Of course, the fulfillment of socialism is precisely what did not evolve in Germany in the 1930s, and the activities of a few cultural workers could not make it happen. Not by chance Meyer deludes himself that he will find in the Soviet Union, in the country of *realized* revolution, that condition that he had tried in vain to construct, and that had been shown to be impossible in the Germany now heading toward Nazism. In what Meyer himself termed a "flight into life,"[36] he wrote, "I am going to work in the Soviet Union, where a true proletarian culture is developing, where socialism was born, and where there exists a society for which we, here, in a capitalist regime, have fought."[37]

the radicalization of building

reproduction and negation:
the cognitive project of
neue sachlichkeit

No firm criterion can draw the line between a determinate negation of meaning and a bad positivism of meaninglessness, as an assiduous soldiering on just for the sake of it. Least of all can such a line be based on an appeal to human values, and a curse of mechanization. Works of art which by their existence take the side of the victims of a rationality that subjugates nature, are even in their protest constitutively implicated in the process of rationalization itself. Were they to try to disown it, they would become both aesthetically and socially powerless: mere clay. The organizing, unifying principle of each and every work of art is borrowed from that very rationality whose claim to totality it seeks to defy.

Theodor Adorno, "Commitment"

The twentieth-century avant-garde's critique of traditional modes of artistic production and reception arises in a context of industrialized mass production. Whereas various transformations of the presumed modernist paradigm have depended on the notion of a removed, inward, self-critical and self-referential artistic (or architectural) practice, one in which autonomy and uniqueness are taken as signs of art's irreducible value as part of a high culture standing over and against "degraded" popularities, mass production is predicated on reproducible operations and objects, which in turn necessitates a reconceptualization not only of the object (re)produced but also of the relationships between the object and its maker and between the object and its reception. The bourgeois humanist conception of the creating or viewing subject is one of a free, active, autonomous, and unified personality appropriate for the freedoms of an emergent capitalist society; and the formal ideologies of humanism reinforce this self-created signification. But industrial capitalism and its chaotic metropolitan experience also engender acute anxieties that challenge the viability of such a conception. In order to criticize and dismantle the humanist subject and its mode of artistic reception, the avant-garde draws upon certain negative aspects of the actual experience of such subjects in industrial society and injects into bourgeois humanist normality the alienating dissonances and contradictions that characterize rapid industrialization in tension with the persistent but now anachronistic ideals of unity and homology.[1] Industrial reproduction is in this sense constitutively involved in the avant-garde's practice of negation.

Moreover, the recurring idealist position in architectural historiography—the successful suppression of everything that is *hors architecture* in favor of strict formal analysis—stems from this same ideology of high art.[2] For the historical avant-garde to militate against this ideology, indeed, presupposed a contemporaneous high art in commerce with a rather entrenched cultural establishment and its claims to authentic aesthetic knowledge. Practices such as dadaism sought to ridicule and destroy this myth of authenticity, to demystify and undermine the legitimizing discourse of the dominant culture, whose ambition it was to salvage the purity of art from the encroachments of technological modernization and mass industrialization. An effort to extend the analysis of some of these delegitimizing procedures into the bounds of architecture "proper" will involve us in a further discussion of the ways in which the architecture of the *neue Sachlichkeit* problematized the notion of autonomous architectural form and the concomitant centrality of the humanist subject. A reading of Hannes Meyer's competition project of 1926–1927 for the League of Nations and Ludwig Hilberseimer's Vorschlag zur City-Bebauung of 1930[3] illustrates two different occasions of negational practice in architecture, and two different ideological consequences. But it will be helpful to begin with an example of an interpretive method in which form is still viewed as autonomous and the subject *thereby* remains at the center of meaning.

That architecture is deeply and inescapably enmeshed in the material world may, on first reflection, hardly seem a contentious proposition, even to those who would insist on an autonomous status for other arts. Yet a transcendent autonomy is exactly what humanist readings of architecture hope for and endeavor to achieve, perhaps especially so in their more sophisticated and critical moments, in which perception is practiced as the detection of various sorts of idealized, conceptual grids hidden within or hovering above the work. In their essay "Transparency: Literal and Phenomenal," for example, Colin Rowe and Robert Slutzky concern themselves with architectural form as "a continuous dialectic between fact and implication." Rowe and Slutzky demonstrate that the brute facts of physical organization can be presented with a significant, inherent ambiguity such that those facts may be read in terms of competing or oscillating mental constructs. Their analysis of Le Corbusier's League of Nations project, and of the opposition it induces between

the reality of deep space and the implication of shallow
space, leads to a conceptual realm where "finally, by a series
of positive and negative implications, the whole area [of the
project] becomes a monumental debate, an argument
between a real and deep space and an ideal and shallow
one."[4] Through the "argument"—the continuous fluctua-
tion between alternative spatial discourses—the building is
experienced not as an inert, mute object, but as a topos
of meanings constituted by a process of cognitive
differentiation.[5]

The consequences of this
kind of cognitive project are important. First there is a distinction between the real, unmediated object in time and
space and the virtual object of the mind, a distinction
dependent on the special capacity of the viewer to organize,
reflect, and interpret. Yet in order to make sense of the
building, the viewer must have recourse to a set of idealized
meanings and categories of which he himself is the generator; each individual must create a transcendental object that
stands in some kind of reciprocal relation to himself as a
transcendental ego. The physical forms are thus subsumed
by their own contemplation, and the goal of this contemplation is the constitution of an ideated, unified form. The
intent is precisely to avoid any of the worldly, circumstantial, or socially "contaminated" content of history, for such

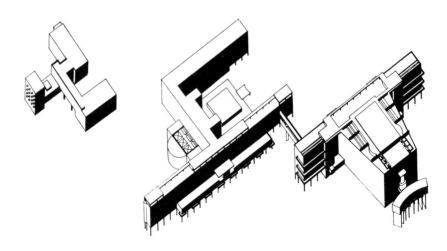

material grounding would impinge upon the subject's interpretive freedom and the ultimate projection of the work toward some specialized aesthetic experience or formal categorization.

Rowe's and Slutzky's reading of Le Corbusier's League of Nations project is a particularly cogent example of what might be called the cognitive project of humanism. Without downgrading the technical brilliance and fruitfulness of this enterprise, I wish to insist on its inadequacy as an understanding of modernism generally. The hegemony of such a humanist ideology has created in the critical establishment a consensus based on a restricted kind of formal analysis of "disinfected" objects. This effectively reconfirms the culture enforcing these restrictions, blinding us to modernism's more anguished occasions, its active engagements in material and ideological struggle. It is an instructive coincidence that we can directly compare Hannes Meyer's most famous design, his League of Nations project, to Le Corbusier's, for Meyer's architecture itself stands as a challenge to the cognitive project of humanism—even before the time when an elite

Le Corbusier's League of Nations project: diagrams by Colin Rowe and Robert Slutzky.

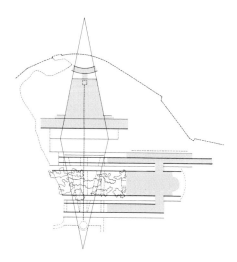

the cognitive project of *neue sachlichkeit*

and rarefied modernism was codified in stark distinction to mass cultural conventions—by problematizing the cognitive status of autonomous form as well as the subject for which that form is a metaphor. In the analysis here I shall maintain an attention to architectural form, but shall try to recast the formal logic by which the avant-garde has conventionally been analyzed in order to include aspects of its practice that have been neglected or denigrated. Meyer's project redirects our attention to those processes of modern life that lie beyond the individual subject, and we can detect this critical attitude within the forms themselves.

The operative technique in the cognitive project of Meyer's *neue Sachlichkeit* is the practice of negation[6]—the dismantling of traditional formal conventions, the production of ruptures and discontinuities, the repudiation of the individual author as the originator of meaning, and the denial to the viewing subject of a space apart from life in which the mind is free to dream, to escape. But negation is not just nay-saying; it is the active constructing of a new perception, the forcing of a new situation through form. Meyer's proposed League of Nations building develops certain architectural corollaries of productivism that follow some of the procedures already announced in the Co-op work. The first is a building system of reiterative spatial and constructional cells—part of an open-ended, nonhierarchical field of spatial and structural coordinates—coupled with plain, tough, essentially modern building materials like "Eternit" (an asbestos cement cladding used in place of a more honorific material like stone), steel, concrete, and glass, with rubber flooring, cork slab walls, and aluminum sheet ceilings on the interior. Such a building system resists the appearance of having been manipulated or mediated by a particular artistic personality or of having been fabricated for a particular (here monumental) purpose. The spatial and constructional elements convey instead their availability to society at large, and the fact that they are the result of certain modes of production, reproducible for a wide variety of uses. It is difficult, then,

to read the building system as representational in any traditional, mimetic sense, or as having been deformed according
to some autonomously conceived formal necessity. With its
emphasis on the material congruence of the building system
and the signification of the work, with its incorporation of
the technical means of its facture into the form of the
object itself, the work is, at least in part, a trace or direct
registration of those materials and procedures of reproduction from which it is constructed. As such, it tends to resist
assimilation in ideational terms, remaining obdurately
external to subjective, aesthetic comprehension. The subject
must rather think through the causal structures and processes operating behind the forms. I shall refer to this condition of the work of architecture as its *factural indexicality*,
by which I mean that the work points to the (reproductive)
processes of its making, seemingly generating its own representation without authorial mediation.

Though Meyer surely
courts a kind of positivism here, I do not intend to construe
his attitude as a deterministic understanding of architecture
as index. What I wish to suggest instead is that his strategy
effectively serves to block any aesthetic contemplation from
a distance. At this point in the development of the productivist avant-garde, factural indexicality means more than an
emphasis on the formal self-referentiality of architecture,
more than a coming to terms with its "medium" or its
"constituent facts." The indexical status of Meyer's project
signifies nothing less than a rejection of any transcendental
conception of the architectural object in favor of a conception of architectural practice as a worldly, engaged activity,
a material intervention and organizing force; an indication
of the potential involvement of the architect with certain
socially developed processes, materials, and standards of
production that, in turn, are identified with social revolution; and an expression of a wish to take part in the work of
negation that is fundamental in other avant-garde practices,
such as constructivism and dadaism.

Compare, for example, Alexander Rodchenko's *Hanging Construction*, part of a series subtitled *Surfaces Reflecting Light* of 1921. The engagement of the sculptural object with the viewer and the real world may be defined in terms of, first, the kinetic potential of the construction—the reflective surfaces register the changing movements of light, air, and touch—and, second, the indexical status of the object—the serially organized form is a product of repetitive circular motions, a kind of simulated mass production emphasizing the causal relationship between the sculptural sign and its enunciative apparatus of reproduction. What I am calling factural indexicality is, then, perhaps analogous to one interpretation of the Soviet avant-garde's concern for an indexical and textural *faktura*. As Benjamin Buchloh has written,

Quite unlike the traditional idea of *fattura* or *facture* in painting, where the masterful facture of a painter's hand spiritualizes the *mere* materiality of the pictorial production, and where the hand becomes at the same time the substitute or the totalization of the identifying signature (as the guarantee of authenticity, it justifies the painting's exchange value and maintains its commodity existence), the new concern for *faktura* in the Soviet avant-garde emphasizes precisely the mechanical quality, the materiality, and the anonymity of the painterly procedure from a perspective of empirico-critical positivism. It demystifies and devalidates not only the claims for the authenticity of the spiritual and the transcendental in the painterly execution but, as well, the authenticity of the exchange value of the work of art that is bestowed on it by the first.[7]

In his development of an architecture conceived according to a factural indexicality with its basis in reproduction, Meyer must have learned from Soviet experiments. Thus the rhetoric of his essay "Die neue Welt" of 1926 echoes constructivist concerns:

Instead of easel-work, we have the drafting machine. Instead of the French horn, the saxophone. Instead of a copy of light reflections,

Alexander Rodchenko, *Spatial Constructions*, 1920–1921: standardized units of wood.

Alexander Rodchenko, *Hanging Construction*, 1920–1921: serialized production.

the cognitive project of *neue sachlichkeit*

we use light itself to create with. . . . Instead of the sculptural imitation of movement, we have movement itself. . . . Instead of lyrics, we have the sound poem. Instead of the novel, the short story. Instead of color tone, we have value of the color in luxes. Instead of sculpture, we have construction. Instead of caricature, photosculpture. Instead of drama, the sketch. Instead of opera, the revue. Instead of frescos, the poster. Instead of painted material, the color of the material itself. ("Painting without a brush" in itself calls for picture construction for manual reasons.) . . . The depreciation of all works of art is indisputable, and there can be no question that the continued utilization of new and exact knowledge in their place is merely a matter of time. The art of felt imitation is in the process of being dismantled. Art is becoming invention and controlled reality. And personality? The heart?? The soul??? Our plea is for absolute segregation.[8]

Meyer's effort in this text to define what he considers to be an adequate artistic sensibility seems interminable; he pushes each signifying practice to its limits, where it turns back into unworked material—tough, emphatic, worldly. The radical quality of Meyer's approach, as of Rodchenko's, a quality continually perceived by audiences as an aggression toward the architectural object's status as high art and toward the individual or class for which that object is a metaphor, lies largely in factural indexicality as a negational operation.

Meyer's League of Nations project seems prompted by the acute awareness that neither the individual subject nor subjective attempts to recover the authenticity of the object any longer have a place in the mass-industrialized city, by the acknowledgment of the absolute incompatibility between the realm of mass culture as a socioeconomic totality ordered by tactility, use, and distraction and the realm of optical, contemplative inner experience. The second proposition of his project thus involves a search for sense within a larger conception of the reality of the metropolis, beyond subjective interiority. Regarding this new frame of meaning, Meyer writes in his essay "bauen,"

all things in this world are a product of the formula: (function times economics).
so none of these things are works of art:
all art is composition and hence unsuited to a particular end.
all life is function and therefore not artistic.
the idea of the "composition of a dock" is enough to make a cat laugh!
but how is a town plan designed? or the plan of a dwelling? composition or function? art or life????? building is a biological process.
building is not an aesthetic process . . .
architecture as an "embodiment of the artist's emotions" has no justification. architecture as "continuing the building tradition" means being carried on the tide of building history.[9]

The statement is first an aggressively rhetorical, materialist refusal of signification based on composition, a refusal of mimetic representation, a refusal of form itself. Second, it is an explicit desire to integrate art with life, or to eliminate the need for art from life, or, in either case, to deny a secondary level of aesthetic meaning beyond the physical traces of rationalized building technique. For to be "carried on the tide of building history" is to conjoin building techniques and technologies with emergent social needs, to interpenetrate technology and the collective body so that the process of building actually becomes biological. Meyer does not seek to propose a set of physical notations that can produce a transcendental object (the virtual object of a humanist reading) as their meaning; the architectural elements articulate an available reproductive *system* rather than a self-involved object. Moreover, history is posited as the driving force of this system. This disprivileging of a preordained, static, aesthetic ideal in favor of a nexus of relationships between modes of production and changing human needs means shifting architecture's meaning *to the outside*, so to speak, where structure is no longer predicated on private, psychological space but rather on public, cultural space.

the cognitive project of *neue sachlichkeit*

We should recall here Walter Benjamin's insight that as one approaches those mediums that are inherently multiple and reproducible, not only does the authenticity of the object as a repository of meaning become reduced, but also the reproductive technique *as procedure* takes on the features of a system of signification. In refusing traditional representational forms, Meyer reevaluated the logic of a particular source of meaning; he did not deny meaning altogether. He saw meaning as arising from the multiple forces of social practice rather than the formal qualities of the auratic art object.

There are representational and formal consequences to this relocation of meaning, nonetheless, and we are led now to consider them. As Meyer states about his project, "Our League of Nations building symbolizes nothing. Its size is automatically determined by the dimensions and conditions of the program. As an organic building it expresses unfeignedly that it is intended to be a building for work and co-operation. . . . This building is neither beautiful nor ugly. It asks to be evaluated as a structural invention."[10] The architect's polemical ambition is the automatic transcription of a socially determined, empirical program into built form. The architect himself is only a switching mechanism who sets in motion the processes of assembling an object made up of use values and visual codes already consolidated by society and structured by continual self-production, thereby negating the controlling action of the artist as the determination of the architectural signification. To this end, Meyer deploys a number of strategies to redirect the cognitive project away from the production of ideated figures or formal unities.

First, the overall configuration is organized in relation to vehicular movement around and through the building, with the pilotis of the assembly building accommodating the access and storage of automobiles, 600 altogether, six times the number required by the competition program. The vehicular provision also

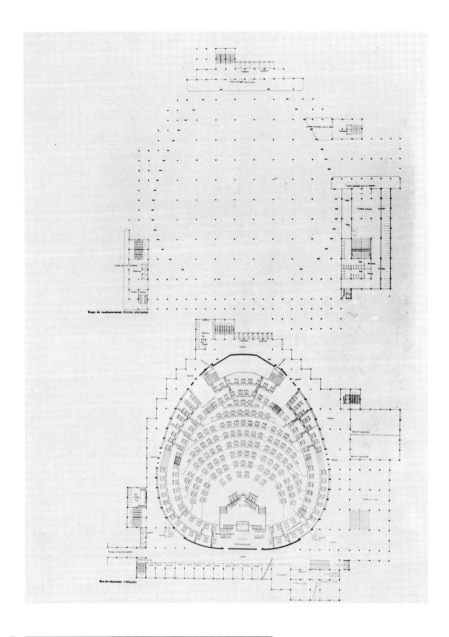

Meyer, League of Nations project, ground plan.

Meyer, League of Nations project, mezzanine plan.

the cognitive project of *neue sachlichkeit*

serves, along with the multiple elevator banks, to categorize and distribute types of users of the building—personnel, journalists, delegates, and the general public. Furthermore, in spite of a competition program with an appendix of ten photographs showing the site's grandeur and pastoral qualities, Meyer's drawings, with their black shadows and depersonalized line work, deliberately refuse the natural site conditions. Instead the project declares itself to be involved in the quotidian but dynamic, mechanized world of which the automobile is the primary agent. If in Le Corbusier's project one senses the attempt to isolate the architectural object in nature, its true ambience being somehow different from the randomly organized, gritty, profane world of driving and parking, the consequence of Meyer's basic organization is to insist that the building is continuous with this space of the world and dependent on it for its existence.[11]

Moreover, unlike Le Corbusier's project with its central axis and stratification of spaces—"the essence of that phenomenal transparency" articultated by Rowe and Slutzky—Meyer's project is egregiously decentered and dissymmetrical. Disparate architec-

Meyer, League of Nations project, site plan.

Hannes Meyer, League of Nations project, 1926–1927, axonometric.

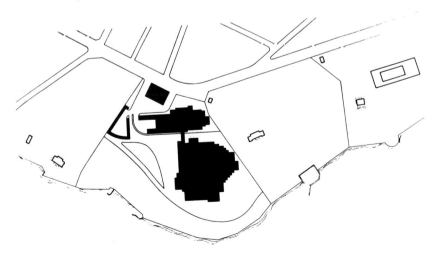

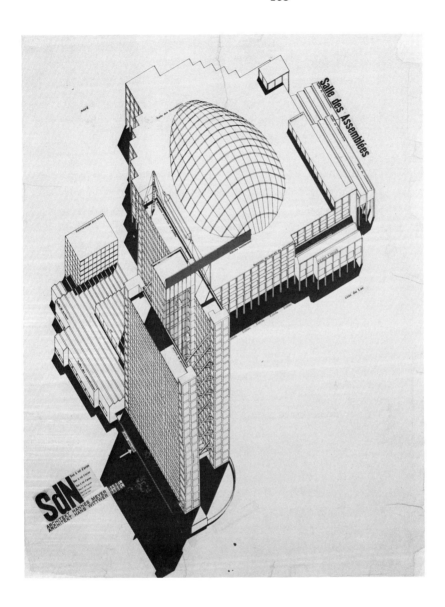

tures, abutting or nesting, articulate themselves from the
same tectonic system. The discreteness of the two halves of
the building, the secretariat tower and assembly hall,
declares the absence of any underlying formal armature that
might in turn engender a series of spatial emanations. The
singular cognitive map that a centralizing datum or ground
would normally provide is thereby obstructed, and tension,
contradiction, and difference define the relationships
between elements.

    Intensifying this percep-
tion within each of the two main halves of the building is
the renunciation of any compositional device that would
organize the diverse parts into a coherent unit, thus further
exaggerating differences within the system. The general
tendency in the fundamental building system toward an
atomization of tectonic parts belonging to a larger but inde-
terminate whole is supported and developed by a secondary
level of architectonic elements—agglomerations of sky-
lighted commission rooms, lecture rooms, offices, a restaurant, and a library; movement systems like the glazed
stairways, elevators, and "toboggan" emergency ramps; and
information-disseminating devices like radio antennae and
illuminated sky signs. The unstable syntax of these elements is determined by their specific functional relations,
"automatically" superimposed on the general system; their
semantics arise from the mass-cultural, industrial city
itself—plain, factorylike, porous, unyielding. Local symme-
tries and unities are deployed in elevation and plan but with
disjunctive relationships to one another. Thus, articulations
within the lattice of the elevations are made to seem randomly distributed over the surface, the stepped plan profile
to seem aleatory and open-ended, and the architectural elements completely detachable and rearrangeable. To be sure,
substantial formal decisions have been made by the architect, but with the effect that we conceive the building not
as an integral formal organism but as an assemblage of
architectural particularities, a montage of discourse, each
part clashing with the rest, defined wholly in terms of their

separate functional and material life. The body of the building thus contorts to assume the forms cast upon it by the forces of the city.

"No pillared reception rooms for weary monarchs but hygienic workrooms for the busy representatives of their people. No back corridors for backstairs diplomacy but open glazed rooms for the public negotiations of honest men."[12] Meyer's own characterization of what Rowe and Slutzky would call the literal (as opposed to their preferred phenomenal) transparency of the League of Nations building captures the sense of a morality effect produced by glass in terms remarkably close to Benjamin's, written the same year: "To live in a glass house is a revolutionary virtue par excellence. It is also an intoxication, a moral exhibitionism, that we badly need. Discretion concerning one's own existence, once an aristocratic virtue, has become more and more an affair of petit-bourgeois parvenus."[13] For Benjamin as for Meyer glass was a material without aura—cold, sober, the enemy of secrets, the enemy of property. Glass is yet another index of Meyer's negational stance.

Finally, Meyer resists as far as possible the creation of any processional space that might result in a monumental unity. The classification of users by parking pattern at ground level allows him to rely on vertical modes of access to all floors above; the interjection of various banks of elevators at strategic points in the plan affords direct access to the vestibules located between the wings of the secretariat or around the periphery of the auditorium. Spaces of reception and passage are pushed to the perforated perimeter in a general avoidance of closure and containment. The viewer walking through the building finds himself always in residual spaces, in the gaps between the primary spatial units, compelled to move, constantly differentiating and recombining spatial experiences, but only in pieces, and only in time.

How can we characterize the strategies deployed by Meyer as a whole? In what is

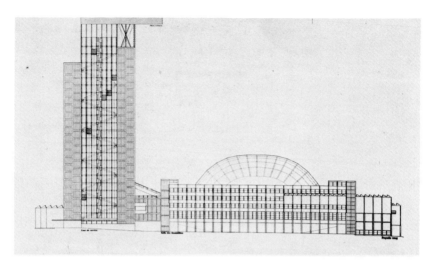

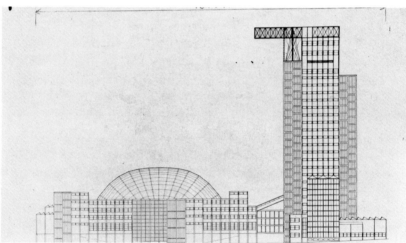

Meyer, League of Nations project, elevations.

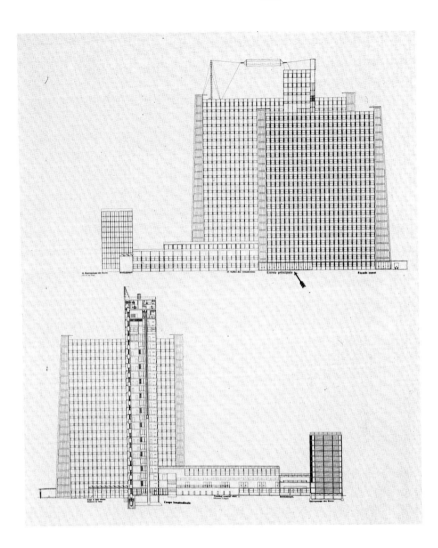

now the canonical interpretation of Meyer's League of
Nations project, Kenneth Frampton suggested, "Meyer
sought to express his egalitarianism through the repetition
of a standard structural module, part of an infinite field of
coordinates. On this field his structural arrangement would
arise in much the same manner as the 'image' came into
being on a Mondrian canvas. The Platonic element for
Meyer was the structural grid."[14] Such an analogy between
the matrix of a Mondrian painting and that of Meyer's
architecture means to claim for the League of Nations project a spatial order that arises from an a priori mental construct; it further implies an equivalence of signification
between form and simple utility. While the analogy to Mondrian is helpful, I would like to offer an alternative one,
which sees the reiterative building system and its relationship to the functional units as comparable to a dada photomontage, with the bits and fragments of the real, profane
world registered on its blank page. My analogy derives from
the fact that both Meyer's system and photomontage induce
the perception of a condition of exteriority.[15]

Ordinarily we discover
meaning in an architectural object or on a pictorial surface
by claiming some sense from the outside world, sublimating
that reality to artistic form, and constructing a unified, integral image of that world within the object or on the surface—a kind of surrogate for the perceiving subject, a
metaphor for the integral self. But in dada photomontage
what we experience more than a unified surface or pictorial
whole are the fissures and gaps between disjunctive representations, and the interferences between signs from different systems. The dada surface does not allow us to impute
to it any formal unity that we can press into service inward;
rather it registers each of a series of intruder objects, securing them in isolation, holding each within a condition of
separateness and difference. Such an atomization of material
is governed by a system of meaning that is extraobjective,
by what Benjamin called the image sphere of "profane illumination." Thus, the dada photomontage, like Meyer's

Raoul Hausmann, *Dada Cino*, 1920.

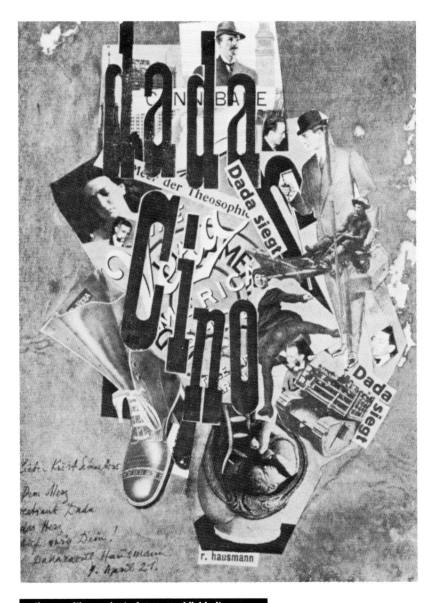

r. hausmann

the cognitive project of *neue sachlichkeit*

building, is less significant as an object than as a procedure. As Benjamin has written, "What [the dadaists] achieved was a relentless destruction of the aura of their creations, which they branded as reproductions with the very means of production."[16]

The medium of photomontage exactly suffices dada's destructive, negational task. It draws its material from those enunciative formations—such as advertising, journalism, and mass production—that were already consolidated by society, just as Mcyer uses mass-produced constructional readymades widely available for building. Dada photomontage exaggerates the chance accretion of fragments of manufactured experience, just as Meyer exaggerates the "automatic" accumulation of diverse functions. By showing reality sequentially and as decomposed—one thing after another and one thing external to another—dada destroys the image of simultaneous presence that is a metaphor for the integral psyche. Dada montage exhausts, overwhelms the individual subject by constituting another place, another history, another way of thinking beyond the self, more powerful than the self. Exteriority, then, is this displacement of sense outward; and dada photomontage is precisely this exteriority given form, a topos of negation and estrangement.

Meyer's League of Nations project involves a more structured, perhaps more abstract version of the notion of exteriority. The architectural medium is understood as a construct encoding sociopolitical and economic processes and functions in the real world that are wholly in place before either the architect or the viewer encounters them, reproducing them for the benefit of the world and according to conditions set by and in the world. The analysis of Meyer's building, then, cannot proceed by means of a reduction of the complex form to a simple, unified diagram or *parti*. The building should rather be seen as a marking or trace of a larger, more complex totality—dense, quotidian, aleatory, exceeding individual, intuitive grasp. This is precisely the same exteriority that

dada photomontage and Meyer's Co-op factography traces,
the factuality of modernity's striated surface. Thus Meyer's
functional markings come to us as a succession of units, as
if from the unreeling of those larger cultural processes, a
serial progression of separate integers whose differences are
not mediated by composition but rather revealed by an
architecture conscious of the irreducibility of its disjunctions. Like the dada photomontage, Meyer's building presents itself less as an object than as a multilayered field of
convergence for the forces and signs of the mass-industrial
city.

In pointing to certain
attitudes common to Meyer and the dadaists, I do not
intend to attribute to either an unselfconsciousness with
regard to form, but rather to query the grounds on which
their formal manipulations are made. The works of Meyer
and the dadaists reflect a wry, derisive awareness of the normative humanist subject they deface and of the humanist
ideology of autonomy they renounce. Just as the dada photomontage adheres to the bourgeois artistic convention of
presenting a unique, fabricated, rectangularly framed object
even as it subversively injects into the singularity of that
object the reproduced and dispersed images of bourgeois culture, so Meyer is driven toward conventional ways of architectural sense-making that are at once unacceptable and
inescapable, vestiges of humanist perceptions that have
become progressively empty but continue to exert their
force. A whole tradition of representation is in crisis, but
the search for meaning is not abandoned. That contradiction, that search, I believe, is what drove Meyer toward an
insurrectionary participation in the discipline of architecture, toward architecture as social practice.

The radical quality of
Meyer's modernism lies in the difficult truth that *things are
just what they are*, utterly shorn of any metaphysical illusions of artistic authenticity, unity, or depth. Suspicious of
subjectivity and the unified whole in which subjectivity
affirms itself, the League of Nations project is a reaction

against the very idea of an autonomous work of art, a refusal of the very possibility of the architectural masterpiece existing in and for itself. With the renunciation of the organizational value of a purely internal formal necessity, the concept of the work as a self-involved object is shattered. The work no longer presents an unbroken and homogeneous appearance, no longer stands complete and suspended, as it were, against the world, but rather falls into the world, becoming one worldly thing (*Sache*) among others. The boundaries between the facts of modern society and aesthetic production are thereby dismantled, and that production returned to its unprivileged place within the totality of social practices.

It is the relentlessness of Meyer's practice of negation that I admire and that I believe is still a viable project for architectural practice—his annihilation of the traditional, hegemonic repertoire of traditional representational form, his fragmentation of form and registration of dissonances, and his shattering of the basis of traditional artistic sublimation, the contemplative humanist subject. But negation is not, of course, unproblematic. For the decoding and dismantling of the older forms of experience, such as the transcendent or the sacred, and the substitution of new forms of standardization, reification, and massification of both subject and object pose crippling problems for architectural pratice; and the *neue Sachlichkeit*'s various attempts to invent new and elaborate formal strategies with which to figure what seemed to be the utter incompatibility between the emerging social structure and individual lived experience, to enact a dialectical reversal of subject and object, are each differently marked by their immersion into a dissipative and all-consuming reality. By 1927 Ludwig Hilberseimer's projects and writings had already emerged as striking illustrations of all the ambiguities and contradictions inherent in this posthumanist avantgarde, of the internal resistances to its self-declared forward movement, seeds of which are present in Meyer's project.

Within the discourse of
Sachlichkeit, the architectural avant-garde in the late 1920s
was to rationalize its program in terms of overcoming the
dialectic, already formulated by Meyer, between part and
whole, molecular and molar, between the elementary cell
and the totality of the physical and social city. In his *Groszstadtarchitektur* of 1927, Hilberseimer writes,

The architecture of the metropolis depends essentially on the solution both of the elementary cell and the urban organism as a
whole. The single room as the constituent element of the habitation will determine the form of the habitation, and since the habi-
tations in turn form blocks, the room will become the decisive
factor of urban configuration, which is architecture's true goal.
Reciprocally, the planimetric structure of the city will have a substantial influence on the design of the habitation and the room.[17]

The metropolis for Hilberseimer is a molar machine involving large-scale social, technical, and economic systems
intercommunicating with architectural elements. The reproducible architectural elements at the molecular level—each
identical in size and shape, without a priori determined
points of focus or termination—translate and relay information received from the global structure of the city, even as
these same elements are, in turn, the prime constitutive
units of that structure. The abolition of the gap between the
urban order and the individual cell eliminates the possibility of attributing significance to the act of selecting or
arranging forms. The auratic architectural object is systematically and utterly defeated by techniques of reproduction
now radically rationalized and expanded.

From this analysis comes
Hilberseimer's Hochhausstadt project of 1924 (first published in *Die Form,* 1926), which he reproduces in his
Groszstadtarchitektur. It is a project menaced with ambiguity. As a first characterization, it may be construed as an
attempt at a complete encoding, within the conventions of
architectural representation, of the condition of exteriority.
The most striking aspect of Hilberseimer's perspective

Ludwig Hilberseimer, Hochhausstadt project, 1924, perspective of a north-south street.

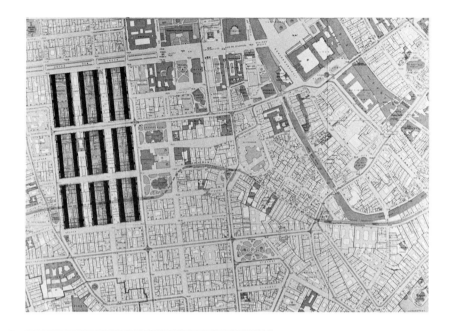

Ludwig Hilberseimer, project for the construction of a city applied to the center of Berlin,
1928, plan.

drawings is their quality of persistence—the relentless repetition of the same cellular blocks without any climax, seemingly without any form or direction that would attest to a
creator's personality, without subjectivity (excepting, perhaps, some vestigial anguish for the suppressed subject in
the drawing's texture, size, and above-eye-level vanishing
point). The formerly self-constituting subject, now disen-
cumbered of all remnants of independent personality, no
longer attends, reflects, or organizes; Hilberseimer's perspective is not the same "view" one has in a humanist perspective where the form of representation functions as a system
of knowledge organized around and for the viewer's own
centrality. The subject—still a concrete individual, but at
the same time part of a more general, collective human
substance, a component in a larger totality of interlocking
mechanical processes and social institutions—is now constituted by the system. And the subject's conscious experience
of interpretation (which used to correspond to its ability to

Hilberseimer standing before a model of a tower made of six fifteen-story buildings stacked vertically, 1927.

reason and reflect) becomes little more than a process of acknowledging the extension of a code without cessation (as if in hyperspace *avant la lettre*), tracing the external network of socioeconomic and historical circumstances that determine and manipulate the subject, recognizing that the network exists beyond the present moment and that one will, in the course of one's mundane involvement, glimpse its return again and again.

On this view, Hilberseimer's project carries to completion a latent tendency in Meyer's work toward an overdetermination of all elements, but, in contrast to Meyer, results in an abolition of contingencies, an assimilation or absorption of all particularity in the raw material into the totalizing structure of the work itself, a collapse of the molecular into the molar. In Hilberseimer's own words, "the general case and the law are emphasized and made evident, while the exception is by contrast put aside, the nuance canceled."[18] Contingency has now become necessity, the part the colophon of the whole, and the mundane facts of modernity have become appropriated, internalized law.

Perhaps, then, it is not surprising that while Hilberseimer's total unification of repetitive cells and the global structure of the city may have been effective in shifting architectural meaning from the aesthetic realm to a deeper logic of the socioeconomic metropolis itself, the architect was hard put to find in this logic a source for invention. It risks little to assert that from the time Hilberseimer committed himself to the totalization announced in the Hochhausstadt, his work virtually ceased to develop and instead became involved with radical repetition. Thus he could propose only the same organization for his Vorschlag zur City-Bebauung of 1930 as he had for his Hochhausstadt of 1924, and for Chicago as he had for Berlin. In 1926 and 1927, he exhibited a project for a tower made of six of his fifteen-story buildings, now stacked.[19] That Hilberseimer should have maneuvered himself into this particular position is quite interesting. For we are led to focus on the apparent fact that logically, axiomatically, such a totalizing organization—one in which the productive, causal source of signification is based on reproduction—*can only be repeated.*[20]

The case is made dramatically in Hilberseimer's Vorschlag zur City-Bebauung. To begin with, there are the anti-illusionistic strategies of the axonometric drawing; the margin of the drawing cuts the outer blocks, and the letters of the title are placed within the margins of the image in such a way as to suppress all effect of depth. But what I wish to concentrate on is the insertion in the drawing of what is apparently a variant scheme. The drawing with its insertion becomes a kind of *mise-en-abîme,* a ceaseless, telescoping fall. For the variant is simply an axonometric reproduction of the Hochhausstadt of 1924, and its insertion places within the field of the representation another representation reduplicated by the first. The insertion serves to focus our attention precisely on the absence of origins.

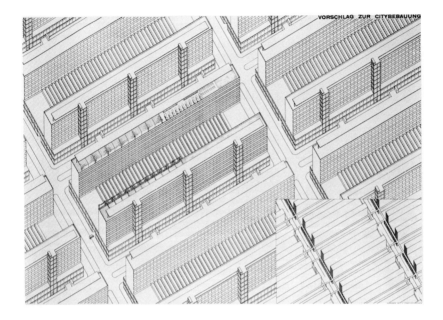

VORSCHLAG ZUR CITYBEBAUUNG

| Ludwig Hilberseimer, Vorschlag zur Citybe-
bauung (project for the construction of a city), 1930;
axonometric with inset of alternative scheme.

What we witness in this *mise-en-abîme* is nothing less than a subtle but definite deconstruction of the notion of function as the origin of architectural form. The notion of functionalism—the originary status of the brute, objective facts of utility intersecting with measured, standardized means of production—has been supposed to provide a fundamental demarcation within modern architecture, one made especially manifest by the *neue Sachlichkeit* of Hilberseimer and Meyer. Yet Hilberseimer's drawing makes it clear that the originary status of function is a fiction.

Between the multilayered functions within the city, the means of production, and the architectural form that is supposed to be their product, there is not the determined correspondence necessary for a notion of origin. On the one hand, the serial, cellular organism that constitutes Hilberseimer's city follows the implacable logic of the city's production cycles. But it is not

transparent to those cycles. It is rather a tissue of representation that reveals only their most salient contours. Hilberseimer's project organizes a metaphor for the city's own
productive and functional procedures, mediating those procedures through the conventions of architectural form and
thus effectively truncating the complex technical, social,
and economic conditions that produced the project, conceal-
ing the "real" origins of its formation by displacing them
with a substitute—an irreducibly architectural form.

Therefore, on the other
hand, the form also precedes the functional and productive
factors, the image precedes the situation it claims to represent. Behind Hilberseimer's representation, his system of
signs, are all those other representations through which the
city's activities and production—its material life—are necessarily described. To the extent that it is architecture,
Hilberseimer's project is inscribed in a particular field of
representations that is already constituted as architectural;
his project summarizes other projects, only the most
obvious of which is his own. Whatever sense we make of
the project has to do with our use of conventions of meaning that allow us to sort the architectural elements into significance. Hilberseimer's architecture thus does not (cannot)
absolutely correspond to material life, but rather translates
it from one sign system (socioeconomic) into another (architectural). *Sachlichkeit,* however much it resisted a basis in
form, was brought into play with formal metaphors, with
the architectural medium in all its quiddity as a vehicle for
certain senses, qualities, and values: architecture seen as the
production of material life, as function. Hilberseimer's
drawing demonstrates peremptorily that form can only represent function when function has first been interpreted as a
possibility of form.

In the standard histories
of modern architecture the originary status of function as a
generator of form and of the active human subject as a generator of meaning have been maintained as presumptions
from which corollaries of authenticity, affirmation, and full-

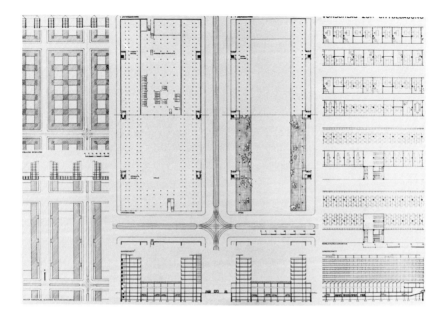

Hilberseimer, Vorschlag zur Citybebauung,
plan.

ness and communicability of meaning follow. The analysis
here leads us to suggest that it is within an altogether different realm that a definition of the historical avant-garde
might be found—in the realm where naive functionalism
and the self-constituted subject are both defeated by the
coupling of reproduction and negation.

Hilberseimer's ultimate
solution is not, however, without even further inherent contradictions. The characterization of Hilberseimer's system
as "total" deliberately emphasizes the term of affiliation of
his project with an emerging tendency in the socioeconomic
structure of the modern world toward radical systematization, a tendency of which fascist political regimes have been
only the most malevolent manifestation.[21] If Hilberseimer's
drawing comprises a sign system for an external network of
socioeconomic and historical circumstances, it does so at a
particular moment in the historical development of these
circumstances. For in the last stages of the Weimar Republic modernization would show its darkest side, and all the

multiplicity and particularity of activities—of production, distribution, and reception—would be coldly rationalized into a single all-absorbing mechanism. And with Hilberseimer's project, so radically linked to the mindset of modernization, this new totalitarian planning of the public realm is operative in the structure of the work of architecture itself. In his drawing all dissonances and disjunctions are absorbed, all differences canceled; the metropolis described here does not permit alternatives. The project is not simply an available, neutral matrix in which monopoly capitalism might incidentally play itself out, absorbing all things, people, and thought into a single-market system; it is itself a form of that system. Now a constraint more than a liberating convention, *neue Sachlichkeit*'s ambition of negation turns back on itself, reentering the work as its opposite—as ideology, as fixed patterns of form, action, and thought, as hypostatized rationalism. The disintegrating ambiguity of Hilberseimer's work stands in poignant parallel to the disintegration of Weimar Germany and its passage into fascism. This is he crisis of modernist culture itself: adversarial, as we saw with Meyer, but, in its drive toward a total organization of the city, conceptually and practically bound up with capitalist modernization and reification, and their convoluted consequences.

So it is that the process of negation tends in the long run to overwhelm avant-garde practice;[22] it quickly becomes cumulative and uncontrollable, and the anthropological rupture it opens is as much susceptible to the invasions of megalomaniacal protofascisms as it is capable of revolutionary discharge. Thus Hilberseimer's work, identifying too completely with the processes and structures of modernization and its promise of progress, as well as its fitful drops into cynicism and self-annihilation, also harbors a psychocultural fear of loss, disintegration, and nullity, which I will later invoke a notion of paranoia to explicate. Perhaps inevitably Hilberseimer's dislocated subject flips over into a faceless functionary of the shifting valences of reification, and his architecture paradox-

ically becomes the very form of closure that Meyer sought
to avoid through his critical assertion of a posthumanist
practice. But who can say that Meyer, too, was not part of
this same trajectory? As Adorno has taught us, reification is
a poison that committed art cannot refuse,[23] and Meyer
took his with some enthusiasm. Without ever straying from
the terrain of architecture, the avant-garde finds itself
deeply implicated in a struggle between adversarial negation
and affirmation of the structure of totalitarian society.

Avant-garde practice is
predicated on reproduction as negation, a strategy that is
inscribed in the very forms in which others would find synthesis and reintegration or self-delighting formal play. In
avant-garde practice negation appears not as a redemptive
effort that blazes the way for a new fullness of meaning, but
rather as an all-encompassing fact, pulling like an undertow,
ultimately swallowing meaning altogether. To pierce
through negation is to find, on one side, emptiness, and, on
the other, totalization: this is the dilemma the avant-garde
confronted constantly, the terms of which it tried constantly to refuse.

ludwig hilberseimer and the inscription of the paranoid subject

Interjection

Herr Bertolt Brecht maintains: a man is a man.

And that is something anyone can prove.

But then, Herr Bertolt Brecht also proves

That one can do as much as one likes with a person.

Here this evening, a man will be reassembled like a car

Without losing anything in the process.

The man will be approached humanely

He will be requested firmly, without vexation

To accommodate himself to the course of the world

And to let his private fish swim away.

And no matter what he is remodeled into,

In doing so no mistake has been made.

One can, if we do not watch over him,

also make him overnight into our butcher.

Herr Bertolt Brecht hopes that you will see the ground

On which you stand disappear like snow under your feet

And that you will notice about the packer Galy Gay

That life on earth is dangerous.

Bertolt Brecht, "Mann ist Mann"

the crisis of humanism, the dissolution of the object

Mies van der Rohe's 1922 skyscraper project comprises two basic architectural strategies. One is a building surface qualified no longer by patterns of shadow on an opaque material but by the reflections and refractions of light by glass. The other is a building form conceived not in terms of separate, articulated masses related to one another by some measurable grid, but as a complex unitary volume that does not permit itself to be read as emanating from a purely internal formal logic.[1] With these two related propositions Mies puts into crisis the cognitive status of the humanist object and the corresponding conception of the subject as an ideal, unified, centered self contemplating the abstract unity of that object. Against the autonomous, formal object of humanism in which the viewer can grasp in purely mental space an antecedent logic, decipering the relationships between its parts and connecting every part to a coherent formal theme, the alternative posited by Mies is an object intractable to decoding by an analysis of what is only immanent and apparent. The glass curtain wall, alternately transparent, reflective, or refractive depending on light conditions and viewing positions, absorbs, mirrors, or distorts the immediate, constantly changing images of city life and foregrounds the context as a physical and conceptual frame for understanding the building. And if this reading of Mies's project is thus far largely phenomenological, it is that very phenomenological reality of the metropolis "reflected" in the project that throws humanist conceptions of the subject into question, even as it is the vestiges of humanist thought that allow the reality to be gauged as unsatisfactory.

An interpretation of the phenomenal context of the Friedrichstrasse—and the post-Wilhelminian, postwar refuse out of which Weimar culture was to be constructed—is offered by Georg Grosz in a drawing of 1918. The drawing recalls Simmel's description of the *Nervenleben* of the metropolis and the fetishization of its products as "the intensification of nervous stimulation" resulting from the "rapid crowding of changing images, the sharp discontinuity in the grasp of a single glance, and the

Ludwig Mies van der Rohe, skyscraper project, 1922, model for study of reflections.

unexpectedness of onrushing impressions. These are the psychological conditions which the metropolis creates." The typical consequence of this *Nervenleben*, according to Simmel, is a blasé attitude—a blunting of discrimination, an indifference to value, a general languor. "In this phenomenon the nerves find in the refusal to react to their stimulation the last possibility of accommodating to the contents and forms of metropolitan life. The preservation of certain personalities is bought at the price of devaluating the whole objective world, a devaluation which in the end unavoidably drags one's own personality down into a feeling of the same worthlessness."[2] *This* is the reality reflected in the surface of Mies's skyscraper, and the context it both focuses and disturbs. The convex, faceted surfaces of the project are perceptually contorted by the invasion of circumstantial images, while the reflection each concavity receives on its surface is that of its own shadow, creating gaps that exacerbate the disarray. These surface distortions accompany and accentuate the formal inscrutability of the volumetric configuration. It is impossible, for example, to reduce the whole to a number of constituent parts related by some internal armature or transformed through some formal operation; no such compositional relationships exist. Neither is it possible to explicate the object as a deflection from some formal type; Mies has rejected the meanings that such mimetic design methods tend to promote. The very body of the building contorts to assume the form demanded by the contingent configuration of the site and to register the circumstantial images of the context. Mies thus invests meaning in a sense of surface and volume that the building assumes in a particular time and place, in a contextually qualified moment, continuous with and dependent upon the world in which the viewer actually moves. This sense of surface, severed from the knowledge of an internal order or a unifying logic characteristic of humanist architecture, is enough to wrench the building from the atemporal, idealized realm of autonomous form and install it in a specific situation in the real world of experienced time, open to all the chance and uncertainty of life in the metropolis.

Mies here exemplifies what we have already seen to be the central strategy of anti-humanist thought: against the a priori categories of rational understanding, in which the mind is supposed to have a pre-formed and permanent structure that parcels out the objects of experience, it is now the temporal, historically developed, and irrational structure of society that is determinant. Adorno—rewriting Marx's dictum that philosophy is not a "matter of logic" (*Sache der Logik*) but the "logic of the matter" (*Logik der Sache*)—puts the point succinctly: "The fetish character of commodities [the reality of the metropolis] is not a fact of consciousness, but dialectic in the eminent sense that it produces consciousness."[3] For Adorno, as for Mies, the renunciation of humanist subjectivity is consequent to an act of "immersion in particularity,"[4] of the subject giving itself over to the object (in Mies's case the city),

Georg Grosz, *Friedrichstrasse*, lithograph, 1918.

Ludwig Mies van der Rohe, Friedrichstrasse project, 1919, photomontage.

crisis of humanism, dissolution of the object

which leads not to the subject's self-discovery but to the discovery of a social structure in a particular historical configuration. Yet Adorno further insists that the subject, though it yields to the object, does not leave it unchanged. Rather the subject actively and interpretively rearranges the elements of reality in an "exact fantasy,"[5] as if to pin down and register the factuality that controls its thought, in a construction of cognitive as well as artistic moment.

It is in this sense of the artistic object as a cognitive-registration mechanism that Mies's skyscraper project can be identified with Kurt Schwitters's Merz-column in Hanover begun around the same time.[6] Both projects share an antagonism toward a priori and reasoned order. Both plunge into the chaos of the metropolis to seek another order within it through a systematic use of the unexpected, the aleatory, the inexplicable. Both are objects in crisis. They attest to the fact that the humanist conceptions of formal rationality and self-creating subjectivity cannot cope with the irrationality of actual experience. In the modern city, such constructs of

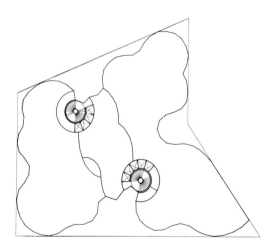

Mies van der Rohe, skyscraper project, plan.

Kurt Schwitters, Merz-column, Hanover, c. 1923.

crisis of humanism, dissolution of the object

rationality fail to function, and the mind, the subject, is consequently unable to perceive a pattern in the chaos. At such a moment, the subject has its one opportunity to escape reification: by thinking through what it is that *causes* reality to appear to be only a collection of fragmented images; by looking for structures and processes operating in time behind what appears to be given and objectified; by constructing, in an aesthetic modality, a cognitive mechanism understood "as a dialectically entwined and explicatively undecipherable unity of concept and matter."[7] Crisis, in short, is converted into a critical mediation between various levels of form and its social context.[8] And the other aspect of Mies's "exact fantasy"—the thick, black, silent elevational drawing—attempts to negate that contextual status quo, asserting itself as a radically different, subversive object within an unsatisfactory social and physical fabric.[9]

The turn to the objective effects of modern industrial capitalism, to its structures and processes understood as factors of form making, and to the construction of some kind of causality among the levels of social experience, new modes and materials of production, and architectural form: this is also the similarity between Mies's 1922 skyscraper project and Ludwig Hilberseimer's Chicago Tribune project of the same year. The distinction between them, however, is the different terms in which these mutual relationships are grasped—the displacement and criticism of the social subtext by form, in the case of Mies (and Schwitters), and the absorption or envelopment of this subtext into form, in the case of Hilberseimer. A definite epistemological shift separates the two: I believe that Hilberseimer's approach amounts to nothing less than the abolition of architecture as a communicative action or representational practice; not only the evacuation of significations and subjectifications from the domain of architecture, but also the negation of all dimensions of critique and conscious resistance available to architectural design.

Mies van der Rohe, skyscraper project,
elevation.

Mies's skyscraper is a
sign still committed to the real—projective, referential,
intrusive, in a negative dialogue with the context of its production, sustained at formal and cognitive levels. Hilberseimer's project, on the other hand, begins not with some
notion of context or situation to which it is a critical
response, but rather with a technical principle dissimulated
as an architectural configuration. The technical principle is
cellular reproduction. As hypothesized by Hilberseimer,
modern building construction requires that each building
unit, each structural and spatial cell, be identical to all others, not just in a linear series but in a multidimensional
matrix of repetitive cells; and the gap between the urban
order and the individual constructional cell is thereby abolished. Thus in Hilberseimer's projects there seems at first to
be a degree of transparency of architectural form to the conditions of its making—building as an exhibition of indus-

trialized technology reduced to an elementary, reiterative structural and constructional system. It is this that has been taken as Hilberseimer's *Sachlichkeit* or functionalism. And, indeed, Hilberseimer's own writings sanction such interpretations. In a section of *Groszstadtarchitektur* entitled "Hochhausbauten," for example, he argues: "Architecture is based fundamentally on an enabling construction [*ermöglichenden Konstruktion*]. More recent architecture, in particular, by virtue of the rationalism that inspires it, has almost completely identified itself with pure structure and construction, whereas in the past, cultural and sacral needs played a much more predominant role compared to the rational use to which the building was to be put." And commenting on Mies's project for a concrete office building in the last sentence of a previous chapter, he asserts, "Form and construction have become the same thing [*sind unmittelbar eins geworden*]."[10]

But it must be recognized that this architecture is not really a demonstration of the technical, social, or economic conditions that produced it. On the contrary, Hilberseimer's architecture substitutes an image of a situation whose simulation it makes possible, collapsing the complex network of colliding forces in which architecture originates in order to present us with a self-generating model that obeys only its own logic. It conceals the real origins and stories of a building's formation with an erased record, a kind of materiality that can communicate nothing detached from itself. And yet it can engender itself. For instance, where Mies renders the context of his building antagonistically—the low, pitched-roof buildings in black silhouette in the drawing; the slightly melting masses in the model—Hilberseimer, in the Chicago Tribune project, reduces the context to two short lines across the page—a horizon or an edge. His building does not measure itself against its context as a negative instance, but rather absorbs the context into its own system; or better, the context itself issues from the same system. And then there are two towers on a base seemingly waiting for a third and fourth, less a plastic manipulation of volume than a reduplication of the modular system indefinitely repeated in ignorance of all circumstance. The signified and the referent are now dissolved by a generalized code that no longer refers back to any real but rather to its own logic. Bluntly put, the signifier becomes its own referent. As Jean Baudrillard has written, "For the sign to be pure, it has to duplicate itself: it is the duplication of the sign which destroys meaning."[11]

There is a lack of articulation here in Hilberseimer's project. The typology of American skycrapers—repetitive towers on a high base as exemplified by McKim, Mead and White's Pennsylvania Hotel in New York, which Hilberseimer published in *Groszstadtarchitektur*—is reduced in the Chicago Tribune project to its most elementary structure.[12] The street facade is distinguished from other sides only by the recess of the door and the slightly lower sill of the windows. At the top of the drawing, where the declarative edge of the building's top would meet the sky, the technique becomes more linear; the two lines that form this edge meet precisely at the border of the paper. This, along with the perspective distortion and tonal reversals, changes the whole disposition of the form, dissolving the volume into two depthless planes and converting the projecting exterior corner into what might be taken as a receding interior. The surface of the glass is gone; now we see only the blankness of the page through the empty openings.

A comparison of Hilberseimer's language of drawing with that of Heinrich Maria Davringhausen's "The Profiteer" (1920–1921) or with Georg Grosz's "Untitled" (1920) is inescapable, and it is a language Hilberseimer was to employ throughout his early career: the reduced surfaces, windows as opaque swaths barely adhering to the exterior surface of the building, the absence of glass from the window openings, the relentless repetition and starkness of the environment. But Hilberseimer defused the critical mechanisms of such painting and drawing and sought to demonstrate the availability of the language for

Ludwig Hilberseimer, Chicago Tribune project, 1922.

McKim, Mead and White's Pennsylvania
Hotel, New York, as published in Hilberseimer,
Groszstadtarchitektur.

use in constructing positive information. His previously
worked out theory of pure form, which I will consider in
more detail later, understands form as that which reunites
the creative process with the conditions of modern building
in a definitive figuration absolved from the need to register
the heteronomy of preliminary operations it claims to comprehend; a single signifier, here the skyscraper, stands for
the multiplicity of forces that are collected in the molar
aggregate. This theory provided a readily available conceptual framework to be fitted out with the floating icons and
atmospheres of the *Grosstadt* as enunciated by his Berlin
colleagues.

These are the visual
effects of Hilberseimer's cellular reproduction, the visible
signs of the closure of his system. But let it be stressed that
what is at issue here is not the exchange of one representation of reality, one "exact fantasy," for another, as with
Mies, but substituting signs of the real for the real itself, a
strategy that subsumes every contingency and defers every
connection with the historical, technical, or social specific-

ity to its simulated double. The very external ground against which figuration may be understood is absorbed into the figure.

So it is with simulation, insofar as it is opposed to representation. The latter starts from the principle that the sign and the real are equivalent (even if this equivalence is utopian, it is a fundamental axiom). Conversely, simulation starts from the *utopia* of this principle of equivalence, *from the radical negation of the sign as value*, from the sign as reversion and death sentence of every reference. Whereas representation tries to absorb simulation by interpreting it as false representation, simulation envelops the whole edifice of representation itself as a simulacrum.[13]

Moreover, it should be made clear that this architectural system of reduplicated molecular elements without origin is viewed by Hilberseimer himself as an elementarist substitute for any metaphysical fullness, or any "cultural or sacral needs" of "community religiousness" as sought by the expressionists. He writes,

The few projects made by Berlin architects for the Chicago Tribune competition fall in [a] period of transition. The projects of Gropius and Max Taut reveal a change from the fantastic to the rational, while that of Bruno Taut is still extravagant in appearance. My own project, though not submitted to the competition, was published in *G* and may be considered, in its extreme puritanism, as a protest against the formal exuberance of the expressionists. . . . As the trend of our time is toward the secular, so is the trend of contemporary architecture. Its themes are all those building types that the expressionists considered inferior to become objects of architecture. . . . To develop adequate types for them according to their purpose and function, the materials used and the structures employed, constitutes the real problem that the elementarists have to solve. This will lead to an architecture that is direct and free from all romantic reminiscences, in agreement with present daily life, not subjective and individualistic but objective and universal.[14]

The protest against expressionism is fundamental to the development of Hilberseimer's theory of architecture, as I will develop later. What is important to note here is the way in which the language of causality found in Hilberseimer's theoretical writings (for example, "architecture is based fundamentally on an enabling construction") gives way in his design work to a different parallelism that holds form suspended from the

Heinrich Maria Davringhausen, *Der Schieber (The Profiteer)*, 1920–1921.

Georg Grosz, *Untitled*, 1920.

crisis of humanism, dissolution of the object

actual constructional-material determinants it claims as its reference, permitting Hilberseimer to elide into the second the terminology of the first: to speak of the logic of simulation in terms of "the laws of matter." There are instances where Hilberseimer's own language betrays the process of dissimulation: "The conformation of material content according to an idea means at the same time conformation of the ideal content according to the laws of matter. In the meeting of both of these moments in a single form architecture is born. . . . *It liberates material and ideal contents from their initial contexts.* And it reunifies them. It joins them according to precise laws."[15] Indeed, the liberation and reunification of subject (idea) and object (matter) according to the "precise laws" of the simulacrum. If the Chicago Tribune project is taken as an instantiation of this "liberation" of subject and object, the degree of abstraction necessary to permit such a sublation can readily be felt. Idea and matter are dissolved into sheer formal relationality, into syntactic categories and dimensional systems. Repetition imposed from without by mass production is met by repetition imposed from within by a formal logic. In contrast to Mies's skyscraper, it is now no longer a question of form providing a way of entering into the real, no longer a strategy of displacement, but of absorption; no longer resistance, but mask. It is when this transformation from causality to parallelism to simulation is fully accomplished that architecture will contribute to the complete suppression of the human subject, of questions of actual experience, context, and history; and, ultimately, an engendering without a subject—without individual human agency or history—will become the posthumanist norm.

Now, this is all very close to what Jean Baudrillard characterizes as the passage from representational objects to the "hyperreality" of our own late twentieth-century present.

The description of this whole intimate universe [of objects]—projective, imaginary and symbolic—still corresponded to the object's status as mirror of the subject, and that in turn to the imaginary depths of the mirror and "scene": there is a domestic scene, a scene of interiority, a private space-time (correlative, moreover, to a public space). The oppositions subject/object and public/private were still meaningful. This was the era of the discovery and exploration of daily life, this other scene emerging in the shadow of the historic scene, with the former receiving more and more symbolic investment as the latter was politically disinvested. . . . But today the scene and mirror no longer exist; instead, there is a screen and network. In place of the reflexive transcendence of mirror and scene, there is a nonreflecting surface, an immanent surface where operations unfold—the smooth operational surface of communication.[16]

Perhaps, then, a case could be made for reading Hilberseimer not as a paragon of modernism but rather as an anticipation of that later and quite different thing we have come to call postmodernism. Certainly the self-generating sequence of forms for which function and construction are mere pretexts, the realization of a formal mechanism, depersonalized and virtually unauthored, in which the seemingly uncontrollable and unverifiable autofiguration obeys a logic of its own—all this is very close, as I have been trying to make it out, to recent work variously called "simulationist" or postmodernist. But I want to argue, to the contrary, for this architecture's historical specificity and limits: that Hilberseimer's architecture can be conceived only as a production of, and a response to, the very particular conditions of the Weimar Republic; that the fissured subjectivity of Weimar modernity reproduces itself in the forms of Hilberseimer's architecture.

First recognizing the determining conditions for a certain historically specific type of subjectivity, which I have broached in the analysis of Hannes Meyer as a radical and potentially critical kind of antihumanism, I see Hilberseimer's modernism itself as increasingly hollowing out such subjectivity, flattening it into a counterflow of undifferentiated surfaces, and rendering its articulation as a critical agency highly problematic. I shall argue that the seemingly contradictory tendencies of Hiberseimer's work—the absorption of objective disjunctions into a single, internally produced formal mechanism, the recognition of chaos as the constitutive condition of artistic production coupled with the redemptive role he assigned to architecture, the search for universal, not to say megalomaniacal, laws for the mass phenomenon—are in fact consistently related through a structure of paranoia. For the primary symptom of paranoia is the projection from an internal economy of a set of images, identifications, and figures that seek to guarantee totality in an intolerable external world. Paranoia occurs when the subject can no longer resist the desultory forces from outside that it regards as threatening; the subject will then withdraw its investment in the outside world and produce an elaborate internal interpretation and systemization of conflicts (through hallucinations) and an imaginary projection of the desired object. Totality is maintained but only as a fiction; the subject is aggrandized but only as an avatar of the forces that would destroy it. "To insert oneself into the machine to find there at last the enjoyment of the mechanisms that pulverize desire—such is the paranoiac experience."[17]

Important for this interpretation are the writings of Hilberseimer published in 1919 in *Der Einzige,* a journal edited by admirers of the nineteenth-century German anarcho-individualist Max Stirner and of his follower (in their opinion) Friedrich Nietzsche; and between 1920 and 1924 in the *Sozialistische Monatshefte,* a newspaper that followed Eduard Bernstein in advocating an accommodating, evolutionary policy of socialism, and for which Hilberseimer was the art critic.[18] Hilberseimer's articles elaborate Nietzsche's *The Birth of Tragedy*—in its views of the epistemological status of art, the notion of the artist as a prophetic leader, and the concept of chaos as the constitutive condition of the eternal return—and assimilate these ideas to Alois Riegl's proposition that the art of all cultures is determined and measured by their *Kunstwollen.*

Several stresses found throughout Hilberseimer's theoretical and critical writings should be distinguished. First is the resolutely epistemological thrust of his concerns. A large part of what is at stake in his essays is an assessment of the status of our knowledge and a characterization of the distinction between artistic and scientific knowledge, or as Nietzsche put it, of "the raging discord between art and truth."[19] Following Nietzsche, Hilberseimer asserts that art has no less a claim to knowledge than science, for "all of science, in the final end, depends on faith. Prerequisite to all of science are believed truths. Ultimate precisions are always affairs of belief and find their roots in religions, which connect inseparably the finite with the infinite." Science delivers the already formed material of thought; it is analytic, searching in the parts and pieces of the external world for knowledge of the whole and tending, therefore, toward specialization and technical proficiency. Scientific knowledge is a form of retrieval, with cool precision, of the images and schema primordially superimposed on the world; and though it aims for objectivity, it remains necessarily partial, subjective, and derivative. In contrast, art, as positive creation, shapes the very raw material of reality; it is comparably primary, holistic, and synthetic, and, "despite its subjective issue reaches the highest objectivity." Artistic knowledge enlarges the world, breaking down the narrow limits of conceptual, rational identities which tend to foreclose on polysemy. Above all,

creation is intuitive, free from laws. Creative work proceeds spontaneously with a legitimacy peculiar to it, derived from creativity. And all science and knowledge, all research and recognition-detection [*Erkennen* (sic)] cannot replace this naive security of creation. The new can therefore never be criticized for not following the old, obsolete laws. Still less can creation itself serve extant laws. It does not know them at all. And if it should know them, it must first have overcome them in order to have come to creation.[20]

It should be underscored that artistic creation is conceived here neither as formative power—as a development from *techné,* craft and artisanry, or science—nor as demiurgic production—as an imposition of form by an individual force—but rather as intuition. Art is ascribed not so much to a talent or faculty, classically conceived and destined to a signifying identification and function, as to compulsion, desire, and will. This is important because it already opens the way to a challenge both of the hubris of conventional bourgeois science with its positivist claim to knowledge, into which much of the *neue Sachlichkeit* fell, and of the humanist conception of artistic creation as mimesis. But it also leaves open the question, to which I will return, of what propels or constrains the will.

Neither is there in Hilberseimer's theory a notion of art as respite from the struggles and sufferings of reality or as withdrawal from knowledge, even though he continued to use words like "banishment" and "magic" to describe artistic activity. Rather, like Nietzsche, he saw science and art as *together* illusory, their epistemological status to be distinguished and judged on a basis altogether different from their descriptive powers. Science and art are both productions of "appearances." Of the two, however, scientific know-how (*Können*) leads us into the worse kind of self-blinded illusion, illusion that does not know itself to be one.

The opposition of science to art is figuratively realized in the antagonisms narrated in *The Birth of Tragedy.* Apollo, without the consciousness forced upon him by the "titanic and barbaric menace of Dionysius," gives birth to Socrates, or more precisely the Socratic principle, which condemns us to the grand self-delusion that the rationality of classical mimesis has priority over intuition. Nietzsche's complaint against Socrates is directed not against reason per se, but against Socratic narrowness in regarding reason as the unique instrument of human knowledge and delivery. Hilberseimer extends this Nietzschean complaint to his own classicizing, formalizing, and functional-materialist opponents.

The art of recent times is still, in effect, only reproductive. The declining culture displaces elementary creation. Under the misunderstanding of what is essential, creativity is exhausted in schematized formalism. It is unspiritual [ungeistig]. Perfection is ultimately purely technical, decaying into bare imitation, going from the accidental to what we have already seen [geht vom Zufälligen, zur Gesehenen aus], leaving chaos in the chaotic. It is formless and arbitrary, exhausted in the superficiality of the thing, remaining content in the so-called beautiful appearance. Unbelievability, external appearance, skepticism, and the analytic are typical for recent times, in which knowledge and ability go over experience and will.[21]

Hilberseimer's theory seemingly implies a contradictory formulation of the structure of aesthetic totalization. He celebrates the Dionysian creative subject—unschooled, unrestrained, naive, natural—as representing the "original ground" (Urgrund) of reality—a primitive and noncontingent substratum of being. The artistic subject reveals the contours of this reality, configures it in an art of invariant meaning—spontaneously and subconsciously created, a "magical banishment," "above time," "incapable of development," and antithetical to the art of the Apollonian self-consciouness that distances us psychically from reality in the arid compartments of beauty and proficiency (Können). "In creatively strong times art is confirmation, banishment, magic. The work signifies this through belief, true ideas, force and will, giving a total world picture [Weltbild]."[22] Thus, Hilberseimer's aesthetic and epistemological formulations set forth an ideal of relatively unrestrained contact with genuine experience (Erlebnis) or total content, and its passage through the creative subject into concrete form, presumably guaranteed by an explicit bracketing of material conditions and causes. Whether what is in question in an art work is the symbol, the singularity, the intuitions, or the illusions, in every case what is established is an ontological and formal purity that transcends such encircling determinants as material, mode,

technique, various historical contexts, rational consciousness, and the discursiveness of ordinary practice. Recall:
"The creator, then, is intuitive, free from law. . . . And all
science and knowledge, etc., cannot replace this naive security of creation."

On the other hand, Hil-
berseimer calls into question both uncircumstanced reality
and, more significantly, the very notion of the antithesis
between reality and its representation. "Extant laws" may
not make art, art may produce rather than repeat reality, but
art does not make itself alone. For while "the will to art
[*Kunstwollen*], just as any will [*Wollen*], is not determi-
nantly subjugated to development," it is, nevertheless,
determined by the conditions of its epoch, and "another
epoch disposes of [*verfügen über*] another will. The formal-
becoming [*Formgewordene*] of this expression just is the
work of art." Hilberseimer understands Riegl's concept of
Kunstwollen as a complex and mediated relationship
between subject and object, a "creative struggle" between
artistic will and material conditions that allows itself to be
understood historically as a special kind of vision, dominant
in a particular epoch. Hilberseimer summarized Riegl's analysis with an often repeated aphorism: "An artwork is a condition of tension brought to harmony."[23]

The form and the mate-
rial conditions of the art work will not be in any easy balance; the will to form needs manifest resistance to maintain
itself. "If the material opposes no resistance to the will to
form, decay enters, evolved through imitation and the ability to play with form, because without resistance no tension
can be maintained."[24] But still less will the material conditions or techniques have determined the form. Hilberseimer
is explicit about this latter point: the problem of the "material functionality" of architecture is finally, as in "primitive" architecture, "a problem of limited relevance."[25] If
"the architectural creation manifests the *Kunstwollen* of an
epoch in its purest form," giving a "faithful picture" of the
"substrate of the respective collective wills of a time,"[26]

then neither material nor technique is by itself capable of modifying this representation in its essence.[27] On the contrary, the autonomy of the *Kunstwollen* assures that its representational demands will be fulfilled even in contradiction of material conditions. And more, the demands of the will of the present epoch, as with any period of transition, are antithetical to the desire for traditional beauty.

The conventional refuses everything new on the grounds of dissonance. Dissonance may exist in music, architecture, sculpture, and painting, but it is because the true art work presupposes it rather than installs it. It is always the new, stressful conditions that diverge from the habitual; therefore, it is the new proportions and constructions that become dissonant perceptions. . . . Where beauty establishes itself, tradition is at hand. One wants to enjoy beauty peacefully. The *Kunstwollen*, however, disturbs this rest. It is radical in its manifestation [*Ausserung*]. It is the constant threat to tradition.[28]

The *Kunstwollen*, according to Hilberseimer's gloss at least, is at once a reaction against positivist science, a disturbance of traditional beauty, and a profound totalization and determinism. And as such, it is a refusal of humanism's celebration of free consciousness, of artistic expression as an activity controlled by an individuated, univocal subject in contact with material essences.

Art produces knowledge of the *Kunstwollen*. But ultimate knowledge is necessarily denied to individual occurrences of art. "[Wills and] ideas are absolute. Their manifestation in works of art, however, is only relative. Therefore, the concretization of the idea has discordance as its consequence." And then, these relationships in our own epoch are "necessarily problematic."[29] There can be no unmediated knowledge of the real. Reality can be known only through its representations and images (*Abbild*), externalized in the space of signification as delimited by the will of a particular present. In his affirmation of a wholly relational and differential view of artistic will that controls that individual creative subject, Hilberseimer not only appropriates Riegl's *Kunstwollen* but also recollects Nietzsche's antihumanism.

A final point to be stressed: for Hilberseimer, the condition for artistic practice endemic to modernism is nothing less than a crisis of cultural legitimation experienced primarily as a loss or breakdown of figurability. Artistic technique has been threatened from the inside by virtuosity and detached academicism, and from the outside by industrialized technology and the specializations of science, with the result that the adequation between form and content—and between both and their essential "oneness"—is no longer possible. "Our age is necessarily problematic. Perfection would appear now as hypocritical, just as comfortable methods neglect to admit of the abyss [*Abgrunde*]." The properties that distinguish artistic discourse as a primal compulsion no longer seem to inhere in that discourse itself. And the human subject is constrained by systems it may have produced but in any case cannot seem to control. "The capitalist economic system has also seized art, and made out of it a specialty production. Academic study enables the effectuation of routine. One learns the métier and makes out of it a distinguished high calling or a profession." Meanwhile, "chaos surrounds us, unformed, but certain to push into form," "chaos, the attendant of civilization that brings all manner of frustration to figural formation [*Bildung*]."[30] What is important for us in this articulation of the inability of a culture to give form to its world is the recognition that the loss of signification, experienced as crisis, is the loss of the paternal fiction of humanist thought, of classical art's heritage and guarantee. But even from this posthumanist vantage ground, Hilberseimer remained diligent, as we shall see, in his search for manifestations of that primitive movement toward the future, and toward ultimate identity of subject and object in a formal utopia whose presence, behind whatever distortion and beneath whatever layers of confusion, may always be detected by the apparatus of artistic intuition.

hope beyond chaos:
expressionism and dadaism

The principal conceptual outline over which all of Hilberseimer's art critical writing is traced is the familiar Hegelian
opposition of the concrete and the abstract, and the nature
of artistic mediation between the two. The opposition is not
a symmetrical one, for the abstract denotes both the brute
facticity of the empirical world—presumed to be preexistent
and already formed material with directly accessible content—and the universal, transcendental, formal categories
that have lost all material contact with that empirical reality. Without mediation, the former falls into the illusions of
a simple positivism, mistaking its own conceptual categories for solid parts and pieces of the real world itself, and
the latter results inexorably in an empty formalism, what
Hilberseimer called the "point zero" of the abstract painting
of suprematism and neoplasticism. Hilberseimer summarized this dialectic necessity: Stripped of rationality, precision, and determination, architecture would be nothing but
an empty play on forms; without idealistic intentions it
would be merely technique.[1]

        The more contemporary
notion of subjective alienation recapitulates the Hegelian
opposition and affords a distinction between modern and
premodern epochs. In the art works of preindustrialized,
religious, nonalienated societies, the artist's raw material
had an immediate meaning; it presented itself as richly
articulate and concrete in its elements from the outset and
required no mediation. In the words of Hegel,

What man requires for his external life, house and home, tent,
chair, bed, sword and spear, the ship with which he crosses the
ocean, the chariot which carries him into battle, boiling and roast-
ing, slaughtering, eating and drinking—nothing of all this must
have become merely a dead means to an end for him; he must still
feel alive in all these with his whole sense and self in order that
what is in itself merely external be given a humanly inspired individual character by such close connection with the human
individual.[2]

In the words of Hilberseimer,

Art is always an expression of a philosophy of life, a symbol of
spiritual experience, a concentration of intuitive knowledge, a portrait of the entire human connection with the cosmos. These conditions are plainly located in the so-called primitive people. In
them endures the unity of the attitude of will and deed. . . . The
essential aspect of art does not point to the development of so-
called high culture but to the primitive creations for which there
was nothing other than idea and material; the primitive creations
still had no models and no restraints. . . . [Such creations] grow out
of their respective materials, using their possibilities completely.[3]

In primitive societies, "there was nothing other than idea
and material": subject and object were one, the Absolute
was immanent in each of its moments. With modernity,
however, everything is changed. The unity of the art work is
broken into aggregates thrown off from their human center
by a strictly means-ends rationality; a dissolution of the
subject is thereby set in motion, a whirling dispersion that
leads out from every subjective opening into the accidental
and incomplete, into brute fact and matter, into abstraction,
into chaos. The very world that constitutes the domain of
the subject also poses a threat to it. The consequent loss of
connection and comprehensibility is the very mark of the
modern experience, one in which the essential concreteness
of life may no longer be immanent to it, but out of reach or
otherworldy or, indeed, wholly missing, one in which the
individual and the outside world can never find absolute
identity or unity, one in which the primacy of the individual subject and its conceptual correlate, a unified and substantial center of experience, cannot be restored but at best
only simulated through quantifiable, reproducible form. Hilberseimer: "What seems essential to the so-called high cultures is, above all, their civilizing consequence. . . . Form
becomes the substitute for intuitive experiences, it makes
possible the illusion [Schein] of an engagement with an
object over which one has control. One tries to replace qual-

ity with quantity, the productive with the reproductive. . . .
Skepticism still remains as the last outlet."[4]

According to Hilbersei-
mer, at present, when individual intuition has been riven
from the collective reality now externalized and rationalized, artistic practice is left to straddle the cleft. The modern artist must mediate between the objective world and its
subjectively comprehensible forms. If art holds to a purely
individual, ungeneralizable subjectivity, it risks falling into
a falsely recreated primitivism.

The worst thing that we possess nowadays is recreated primitiveness. . . . In painting this is the tendency represented by the groups
around Pechstein, Heckel and Schmitt-Rottluff, intoxicated by
effects, attracted by the Ash Wednesday of Lent. Study voyages to
the South Seas are no substitute for creative energies. . . . Wanting
to be primitive in one's creating without really being so: this is the
most monstrous of mistakes. One can, of course, be primitive in
one's own means, but not in one's own objectives. The result is the
most vulgar of artistic workmanship.[5]

If, on the other hand, art disengages itself completely from
subjectivity and (truly) primitive intuition, it tends to
become absorbed by ever more complicated, self-regulating
mechanisms of the discipline, and by categories of abstract
knowledge rather than concrete experience. When an artistic practice maximizes stylistic development rather than
creation, when "know-how" (Können) and refinement, habit
and reproduction, triumph over primitive imagination and
material, and the bonds with the subjective realm are thus
broken, then the necessary tension between form and matter is eased, and the primitive "desire for form" is collapsed.
"One suddenly understood the fundamental importance of
primitiveness as against that reproductiveness that turned
into habituation and dominion over materials, killed will-
power, and saw good in the mere development of knowledge
and the work of art."[6] Neoplasticism and suprematism,
according to Hilberseimer, have thus guided modern
abstract art to the point of total annihilation of its material

and to extreme formal concentration, just as Renaissance painting had done in its epoch. Pictorial stereometries risk becoming depleted planimetric elements, rhythmical games on the surface of the canvas. This is the "zero point of art"[7] of our own disenchanted present.

Thus we see that, for Hilberseimer, the brute facticity of simple empiricism or "engineering" and the formal universals of nonobjective painting are obverse conditions of equal abstractness, out of touch with concrete reality, whereas the monadic subjectivity of expressionism is that abstraction's inverse, a false primitivism. What is necessary, then, is a constantly articulated "state of tension" between the subjective will to art and objective reality. When considering in one of his last works (1972) the possibility of transforming life into an organic work of art, Herbert Marcuse concluded that "no matter in what form, art can never eliminate the tension between art and reality. Elimination of this tension would be the impossible final unity of subject and object: the materialist version of absolute idealism."[8] Tension may be construed as nonantagonistic and nondestructive, but it can never be eliminated. Half a century earlier, Hilberseimer could have agreed with Marcuse: according to Hilberseimer, while art attempts to "humanize those *unheimlich* metaphysical experiences" in the "vision engendered in the moment of ecstasy," "the true work of art is the result of a state of tension" between that subjective vision, that primitive will, and objective reality.[9] We are led, then, to consider such a dialectical vision of artistic mediation in the two primary moments of art reviewed by Hilberseimer, expressionism and dadaism.[10] I shall attempt to articulate these two moments according to the various possible relationships between subject and object entailed by each, and then to construct out of Hilberseimer's often aphoristic and elliptical assertions the implied synthesis of a more "truly" primitive moment of completion against which all historical stages of art are evaluated. We will come to see that this synthesis is necessarily contradictory in terms of the subject it constructs: a subject at once dispersed into present actuality—a product of a present condition that Hilberseimer designates as chaos—and yet, through the excercise of artistic will, capable of discovering within that very chaos of the present ciphers of a possible future.

A preliminary indication of Hilberseimer's conceptualization of the primitive is his dissent from the "false primitivism" and romantic-expressionist pronouncements of the Arbeitsrat für Kunst. Although an early supporter of the group, which was led by Bruno Taut and later Walter Gropius, Hilberseimer withdrew his participation by the summer of 1919, after submissions by him and Mies to the Ausstellung unbekannter Architekten had been rejected. Hilberseimer was to recall these events later:

In the spring of 1919 the "Arbeitsrat für Kunst" organized at Berlin an exhibition entitled "Unknown Architects." It is perhaps interesting to note that neither Mies van der Rohe nor I myself was able to take part in this exhibition. The jury refused to accept our designs, probably because their clarity and soberness from an architectural point of view was at odds with the romantic spirit that reigned over the exhibition. During the same period the "Arbeitsrat für Kunst" published a manifesto that carried some of Walter Gropius's and Bruno Taut's declarations on architecture that were characteristic of the dominant tendency in that period and that clearly illustrate the expressionism in architecture. . . . While Bruno Taut, under Paul Scheerbart's influence, busies himself with the transformation of the surface of our planet, the other expressionist architects, Hans Scharoun, Max Taut, Hans and Wassily Luckhardt, and Hermann Finsterlin, content themselves with applying their ideas and principles to single buildings or groups of buildings. Their studies consisted of sketches, drawings, and models that generally concerned religious buildings, theaters, and auditoria. Some of these projects were nothing other than formal exercising of their imaginations. As we have already said, they believed that this type of architecture, considered primitive and primeval, had the faculty of either reawakening religious feelings or

Wassili Luckhardt, *Monument to Joy*, 1919.

of deepening and consolidating them. These ideas were received with ever increasing skepticism.[11]

Hilberseimer articulated his skepticism about expressionism in a number of his art critical essays of 1919.[12] According to him, expressionist art is the necessarily false attempt in modernity to recapture some of the quality of a lost primitive past, the attempted reconciliation between matter and spirit, between daily life and life's essence. Expressionism's promise of a future of reconciliation and happiness—a utopian alternative to the present degraded social existence—is bound up with its romantic retention of previous instances of joy and fulfill-ment recoverable through some notion of anamnesis, "a conscious inclination toward the past," as Hilberseimer put it. And yet the formal activities of the expressionists project their desire for a reconciled community of man into a psychic space not so different from the present save for the eruption of particular desired affects presently lacking—the quasi-spiritual disposition aroused by Gothic colored glass, curved lines, crafted details, and continuous metamorphoses of light and colors. Such affects amount to fetishization—psychophysical displacement and libidinal overvaluation—a falsely "recreated primitiveness" and "infantilism" that conjures up a condition longed for, in all its plenitude, while at the same time holding the actual material of the world in suspension, with no real attempt to change it.

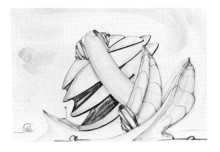

Hermann Finsterlin, *Glass Dream*, 1920.

The fantasies of the freed individual psyche and uncoerced subjectivity maintain faith in a moralized and mythicized future where that most untrue attribute of the present, alienation, has disappeared. Yet the very concept of expressionism presupposes a painful split within the individual subject. As Fredric Jameson has written,

Expressionism requires the category of the individual monad, but it also shows us the heavy price to be paid for that precondition, dramatizing the unhappy paradox that when you constitute your individual subjectivity as a self-sufficient field and a closed realm in its own right, you thereby also shut yourself off from everything else and condemn yourself to the windowless solitude of the monad, buried alive and condemned in a prison-cell without egress.[13]

Furthermore, in expressionism that paradox now finds its analogue in the object itself, in expressionist strategies such as the symbolism of the crystal, the empathetic content of contorted surfaces, the projection of the consolidative *Stadt-krone*, or the withdrawal into the protective cave.[14] The subject having been split from its object by the logic of social reification, the object must now be reconstructed by expressionism in such a way as to bear the place of the subject within itself. The differential play between subject and object that normally takes places along the axis of viewer and representation is now made visible in the corporeal con-

tortions of built form. The anguish of the metropolitan
experience is externalized in the work of architecture as an
outward projection and formalization of an inward despera-
tion for freedom. A typical statement of the period expresses
this desire:

Freedom of the subject, as a corrective and confrontation to the
conservative social art practiced with the unstable ethic of commercial interests. Freedom and authentic life for the individual. . . .
It wants to transcend the commonplace, which means freedom
from it. It tends to recognize the forms of expression of counter-art,
that is to say, of the art of those regarded as infantile or sick,
according to its own laws, not as a rational product of consciousness, but rather as an expression subjected to its own particular
laws.[15]

According to Hilbersei-
mer, the nostalgia for past totalities, the welling up and formal dramatization of subjective protest against the objective
universe that threatens to crush the individual, along with
the provincialism of presentness, what he called "the
unshakable belief in one's own face," these expressionist
tendencies effectively block the possibility of any genuine
opening onto the future, of imagining a future that might be
constitutionally (rather than affectively) different from the
present. Expressionism's eschatological vision of the
uncoerced self is generated by a thoroughly despairing
understanding of the actual possibilities of historical life. Its
hope is placed rather in the myth of absolute presence—the
notion that being is a kind of plenum in which there exist a
fullness and wholeness partaken by past societies, and that
for this reason something like a substantial and meaningful
present is ontologically possible and imaginable but actually
unachievable, that any hope for the damaged subject must
remain in the future. The expressionist anxiety before the
future ends up, paradoxically, by glorifying both past and
future and hypostasizing the present.

So it is that Hilberseimer here identifies expressionism's Platonic side, for the most tenacious version of absolute presence and anamnesic thought is the Platonic doctrine of memory as a return to sources of plenitude lost since birth.[16] "Thus primitivism, exoticism, and infantilism arose within expressionism. . . . All these intentions that link themselves to the past are but attempts to substitute an intellectual rapport with the past for the *lost tradition.*" But more important, it is here that Hilberseimer rejects the possibility of a return to plenitude and counters the Platonic doctrine of *memory as a return to significant objects* with the Nietzschean imperative of *chaos as the production of significant appearances.* It is this latter that is, by Hilberseimer's lights, truly primitive. He continues, "But [this expressionist return to the primitive] is far from a return to nature. Expressed in all these aspirations is the search for the law that the art of the past manifests in almost all of its works. But every link to the past is destined to lead to eclecticism. The true [or truly primitive] work of art will always be born *only from the chaos of time.* Only in this way can its image take on sense."[17]

Hilberseimer's notion of chaos as a constitutive condition for meaning in modernity cannot be overemphasized, for it occurs, often conjoined with primitivism, again and again in his criticisms, and is the hinge on which his concepts of artistic mediation and subjectivity turn. It is one of the principal themes in the Nietzschean thought from which Hilberseimer borrowed. At once a relational condition organizing phenomena, manifestations, and dissimulations, and the intolerable, depthless, groundless reality of being, chaos is neither disorder waiting for organization nor meaninglessness waiting for the imprint of sense. Rather chaos is already interpreted being, not so much a perversion of some original harmony as the constitutive condition for any existence whatsoever and the primitive determination of will to power. And then, it is "nature" (as in Hilberseimer's "return to nature" above)

that determines being itself as the significant manifestation
of chaos.[18]

In Nietzschean thought
chaos is related to epistemological as well as ontological
concerns, and it is through the former that we are afforded a
route into Hilberseimer's art criticism. For Nietzsche, philosophical interrogation arrives not at truths corresponding to
things-in-themselves—solid essences of reality that issue
signs of themselves, that produce their own noumena—but
at senses constructed by interpreting subjects from a flux of
"appearances." Knowledge is essentially active; it is belief
and conquest; and as such its particular structure, including
the principles and categories of logic, is not an adequation
to preformed objects but rather to the will to power.

Appearance, as I understand it, is the true and unique reality of
things; it is what all existing predicates belong to, and what to
some extent could best be designated by the sum of these predicates, and this would even include contrary predicates. But this
work plainly signifies a reality that is *inaccessible* to the operations and distinctions of logic, an "appearance," therefore, in relation to "logical truth," which—it must be added—is only possible
in an *imaginary* world. I am not claiming that appearance is
opposed to "reality"; on the contrary, I maintain that appearance is
reality, that it is opposed to whatever transforms the actual into an
imaginary "real world." If one were to give a precise name to this
reality, it could be called "will to power." Such a designation, then,
would be in accordance with its internal reality and not with its
proteiform, ungraspable, and fluid nature.[19]

To construct any system
of value or any sort of logic from will to power is to relate it
to the desires and needs of a subject—desires for categories
of good and bad, for stability, order, causality, finality, unity,
identity. As Michel Haar has written,

Logic rests upon a useful and necessary falsification, being born of
the vital need to lean upon identities despite that fact that nothing
real is reducible either to unity or to identity. Therefore, "truth is

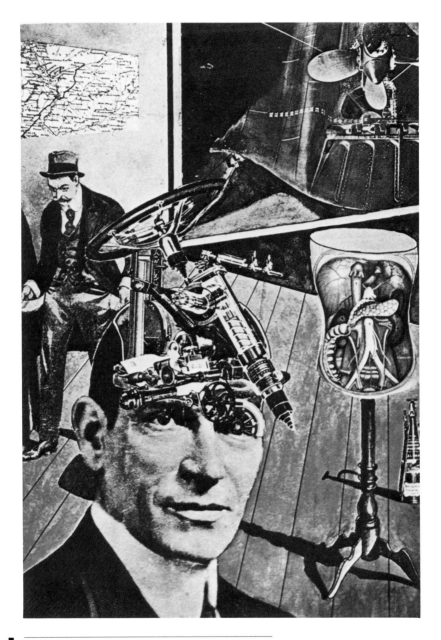

Raoul Hausmann, *Tatlin at Home,* 1920.

that kind of error without which a certain kind of living being cannot live" [Nietzsche]. But truth is, in addition, falsification of the False, for the "in itself," namely "pure becoming," presents itself to us as Chaos—i.e., as non-(logical)-truth, eternal and infinite.[20]

All existence is interpretation; the subject constitutes sense by an interpretive engagement. "Ultimately, the individual derives the values of his acts from himself; because he has to interpret in a quite individual way even the words he has inherited. His interpretation of a formula at least is personal, even if he does not create a formula: as an interpreter he is still creative." It should not be thought, however, that this entails a conception either of centralized, unified subject or of a limiting case of interpretation. On the contrary, "we are a pluality that has imagined itself a unity."[21] The world has become infinite; there are only interpretations of interpretations, meaning that we cannot refuse it the possibility that it lends itself to an infinity of interpretations.[22]
                                    So truth designates
chaos. But chaos is too hostile to life, too terrible to be apprehended. Chaos can only appear as masked in interpretation, veiled in appearances. "It would be possible that the true constitution of things was so hostile to the presuppositions of life, so opposed to them, that we needed appearance in order to be able to live."[23] So every interpretation is always already a dissimulation, a concealment, a deferral, a mask. "We no longer believe that truth remains truth when the veils are withdrawn; we have lived too much to believe this."[24] Every interpretation is an ontological dispersal—a necessary refusal of unity, essence, and identity—and an epistemological "scrawl" (the word is Nietzsche's)—the production of sense that is partial, contingent, superimposed, and shifting. "Insofar as the word 'knowledge' has any meaning, the world is knowable; but it is interpretable otherwise, it has no meaning behind it, but countless meanings—'Perspectivism.'"[25]
                                    Chaos, then, designates,
in turn, the horizon of forces against which various interpre-

tive perspectives are drawn and, at the same time, the instance when, all values and logics having imploded, the will to power returns to itself. The incessant passage of the eternal return—the reiterative power of appearance to affirm itself—is inscribed in chaos and directed against the essential unity in things, against identity. Neither is the will to power a substrate behind the constant issue of appearances; appearances do not conceal *something*; there is no solid essence of will that accounts for them. The will to power is just, in Nietzsche's words, "the last instance which we could go back to," like a wall of light infinitely far behind the successive appearances of galaxies coming into being, an instance rather than an essence. And the eternal return is not the recurrence of the same essence in different guises but the instantiation of ever divergent appearances without an ultimate goal. "Universal chaos of the sort excluding all activity having a final purpose does not contradict the idea of circular movement: it's just that this movement is an arational necessity."[26] The inclusion of chaos in the necessity of the circle of the return constitutes the perfection of circle as always already a defect. The totality of the return is a fractured totality.

This emphasis on chaos distinguishes Hilberseimer's theory from the altogether different, antiurban Nietzscheanism of both *Jugendstil* and expressionism. Hilberseimer's early contact with the disquietude of the radical art circles in Berlin, such as the *G* group, the Novembergruppe, the Ring, and for a brief period Die Kommune, gives further specificity to his understanding of possible new sensibilities springing not from a false sense of the fullness of the past, but from the chaos of the present.[27] Hilberseimer was associated with the Berlin dadaists, such as Hans Richter, Hannah Höch, and Raoul Hausmann, as well as with Otto Dix, Kurt Schwitters, Theo van Doesburg, El Lissitzky, Viking Eggeling, and Carl Einstein[28] throughout the 1910s and 1920s. Richter published the magazine *G: Zeitschrift für elementare Gestaltung*, to which Hilberseimer contributed articles. "This circle," Richter

wrote, "included Arp, Tzara, Hilberseimer, Doesburg, but
soon also Mies van der Rohe, Lissitzky, [Naum] Gabo,
[Anton] Pevszner [*sic*], Kiesler, Man Ray, Soupault, [Walter]
Benjamin, Hausmann, etc."[29] The first issue of *G*, in July
1923, announced its refusal of romantic subjectivity in
rather harsh terms. "The basic demand of creative figuration
[*Gestaltung*] is economy. Pure relationship of power and
material. This depends on elementary means and a total
command of means. Elementary order. Regularity. We have
no need for the sort of beauty that attaches itself like tinsel
to our very being; rather we need [to realize] the internal
order of our being."[30] Richter described Hilberseimer as
"one of my oldest friends, since 1912. . . . As a friend he
was in some ways an anti-friend, a man never satisfied and

Cover of *G*, no. 4 (March 1926).

a bastion contrary by profession; a just man who was quite convinced he was in the right."[31] Hilberseimer's work was of interest also to Schwitters. In 1925 he published Hilberseimer's *Groszstadtbauten* as numbers 18–19 of *Merz*.[32] In *Kunst und Zeiten,* 1926, he lists Hilberseimer among those artists with whom he sympathized and notes that Hilberseimer's "steps take him from the dry premises of rational thought to proper figuration."[33] And in an article on the Weissenhof Siedlung in Stuttgart, Schwitters criticizes the trendiness of Peter Behrens and Hans Poelzig, who produced "pretty Italian villas" in the "new style," and identifies a "danger" in Le Corbusier because he is a genius dedicated to romantic excess. In contrast, Schwitters praises the Weissenhof projects of Hilberseimer as "basic, normal, and devoid of daydreams."[34] As a final instance of the art world's interest in Hilberseimer's work, it should be noted that in 1924 some of his drawings were exhibited in the Novembergruppe section of the Grosse Berliner Kunstausstellung and in the gallery Der Sturm. Hilberseimer's explicit identification of his work with the elementarists against the expressionists[35] is an identification with this circle of post-dadaist artists and with the postanthropomorphic, automechanical consciousness they sought through elementarism and the formal vernacular of the impersonal present. As Hausmann wrote in his "Presentist" manifesto published in *De Stijl* in 1921, "Naive anthropomorphism has played out its role. The beauty of our daily life is defined by the manikins, the wig-making skill of the hairdressers, the exactness of a technical construction! We strive anew towards conformity with the mechanical work process: we will have to get used to the idea of seeing art originating in the factories."[36]

Hilberseimer's estimations of dadaist and post-dadaist art movements were recorded in his art critical writings. In his essay "Anmerkungen zur neuen Kunst" of 1923, he summarizes the dadaist experience simply: "Dadaism brought with it a general activity that had a vivifying effect on art. Its effect in Ger-

many has been essentially political."[37] But in "Dadaismus"
of 1920, his characterization is put more precisely in terms
of subjectivity and dadaism's adversarial relationship with
bourgeois culture: "[In dadaism] the ancient feelings of security are dissolved and replaced by an animated world, by
restlessness, by excitement. The I, now set free from meaningless bonds, 'flows freely into the cosmos.' Dada destroys
the idols of culture and scorns the serious tedium of art."[38]

For Hilberseimer, dada
fulfilled the contestatory obligation of art to resist the security of habit and explode the nostalgias for a no longer possible romantic reconciliation between subject and object.
Furthermore, there is no reason not to allow that Hilberseimer fully understood the dadaist politically motivated
destruction of aesthetic autonomy and aesthetic pleasure in
the service of a specific cultural critique of the Weimar
Republic of circa 1920. It is precisely the critical-negational
aesthetic practices and forms of expression adopted by the
dadaists, their rejection of art's traditional role as the "production of specialties," that indicts any attempt to fall back
into a falsely primitivist reproduction of a reconciled world.
So it is that the "truly primitive" impulse of Hausmann,
Dix, or Grosz can measure up to the realism of "a pictorial
practice that will not be a mimetic reproduction of nature
but, rather, criticism, parody, drama, and a new order springing from chaos."[39]

Berlin dada was, as Hil-
berseimer recognized, first and foremost a politico-ideologi-
cal weapon, with *der blutige Ernst* (bloody earnestness) as
Carl Einstein's journal title claimed, aimed at well-defined
targets, an instrument of derision and ridicule dedicated to
the destruction of bourgeois chauvinism and the autonomous artistic practices that it fueled. The range of hybrid
art forms produced by the Berliners between 1919 and 1923
reveals more than an elaboration of cubist compositional
techniques; the dadaists were aware of their assemblages,
cabaret productions, *Klebebilder* (glued pictures), and photo-
montages as forms for a new politicization of intellectual

work, one that would give audiences to understand what kinds of future psychic and social regeneration might be available by reordering their perception of the historical present.

What distinguishes dada from most other modern movements in art, and what is important for our consideration of Hilberseimer's conception of dadaist practice, is not the reductive thesis that "it's all political" (or as Max Ernst dismissed dada, "C'est vraiment allemand. Les intellectuels allemands ne peuvent pas faire ni caca ni pipi sans idéologies"); instead, it is the acute awareness that affiliations between art and cultural authority obtain *both* in the case of art's direct dependence on the institutional ideological apparatus and in the unlikely condition of art's total autonomy. Dada understood art as belonging not to some free-floating *Geist* or to some self-governed, coherently determined domain, but to a worldly intellectual endeavor—enmeshed in circumstance, historical contingency, and currents of thought; connected in complex ways to power, social class, and economic production, to the dissemination of values and world pictures. What must be made clear is the proposition that culture itself—or thought, or art, or what used to be called the superstructure—was for dada, as for Hilberseimer, a quasiautonomous and reciprocally effective extension of politicoeconomic reality. To adopt the language of Edward Said, "One could go so far as to say that culture . . . is what gives the State something to govern."[40] Through a ferocious decomposition of the images of the dominant values, dada attempted to oppose the self-affirming machinery of culture as well as to reject "art's traditional role as the 'production of specialties'" that encode the culture's values.

The terms with which dada defined the political instrumentality of art are important in coming to a characterization of "a pictorial practice that will not be an imitative reproduction of nature but, rather, criticism, vital parody, drama, a new order springing from chaos." After 1920 the Berlin avant-garde was becoming progressively disillusioned with the political revolution. *Junker* militarism and nationalism had proved far stronger than radical intellectuals with international associations had originally expected. The entire cultural establishment in which dada was enmeshed quickly became suspect in a way that Lunacharsky's Narkompros organization, on which the proto-dadaist members of the Arbeitsrat für Kunst seem to have modeled some of their more positive notions of engagement, was not. Society and culture were viewed as fundamentally nonorganic entities, products of a system, a ruling order that was progressively replacing technologies and spaces controlled by and for man with ones spontaneously elaborated—of both wonder and fear, of civilization and death, with potentials for destruction as well as new forms of life—that began to overwhelm man. Georg Grosz saw it as

complete insanity to believe that Spirit or people of spirit ruled the world. . . . Our only mistake was to have been seriously engaged at all with art. Dada was the breakthrough, taking place with bawling and scornful laughter; it came out of a narrow, overbearing and overrated milieu. . . . We saw then the insane end products of the ruling order of society and burst into laughter. We had not yet seen the system behind this insanity. . . . Then, there would be no more laughing.[41]

Hannah Höch's 1920 poster "Schnitt mit dem Küchenmesser Dada durch die letzte weimarer Bierbauchkulturepoche Deutschlands" (Cut with the Dada Kitchen Knife through the Last Weimar Beer-Belly Cultural Epoch of Germany) cuts a cross section through the cultural tissue of Weimar industrialization; while the portraits of Grosz and Dix present, among other things, a preoccupation with the horror and disgust of the destruction of the war (a war viewed as propagated by an overwhelming technology and the lies of bourgeois rationalism) and "oppose with irony and cynicism the constraints on difference [*Variétéhafte*] of our profiteering world,"[42] as Hillberseimer wrote. The artist, according to Grosz's self-

Hannah Höch, *Cut with the Dada Kitchen Knife through the Last Weimar Beer-Belly Cultural Epoch of Germany*, 1919.

Georg Grosz, _Meta-mechanische Konstruk-_
tion, 1920: "Daum" marries her pedantic automaton
"George" in May 1920, John Heartfield is very glad of
it.

portrait, is a "pedantic automaton," at once a product of a mcchanized, commodified culture and its most violent enemy. Similarly, Hausmann's "Tête mécanique, L'Esprit de notre temps," and his portrait of the artist, "Tatlin," with their isomorphism between man and machine, are more ambivalent, accidental, "oneiric," accumulations of ready-made images than they are organized affirmations of machine art. By Hausmann's own account, he was inter-ested in demonstrating that "everday man has nothing but the capacities that chance has glued to his skull, on the exterior [_extérieurement_], the brain was vacant";[43] that is, in showing that the possibility for private redemption had been foreclosed by the penetration of the mechanization and massification of the market into the most remote regions of the self, in showing the reduction of the individual, at once exalted and ridiculed, to a nullity.

Dada demonstrates that artistic production in society has an inescapable dialectic relationship with those mass-cultural formations that govern collective perception. It would not seem possible after dada to presume that aesthetic perfection and disinterested contemplation possess a transhistorical value that places them outside or beyond the material determinations of history. But more, dadaist practice appropriates the very terms provided by capitalist society to perceptually interpellate the viewer—advertisements, journalism, commercial products—and uses them in an insurrectionary form of affiliation with that society, adhering to the bourgeois artistic convention of presenting unique, fabricated, rectangularly framed art objects even as it subversively folds into the singularity of those objects the dispersed images of bourgeois culture. In this way, dada can be said to *repeat* reality but not to *duplicate* it; or in Nietzschean terminology, to construct appearances of the real against the horizon of chaos. In so doing, it would abolish idealist and humanist ideologies by dismantling the increasingly entrenched notion of the viewing subject as an ideal, unified, centered self, undivided by conflicting psychical enticements or material appetites, unencumbered in its contemplation of the abstract unity of the autonomous art object that was to be both an inducement to and a metaphor for a position of transcendence and mastery. For dada, the human subject, to put it now in Althusserian language, is structured like a mode of production, and as such cannot be the centered subject of bourgeois epistemology and aesthetics, but is instead precisely decentered to the degree that it is the bearer of different and often contradictory structures.

Hilberseimer understood this, but it must be underscored here that the critical dissonance, shock, and what he called the *Wahrheitsfanatismus* of dadaist activities, as well as the concomitant assault on the human center as the origin of sense, are interpreted by Hilberseimer as directed toward a possible future. In speaking of dadaism, Hilberseimer evokes Nietzsche's lesson of a world "where we will be able to be original, something like parodists of the history of the world and God's clowns; to the point where, perhaps, our laughter possesses a future, out of the so many things belonging to the present time that are condemned to oblivion."[44] If one cannot avoid or refute the generative experience of chaos, one can nevertheless mediate it, transforming it into that elementarist anticipation which is its correlative. Indeed, artistic practice for Hilberseimer just *is* such mediation: "the formal-becoming of this expression [of the will of the epoch, which is chaos] just is the work of art."[45] Hilberseimer quotes Raoul Hausmann to verify his own thesis:

Raoul Hausmann, *Tête mécanique, L'Esprit de notre temps*, c. 1921.

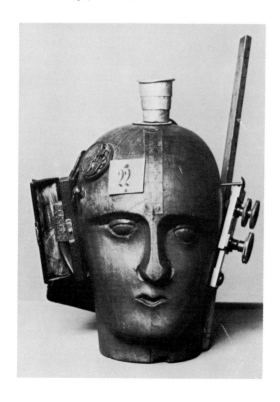

Times of decay, of stagnation, are at the same time epochs of new stimulation [*Neubelebung*] to becoming. One breaks open the old to enable the new to be formed. [We are] suspended between two worlds. In these times the productive energy is inclined toward the grotesque and satirical, toward [as Hausmann says] "the laughing or ironic elevation of men over their no-longer-appropriate responsibilities. So, too, the tendency in art—the objectification [*Gegenständlichkeit*] will lose sense, so to speak, through the presentation of its refusal to correspond with the sense of events. By emphasizing the ridiculous, the senseless, the repulsive . . . , through the figuration [*Gestaltung*] of the deficiencies of the world, we are allowed to anticipate a higher world. By way of representations, the sculptor must support such consciousness.". . . From this paradox it follows that the senseless, repulsive, and hideous will let the genuine and real step forward.[46]

Out of the banality, the senselessness, the triviality of the present emerges the hope for a future. Hilberseimer wishes to locate the positive within the negative itself: to grasp that the negative present may serve as a means of projection to the future, the "real step forward," that reveals itself through it; that the negative is the very authentication of the positive; and that chaos is the constitutive condition of a new order. The lacerating ambiguity of Hilberseimer's position derives from his wish to preserve the chaos-negating power of subjective intuition without collapsing into either the mysticism or individualism of expressionism; and this crossed by his equally intense insistence that the motor of that intuition is immanent in the very chaos of the world.

And so we can finally characterize with some precision the concept of the subject that emerges in Hilberseimer's account of expressionism, dadaism, and other artistic practices by which he was surrounded. It is a subject that can be fitted into both a vision of effective human agency and some more radical notion of a subjectivity dispersed into the realms of industrialization, standardization, mass reproduction, and consumption. That is, Hilberseimer understands the epistemic subject of modernism as *at once* the particular constitution of knowledge, history, and discourse in a historically specific and individual human agent, *and* the no less circumstantially dense plurality of forces that has passed from both an arrogant bourgeois humanism and expressionist sentimentalization of individual distress to a new, postindividualist, posthumanist framework. The subject as seen by Hilberseimer is continually interpellated or called upon to take multiple and contradictory subject positions, yet it is capable of binding these positions together into "a new order springing from chaos." "The I, now set free from meaningless bonds, 'flows freely into the cosmos.'" As a human agent the artistic subject preserves the potentiality of negativity and resistance in its capacity to mediate between an unsatisfactory external world and the anticipation of other experiences; whereas the dispersed subject is destined to resolve itself in a superior, if vaguely articulated, Nietzschean consciousness.

Such paradoxical, primitive, liberated energies as those invoked by Hilberseimer are nothing less than a search for new constitutions of reality. Chaos as the constitutive condition of the present reality; the present as the only reality from which art might emerge; art as the formation of a conciousness whose horizon is determined not by a mystique of the past but by forms that reveal the essential movement of human reality toward the future: Hilberseimer corrects expressionist anamnesis precisely along the lines of Ernst Bloch's notion of *anagnorisis:*

The doctrine of *anamnesis* claims that we have knowledge only because we formerly knew. But then there could be no fundamentally new knowledge, no future knowledge. The soul merely meets in reality now what it always already knew as idea. That is a circle within a circle and just as inaccurate as the other theory (*anagnorisis*) is revealing: that the new is never completely new for us because we bring something with us to measure by it. . . . *Anam-*

nesis provides the reassuring evidence of complete similarity; *anagnorisis*, however, is linked with reality by only a thin thread; it is therefore alarming. *Anamnesis* has an element of attenuation about it; it makes everthing a gigantic *déjà vu*, as if everthing had already been, *nil novi subanamnesi*. But *anagnorisis* is shock.[47]

Hilberseimer could not have known of this formulation made by Bloch in 1968 or of his magnum opus *Das Prinzip Hoffnung* (1954–1959); nor have I found any evidence that he read Bloch's earlier *Geist der Utopie* (1918 and 1923). Yet the evocation of Bloch's thought is not arbitrary in the context of this examination of Hilberseimer's critical writings. For Bloch provides a way of conceptualizing the future and its relationship to the present and the primitive that is suggestive for an interpretation of Hilberseimer's own epistemology of art.

Bloch spent most of his intellectual life developing what he came to call his ontology of "not-yet-being" or philosophy of hope and articulating a nonhumanist hermeneutics of restoration for the alienating and antagonistic cultural experiences of the present.[48] For Bloch, the present totality was not a homologous set of relationships and functions with one genetic center, such as the Marxist mode of production or the Lukácsian metasubject returned to itself as the maker of history, but rather a kind of horizontally deployed grid, what Martin Jay has called an intensive, "latitudinal totality" in which past, present, and future—along with the mysteries of each—are spread out on the same conceptual plane. However homogeneous it may have appeared in reductive analyses of socioeconomic essentiality (Bloch was critical of Marx on this point), present reality, according to Bloch, comprised distinct, eccentric, and irreducible spheres such as religion, nature, reason, and art, as well as socioeconomic relations, which were not mere alienations produced by capitalism but were rather a "consequence of the laboriousness of the founding of the Kingdom [*Mühseligkeit der Reichsgründung*], which expresses itself in the temporal process, as well as spatially in the creation of spheres."[49] Furthermore, even while apparently complicitous with the unfulfilled present, these *ungleichzeitig* (nonsynchronous) spheres also contained "*declining remnants* and, above all, uncompleted *past*, which has not yet been 'sublated' by capitalism,"[50] as well as emergent intimations of the future—*Spuren*, or figural traces, marks, and surplus signs of the "not-yet" that destabilize the dominant trends of the present. Suspicious of claims that the past contained some archaic heritage of plenitude, or that some original meaning could be recovered from the memory of that past, Bloch stressed the interpenetration of present actuality and utopia—the present gives us raw material for a hope for plenitude in the future. "The real of the essence is that *which does not yet exist, which is in quest of itself in the core of things, and which is awaiting its genesis in the tendency and latency* [Tendenz-Latenz] *of the process.*"[51]

As Fredric Jameson has argued, Bloch's utopia is, above all, a formal one.[52] And it is therefore of little surprise that he finds in the forms of art works and artifacts of daily life (including buildings and their furnishings) the most persuasive examples of attempts of the subject to rejoin in immediate experience with the things of the world, and to anticipate other possiblities. "Every great work of art, above and beyond its manifest content, is carried out according to a *latency of the page to come*, or in other words, in the light of the content of a future that has not yet come into being, and indeed of some ultimate resolution as yet unknown." The very form, structure, and appearance (*Schein*) of the work themselves "*represent an ontological anticipation* [Vorschein] *of the real which both transcends that limited and temporally developing object of the work and intends it at the same time*, an ontological anticipation precisely representable in an aesthetically immanent way. Here is illuminated what dull or habituated sense still scarcely sees, both in individual events and in social or natural ones."[53]

Occasioned by the same social milieu and historical moment as Bloch's *Geist der Utopie*, Hilberseimer sought to redirect the historical trajectory of culture from the disasters that had befallen Europe since the First World War, and, through the apparatus of hope, to discover behind the distortions of present appearances the hidden ciphers for a transfigured world—basic, primal figures (whose forms we will see shortly), latent aesthetic potentialities of the primitive moment of subject-object identity. Hilberseimer: "Our age is necessarily problematic. Perfection now would be judged hypocrisy, just as comfortable techniques retreat from the admission of the abyss." But "precedent teaches that every creative age follows from such a relaxation, loosening, and disintegration, like a perpetual antagonist. . . . Every revolution that disentangles a dismantled tradition is nothing less than the anticipation of a new becoming. . . . We live for as yet unfulfilled, unconcluded horizons, a future pregnant with hope."[54]

With a hope now placed in the redemptive power of form itself, Hilberseimer sought to fill the hole opened up in the symbolic order (in the field of the signifier) by the chaos of modernity. We must now return to an examination of Hilberseimer's proposed forms of this hope, to the *Spuren* and ciphers for a future to arise out of the foreclosure of signifiers in the present.[55] It is when these ciphers are fully conceptualized that Hilberseimer's art historical writings can be crossed with his design projects, and his architectural production can be fully understood.

groszstadtarchitektur and *weimar-stimmung*: the construction of the paranoid subject

The subject is an effect of a system of differences and deferrals, not a unified consciousness but a variable and dispersed entity whose very identity and status are constituted in social practice. "[This] confirms that the subject, and first of all the conscious and speaking subject, depends upon the system of presence, that the subject is not present, nor above all present to itself before *différance*, that the subject is constituted only in being divided from itself, in becoming space, in temporising, in deferral."[1] These words of recent critical theory accord strikingly with Hilberseimer's perception of the subject, split between intentional human agency and dispersion across systems beyond the horizon of intention and presence. The artistic will of the individual, which would seem to be the most certain sign of the self's identity, is in fact the obliteration of that identity, the disappearing of the self in the autonomy and determinateness of the *Kunstwollen* that extends before and beyond the individual even as the individual seems to emerge. "The I, now set free from meaningless bonds," is the I that "flows freely" into—is dispersed into—the structure of will.

The psychic dissolution perceived by Hilberseimer is, as we now know, the very condition of subjectivity under industrial capitalism. The lived experience of individual consciousness as a fissured, compartmentalized, subjugated, and reified condition, coupled with the hope of some radical utopian agency of mediation and colligation, is not a mere confusion to be resolved either by reasserting a notion of monadic and autonomous individuality or by voiding the category of the subject altogether. Rather the articulation of such an experience conjoined with such a hope conveys the precise historical moment at which the whole range of problems and questions constituting Hilberseimer's problematic is cut through, the concrete cultural situation in which the emergence of his inscription of the posthumanist subject can be understood. For if Hilberseimer's writings often attempt to sound timeless and universally valid, his theoretical position, as I have attempted to locate it, can be conceived only

as a production or a displacement of the very particular
Stimmung of the Weimar Republic, an encounter between a
signifying practice and socioeconomic practices enclosed by
the same boundaries of that time and place. Hilberseimer's
ambivalence toward the metropolis—the disenchanted
euphoria, comprising almost equal measures of anxiety and
elation, that finds its object in Berlin, the principal city of
the early twentieth century and the focus of industry, production, consumption, and all manner of worldliness—is
just the ambivalence and paradox of Weimar culture, where
modernity and negativity, higher consciousness and alienation, sobriety and unhappiness, authenticity and depthless-
ness, become almost inseparable. As Peter Sloterdijk writes,

The Weimar Republic is one of those historical phenomena
through which we can best study how the modernization of a society has to be paid for. . . . In the intelligentsia, which consciously
went through and participated in the process, there is no longer
anywhere a "false consciousness" in the simple sense but rather
dissolute consciousness on all sides. . . . Weimar art cynics train
themselves to play masters of the situation, while the situation in
fact is one in which things have gotten out of control and sovereignty is no longer possible. . . . They impudently place their poses
against the equally overwhelming and mediocre destiny of the
period: cynically allowing themselves to be swept along—Hey,
we're alive. The modernization of unhappy consciousness.[2]

In his study of Weimar
culture, Sloterdijk uses Heidegger's concept of "Anyone" to
characterize the Weimar *Stimmung* in terms of the conditions and constructions of subjectivity. Without seeking to
make Hilberseimer's work a homologue of Heidegger's, it
will be helpful here to draw a comparison between their
respective theories of subjectivity—both of which turn on
the deliberate confrontation with the objective conditions of
the "everyday" metropolitan experience—in order to further
characterize Hilberseimer's effort to find material for the
construction of a new consciousness that might replace a
dysfunctional and discredited humanism. Sloterdijk elabo-

rates Heidegger's turn toward the everyday in a series of passages that are suggestive enough for my analysis to quote here at some length:

[Heidegger] eavesdrops on the "subject" in the banality of the everyday mode of being. The existential ontology, which treats Anyone and its existence in everydayness, attempts something that would not have occurred even in a dream to earlier philosophy: to transform triviality into an object of "higher" theory. . . . A philosophy thus appears that participates ambivalently in a disillusioned, secularized, and technicized zeitgeist. . . . What is the rare being that Heidegger introduces under the name of Anyone? At first glance, it resembles modern sculptures that do not represent any definite object and whose polished surfaces do not admit of any "particular" meaning. Still, they are immediately real and firm to the touch. In this sense Heidegger emphasizes that Anyone is no abstraction—roughly, a general concept that comprises "all egos"; instead, he wants to relate, as *ens realissimum*, to something that is present in every one of us. But it disappoints the expectation of personalness, individual purport, and existentially decisive meaning. It exists but there is "nothing behind" it. It is there like modern, nonfigurative sculptures: real, everyday, concrete part of a world but not referring at any time to an actual person, a "real" meaning. Anyone is the neutrum of our ego: everyday ego, but not "I myself." It represents in a certain way my public side, my mediocrity. I have Anyone in common with everyone else; it is my public ego, and in relation to it, averageness is always in the right. As inauthentic ego, Anyone disposes of any highly personalized decisiveness (*Entschiedenheit*) of its own. By nature, it wants to make everything easy for itself, to take everything from the outside and to abide by conventional appearances. In a certain respect, it also behaves in this way toward itself, for what it is it"self" it also accepts, just like something it finds among other things that are simply givens. This Anyone can thus only be understood as something nonautonomous, which has nothing of itself or solely for itself. What it is is said and given by others; that explains its essential distractedness (*Zerstreutheit*).[3]

From this formulation come the initial points I should like to draw out in relation to Hilberseimer's construction of the posthumanist metropolitan subject. First, banality, triviality, and everydayness are now the proper material for a theory of art and architectural production. This much Hilberseimer gathered from dada. A rarefied and autonomous aesthetic is no longer possible in the modern city, whether for pleasurable aloofness *or* for resistance; instead a practice enmeshed in the everyday lifeworld is demanded. Second, the subject itself, to the extent of its relation with the structure of the everyday, cannot be thought of as autonomous. Objectively structured like a mode of production, the subject is not so much an abstraction as a *neutrum*. The character of the subject is given from the outside, and contradictorily. And consequently it is, precisely, *distracted*. It is, at bottom, against this distraction that expressionism, unsuccessfully by Hilberseimer's lights, attempted to militate. Finally, as Sloterdijk demonstrates, the concept of distraction (*Zerstreuung*) is explicitly linked with postwar Weimar culture.

No other word is so saturated with a specific taste of the mid-twenties—of the first German modernity on a large scale. Everything we have heard about Anyone would be, in the final analysis, inconceivable without the precondition of the Weimar Republic with its hectic postwar life feeling, its mass media, its Americanism, its entertainment and culture industry, its advanced system of distraction. Only in the cynical, demoralized, and demoralizing climate of a postwar society, in which the dead are not allowed to die (because from their downfall political capital is to be made), can an impulse be diverted out of the "zeitgeist" into philosophy to observe existence "existentially" and to place everydayness in opposition to "authentic," consciously decided existence as a "being unto death." Only after the military *Götterdämmerung*, after the "disintegration of values," after the *coincidentia oppositorum* on the fronts of the material war, where "good and evil" dispatch each other into the "beyond" did such a critical "reflection" on "authentic being" become possible. In this period, for the first time attention is drawn in a radical way to the inner socialization.

This period senses that reality is dominated by spooks, imitators, remote-controlled ego machines. Each person could be a double (*Wiedergänger*) instead of itself. But how can one recognize this? In whom can one still see whether it is "it-self" or only Anyone? This question stimulates in existentialists deep cares about the important but impossible distinction between the genuine and the nongenuine, the authentic and the inauthentic, the articulated and the inarticulated, the decided and the undecided (which is simply "as it is"). [Heidegger put it this way:] "Everything looks as though it is genuinely understood, comprehended and said, but basically it is not, or it does not look as though it is, but basically it is."[4]

Sloterdijk makes it clear that the ambivalence of Heidegger's language in this last quotation, an ambivalence born of the acute recognition of distractedness, should not be understood cognitively (in the terms of science or information or knowledge) but rather existentially; it is the existential pathos of the ambivalence that must be grasped. It is this sort of ambivalence that leads Heidegger (and, I am arguing, Hilberseimer as well) to search for authenticity in the very inauthenticity of Weimar, to search for a mode of existence other than the present *in the very conditions of the present.* "The Other can initially be asserted only by simultaneously averring that it looks precisely like the One; seen from the outside, the 'authentic' does not distinguish itself from the 'inauthentic' in any way." What society gives us as an existential reality—a firmly ensconced structure of reification—already binds us to inauthenticity. And yet a difference can be made, though the difference must needs look much the same as the condition it opposes: hence, the dimension of resistance, hope, and redemption found within ambivalence.

As long as ambivalence is at least still asserted as a fundamental feature of existence, the possibility of the "other dimension" remains formally salvaged. With this, Heidegger's movement of thought (*Denkbewegung*) seems to already exhaust itself: in a formal salvaging of the authentic, which of course, can look exactly like the "inauthentic." . . . Alienation, we learn, does not mean that existence had been wrenched from it"self", but rather that the inauthenticity of this alienation is from the start the most powerful and the most primitive mode of being of existence. In existence there is nothing that, in an evaluative sense, could be called bad, negative, or false. Alienation is simply the mode of being of Anyone.[5]

This characterization of subjectivity in Sloterdijk's extraordinary explication of Heidegger's philosophy merges with the conditions of subjectivity already described in the distinct but related aesthetic practices of expressionism and dadaism as construed by Hilberseimer. And Weimar is the primary locus of the development of these conditions, which I have taken the terms reification, rationalization, and alienation to denote. It is in this sense that we can reassert that Hilberseimer's theoretical production is fundamentally a historical act.

With the publication of his book *Groszstadtarchitektur* in 1927 Hilberseimer fully thematizes what had only begun to emerge in his consideration of dadaism and expressionism: the external economic structures and modes of production of which the subject (as well as the subject's distraction) is an effect. Furthermore, with the publication of the Hochhausstadt project in *Groszstadtarchitektur* we find more fully explicated the relationship between structural causality and architectural form, along with the proposal of the possible, if as yet only imperfectly realized and only vaguely discernible, future architectural form. It is here, then, that Hilberseimer's theory of the subject as I have constructed it from his writings can be rejoined to the consideration of his architectural projects. The theoretical and historical moment of Hilberseimer's production is just this exigency to construct the new form, the new order, the utopian configuration of *grosstädtische* society, from the chaos of the present. Hilberseimer maintains an ambivalent commitment; indeed, he "asserts" an ambivalence toward that hegemonic mode of production of his own present, which, as he understands it, both intends

247

LUDWIG HILBERSEIMER

BAUBÜCHER BAND 3

GROSS STADT
ARCHITEKTUR

JULIUS HOFFMANN
VERLAG / STUTTGART   MIT 229 ABBILDUNGEN / KART. M 9.50

Cover of Hilberseimer, *Groszstadt-architektur* (1927).

groszstadtarchitektur and weimar-stimmung

and anticipates the future to be diverted out of the waste products of bourgeois humanism.

Hilberseimer begins his book with a concise characterization of the *Grosstadt* that joins its identification as a multinational economic organism to a description of its psychological effects.

The present type of large city owes its birth above all to the economic form of capitalist imperialism, which is in turn closely connected to the evolution of science and of production techniques. Its possibilities surpass by far the sphere of the national economy, and its influence is reflected ever more strongly on the world economy. With the maximum concentration and an extensive and complete organization it achieves a superabundance of intensity and energy: as soon as production does not find a sufficient outlet for its own exigencies, there is a move toward overproduction and toward antagonism with other countries, and a tendency to the stimulation of needs rather than to their satisfaction. Thus the large city appears primarily as the creation of omnipotent large capital and therefore is imprinted with anonymity. Furthermore, it is a type of city with its own socioeconomic and psycho-collective bases, in which is found at the same time the maximum isolation and the densest crowding together of its inhabitants. In it, an enormously intensified rhythm of life [*verstärkter Lebensrhythmus*] very rapidly represses every local and individual element.[6]

One cannot but connect this characterization of metropolitan anonymity, intensity, and leveling with Simmel's *Nervenleben*, conceived as a result of the bombardment of undifferentiated, free-floating, and contradictory images all generated by the monetary economy.[7] According to Hilberseimer, though the advanced capitalism of the bourgeoisie had brought this city into being, the bourgeoisie had not been able to control it. Through parasitic, speculative enterprise, the city had fallen into disorganization. Only in a "socially ordered society where production corresponds to the needs of men, not the greed for profits of privileged individuals, will the metropolis become a meaningful organism."[8]

And so the *Grosstadt* is also, for Hilberseimer, a productive organism in its own right.

The great cities . . . were stamped as parasitic with respect to the rest of the country and considered as organisms capable only of consumption and not of production. Their true nature has been completely misconstrued, and the fact ignored that it is precisely the large cities that automatically increase the productive process, taking over with ever-increasing rapidity and ability the direction of the economy and contributing in a substantial way to the material and spiritual productivity of the country.[9]

Hilberseimer here reveals the profound influence exercised on radical culture by the intelligentsia of "democratic capitalism." Inevitably he cites Henry Ford, the apostle of assembly line techniques, scientific management, consumerism, and productive capital, whose autobiography of "enlightened" capitalism, *Mein Leben und Werk*, had appeared in German in 1923. But it was Walter Rathenau who had already seen that, within the expanding cycle of production and consumption, "mechanical production has elevated itself to an aim in itself,"[10] and had already expressed an ironic disdain for the person who would futilely try to hold to old beliefs and values:

Now he strives with cunning to regain what has been lost and plants little shrines in his mechanized world, just as roof gardens are laid out on factory buildings. From the inventory of the times, here a cult of nature is searched out, there a superstition, a communal life, an *artifical naïveté*, a false serenity, an ideal of power, an art of the future, a purified Christianity, a nostalgic preoccupation with the past, a stylization. *Half believing, half dissembled*, devotion is given for a while, until fashion and boredom kill the idol.[11]

What is more, Rathenau's description of the large cities that "shoot their petrified street-threads over the countryside," and of massive constructions that directly and indirectly serve production,[12] are echoed in Hilberseimer's expansion of metropolitan laws such that "from the building of the city one arrives at the building of the country." According to Hilberseimer, "From the fusion of national or multinational states we will arrive at economic unions: for us, above all, the fusion of the European continent, today politically torn apart, into a single economic entity, will constitute the premise for an avant-garde urban policy in a productive sense, which will finally lead to the solution of the problem of the *Grosstadt.*"[13]

But what must be underscored in the present context is Rathenau's cogent description of the laboring subject as an epiphenomenon of the apparatus of production: "Labor is no longer an activity of life, no longer an accommodation of the body and the soul to the forces of nature, but a thoroughly alien activity for the purpose of life, *an accommodation of the body and the soul to the mechanism.*"[14] If the subject does not wish to be merely a cog in the city-machine, it must stretch itself out across the machine in unresisting accommodation. Here, again, the assertion of capitalism and mass reproduction— taken together as the sign of the determination to crush the individual and to pass from the sentimentalization of individual distress to a new, postindividualist framework— emerges as a primary constituent of Weimar modernity, even as it calls into question, as thoroughly as Hilberseimer's art critical writings, any expressive or reflective model of subject construction.

For Hilberseimer, as for Rathenau, advanced capitalism harbors contradictory forces. It is, on the one hand, the structural precondition of modernity, whose force blasts subject from object and recolonizes the fragments of each in terms of purely instrumental and functional categories (thus promoting what Hilberseimer saw as the overdevelopment of science, know-how, and technique). It is, at the same time, the proleptic basis for at least the figural projection of a future restructuring of experience. Capitalism is itself the only force capable of organiz-

ing and harmonizing the dissonance of an otherwise random
concatenation of objects and events into a rationalized totality. The "evil" of the *Grosstadt* is in capitalistic "abuse,"
not in capitalism's substance. For capitalism itself is but an
obscured form of reason, and its productive attributes—
rationalization, Fordism, Taylorism, planification—along
with its corresponding massified subjectivity constitute
what we might call Hilberseimer's "concrete utopia."[15]

Here, too, the full ideo-
logical force of Hilberseimer's proposition of the Hochhausstadt can be felt—properly ideological just to the degree that
it produces an entire image and structure of subject-object
relations in an irreducibly aesthetic, that is to say imaginary, modality. Without ever leaving the terrain of the
architectural project, Hilberseimer's total solution for the
city projects an understanding and experience of an actual,
concrete, historical situation of everyday social life that is
intolerable but inescapable. One might speculate (in order to
make the point more vivid) that the inhabitants of Hilberseimer's Hochhausstadt are the very postindividuated metropolitan subjects cynically portrayed in the drawings and
paintings of Grosz, Dix, and Hausmann, or in Heidegger's
picture of "Anyone." The vocation of architectural theory,
then, is to produce the image, the referent, the *Stimmung*—
the matter-of-factness, the new "intensified rhythms of
life,"[16] the new ascetic, desacralized, and disenchanted
objects, as well as the marked and expectant absence at the
heart of the actual, perceptible spaces in this city—in short,
that very lifeworld of intolerable ambiguity, contradiction,
and abstraction of which theory can then claim to be the
opposition, resolution, and displacement. Hilberseimer, once
again, confirms that any future solution has its precondition
in present fact.

The chaos of the city of today can be opposed only by attempts at
theoretical systematization, having the purpose of *enucleating from
actual situations*—in a totally abstract way—the fundamental principles of urban planning, thereby arriving at the fomulation of gen-

eral norms that then permit the solution of determined concrete problems. Only the abstraction of the specific case enables us, in fact, to demonstrate how the disparate elements that make up a large city can be placed, in an orderly way, in relationship with the whole.[17]

While Hilberseimer in his art critical writings had argued against the overly abstract pictorial representations of neoplasticism and suprematism, it is the elementarist architectural abstraction of metropolitan actuality that is now staged as the path to concreteness. Though the Hochhausstadt has usually been interpreted in purely technocratic, functional, and organizational terms,[18] it seems to be more correct in the larger context of Hilberseimer's theory of art—which in general tends toward an ever greater degree of formalization if not abstraction—to construe it as a logical and necessary progression of his thought toward a more purely and completely formal incarnation. In the conjunction of Hilberseimer's theory with his projects for metropolitan architecture we will see that his "enucleations" from actual situations are nothing less, and nothing more, than elementary signs, *Spuren*, for an architectural "not-yet."

As early as 1919, in one of the few preserved examples of his early work, Hilberseimer had organized his ideas for a *Kleinstadt* in a delicate but austere drawing in one-point perspective.[19] In technique it followed Heinrich Tessenow's drawing style used for representing his *Heimatstil* rural buildings, and Friedrich Ostendorf's theoretical insistence on reduced, symmetrical building forms determined by functional program and the spatial implications of concomitant streets, plazas, and gardens.[20] The enfilade of repetitive single-family houses converges toward a public building differentiated from the residences only by the organization of its windows. The scheme is striking in its reduction and indifference, and it was to serve as the formal armature from which Hilberseimer was to develop all of his later urban proposals.

But it was his personal contact with and his analyses and absorption of the most advanced experiments of the elementarist avant-gardes that provided Hilberseimer with the conceptual mechanisms necessary for a decisive shift away from the classicizing tendencies and stylistic influences of Tessenow and Ostendorf, and toward his ultimate solution.[21] For Hilberseimer, it was Cézanne who had initiated the shift toward *elementare Gestaltung* in his revelation of "the sphere, the cone, and the cylinder; using these starting points nature can be molded into new figures. His pictures enable one to perceive once again what an organism is, what figuration is. . . . For the first time his work rises above the chaos of the confused world."[22] Cézanne "opened the way to cubism," which continued this development:

Cubism is essentially a structure of planes mediating contrasting subdivisions. It has recognized the particular ordinance of the work of art, like an extraordinary organism with iron-clad laws of structure. It has consciously touched on the elements of all formations, returning to geometric-cubic form. It has recognized the identity between matter and form. In cubist works, in fact, one sees the contrasts of manufacture and varied materials forced into unity by compositional points of view. An artistic principle, which [Schwitters's] *Merzkunst* has systematically elaborated.[23]

I should underscore here the mediating role between art and reality that Hilberseimer ascribed to cubism and the Merz work. As well as Schwitters, it was Archipenko who for Hilberseimer recapitulated this overall scheme of development, beginning as an expressionist sculptor, then developing his "dynamic-constructivist fantasies" through analogies with and syntheses of the forms of "New York skyscrapers, glass constructions, of the machine and the airplane. . . . Through the reduction to the fundamental he came to his synthesis of form."[24] And finally, whereas "suprematism carried nonobjective art to its ultimate possibilities" and "[sought] the point of nothingness in art," it was the constructivists who had "traveled a new path. That of reality."

From construction in painting the constructivists have moved on
to the construction of objects. To architecture in the broadest sense
of the word. Constructivism is the logical consequence of methods
of work that are based on the collectivity of our time. Thus it has a
base that is of a general rather than a subjective nature. It perceives
the subordination of art to society without reserve, as of all of life.
It seeks its elements in the expressions of our mechanized and
industrialized time. Mathematical clarity, geometrical rigor, functional organization, extreme economy, and the most exact possible
constructiveness are problems that are not only technical but also
eminently artistic. They determine what is properly essential in
our epoch. The constructivist method brings any object into the
ambit of formation. Not suppressing liveliness, but forming a reality. The works of the constructivists, when all is said and done, are
nothing but experiments with materials. They consciously work
toward a solution to the new problems posed by material and by
form. Theirs are merely works of a transition toward functional
architectural constructions. The ultimate goal is a well-disciplined
preparation for architecture.[25]

It was Hilberseimer's introjection of the formal experiments
of the avant-garde, already analyzed in his art critical writ-

**Ludwig Hilberseimer, Kleinstadt project, c.
1905.**

ings, that sponsored this movement toward elementary form and enabled his subsequent architectural designs.

To develop adequate types for [the buildings of which our cities consist] according to their purpose and function, the materials used and the structures employed, constitutes the real problems which the Elementarists have to solve. This will lead to an architecture which is direct and free from all romantic reminiscences, in agreement with present daily life, not subjective and individualistic, but objective and universal. . . . Clarity, logic, thoughtfulness will lead to a unification. All architectural work, as different as it may be, is the result of the same spirit, an unfolding of it.[26]

In *Groszstadtarchitektur,* Hilberseimer projected his evolutionary schema toward its ultimate destiny in elementarist architecture.

Like every discipline, architecture, too, is confronted with the pressing need to define its fundamental principles and the means at its disposal. In this regard, painting has carried out a valuable preliminary task by focusing attention for the first time on the fundamental forms of every art: geometric and cubic elements, which represent a maximum of objectification. The simple solid bodies— the cube, the sphere, the prism, the cylinder, the pyramid, the cone—pure compositional elements—are fundamentals of all architecture. The exactness of their definition requires formal clarity and imposes order on chaos, in the most concrete ways.[27]

Late in 1923 Hilberseimer designed his second scheme for dwellings, the Wohnstadt for 125,000 people, first published in 1925 by Kurt Schwitters as *Merz* nos. 18/19 and later in *Groszstadtarchitektur.* It is stylistically altogether different from his earlier Kleinstadt project. A related drawing, published as an illustration of his "Der Wille zur Architektur,"[28] provides what can be taken as a model for the public building shown at the center of the Wohnstadt perspective, and is itself the "same" building as the Chicago Tribune save some volumetric redisposition of its repetitive constructional cells. Hilberseimer's repetition works at a structural level as well

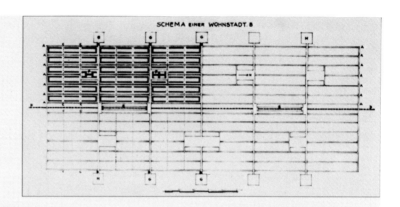

SCHEMA EINER WOHNSTADT. B

STRASSEN-ANSICHT.

BLOCK-ANSICHT.

KÜCHE

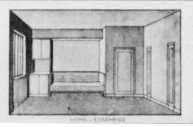

WOHN- u. ESSZIMMER

SCHLAFKABINE

as an imagistic one. The Wohnstadt project comprises walk-up apartments organized on a *Zeilenbau* system, with thin slabs oriented north-south and commercial spaces housed in lower blocks along the wider east-west streets. Rapid transit lines are sunk along the axis of the plan, connecting the residential satellite town to the main city, which was to be for work and business only. The apartments are minimal, modeled on American hotels. But what is remarkable is how the definitive perspective of the project repeats that of the Kleinstadt project of 1919—in the construction of the perspective, in the functional disposition of the public building and the residences, and in the street space defined by the buildings. Here we return to the radical repetition and denunciation of invention with which, as we have seen, Hilberseimer was involved throughout his career, but now we see it within the very gestation and formation of the project.

Here, too, we witness Hilberseimer's version of what Bloch called *Spuren*, or

Ludwig Hilberseimer, Wohnstadt project, 1923: plan, perspective of street, residential blocks, perspectives of interior cells. Published in *Groszstadtarchitektur* and *Groszstadtbauten*.

Georg Grosz, *Diabolo-player*, 1920.

groszstadtarchitektur and weimar-stimmung

figural traces and signs of the latent "not-yet" that arise out of, but seek to undermine, the dominant trends of the present. Recall Bloch's suggestion that these *"represent an ontological anticipation of the real that both transcends that limited and temporally developing object of the work and intends it at the same time,* an ontological anticipation precisely representable in an aesthetically immanent way."[29] Hilberseimer's *Spuren* are "the cube, the sphere, the prism, the cylinder, the pyramid, the cone—pure compositional elements" whose exactness of definition and formal clarity "imposes order on chaos, in the most concrete ways." These elements are not archetypes of an older, preindustrialized, and socially more stable culture, but nothing less than the forms of modern collective intelligence itself, the shared experience of industrial capitalism gathered up into images. In the Wohnstadt the "valuable preliminary" elementarist studies analyzed by Hilberseimer find their architectural analogue in the reiterative cell and converge with the distracted subjectivity given by Weimar culture. All of which produces architectural *Spuren* structured on radical repetition, seriality, and asserted ambivalence toward the actual situations from which they emerge.

In architecturalizing the elementary forms of the pictorial avant-garde, Hilberseimer also reconnects his research with the most advanced urban planning projects of the time. It is the Wohnstadt and Le Corbusier's Contemporary City of Three Million of 1922 that stand between Hilberseimer's Kleinstadt project of 1905 and the Hochhausstadt of 1924.[30] According to Hilberseimer, the failure of Le Corbusier's project was in its faulty calculation of possible densities of the residential area and its inability to solve the traffic problems; it was these shortcomings that prompted Hilberseimer's critique of Le Corbusier's effort. Hilberseimer's project relates the residential and commercial functions by superimposing fifteen-story apartment slabs on five-story commercial volumes in 600 meter by 100 meter city blocks and coordinating the pedestrian and vehicular traffic specific to each in separate levels.

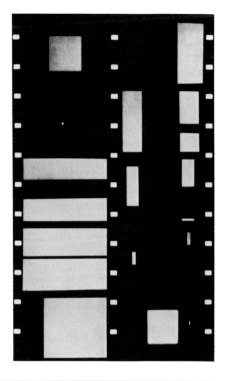

Hans Richter, *Rhythm 21*, 1921, frames
from the film.

Hannes Meyer's conceptualization of nomadic space is here
made fully concrete, for the elevators and rapid transit systems and the coordinated places of dwelling and work eliminate the need (and the possibility) of bourgeois domestic
entourage. But what is most striking is, again, the repetition
of the Kleinstadt and the Wohnstadt project(s), now with
almost no modification of the latter other than an increase
in size, the separation of traffic, and the addition in the perspective of metropolitan people walking the streets of the
city, evenly dispersed by the flow of the city's forces. This
last addition is a pictorial adjustment that thematizes what
was already implicit in the earlier projects: that the constitution of the metropolitan subject is fundamental to this
architecture. The differential play of subject and object now
finds literal representation.

Georg Grosz, *Berlin C,* 1920.

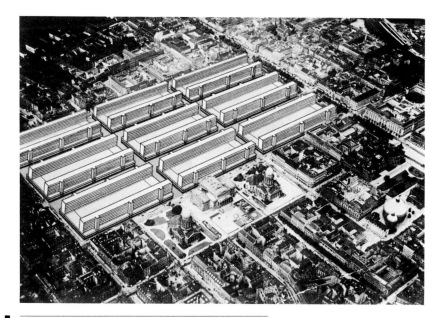

Ludwig Hilberseimer, project for the construction of a city applied to the center of Berlin, 1928, photomontage.

In Hilberseimer's constant repetition of his own project we find confirmation that, in the long run, the content of the new architecture stands judged by its form, which is the most certain index to the actual, experiential possibilities of that social moment from which it springs. Hilberseimer's evolutionary schema involves a constant movement away from the nonsynchronous and complicated factuality of society and toward the various determinate, elementary traces to which society's content can be reduced, and whose conceptual limits and inadequacies stand as immediate figures of the limits of the concrete social situation itself. I have been describing the force of this movement as reification, but we must find another interpretive language with which to comprehend the now superattenuated link between architectural form—understood as a system of signs that is "semi-autonomous" (in an Althusserian sense)—and the cultural sphere or "structural totality" that is its ultimate referent. And if

Hans Richter, *Ghosts Before Breakfast,*
1927–1928, frames from the film.

assertions of "a free play of signifiers" or "the discourse of the simulacral" (à la Baudrillard) seem premature, we must nevertheless find some way to explicate a signifying practice like Hilberseimer's, which generates formal patterns and subjectivities but, emptied of the ballast of interiority and plenitude, seems nevertheless to hover above the everyday lifeworld in midair.

Siegfried Kracauer once defined the intention of his critical analyses of the "surface manifestations of an epoch" that resemble "the *aerial photographs* of landscapes and cities for [they do] not emerge from the interior of a given reality, but rather appear above it."[31] He wrote, "Spatial images [*Raumbilder*] are the dreams of society. Wherever the hieroglyphics of these images can be deciphered, one finds the basis of social reality."[32] For Kracauer, the aesthetic topography of mass culture is the surface that reveals the movement of society within a historical context, and what he called "the mass ornament" was, in the Taylorized culture of Weimar, "the aesthetic reflex of the rationality aspired to by the prevailing economic system."[33] I propose Kracauer's notion of the mass ornament as the concept with which to frame my conclusions about Hilberseimer's work.

Kracauer's characteristic example of mass ornament is the Tiller Girls, an American dance troupe that began performing in Berlin during the period of inflation.

Not only were they American products; at the same time they demonstrated the greatness of American production. I distinctly recall the appearance of such troupes in the season of their glory. When they formed an undulating snake, they radiantly illustrated the virtues of the conveyor belt; when they tapped their feet in fast tempo, it sounded like *business, business;* when they kicked their legs high with mathematical precision, they joyously affirmed the progress of rationalization; and when they kept repeating the same movements without ever interrupting their routine, one envisioned an uninterrupted chain of autos gliding from the factories into the world, and believed that the blessings of prosperity had no end.[34]

The Tiller Girls in Berlin, 1920s.

Like the constellations of Tiller Girls, Hilberseimer's mass ornament generates a correspondingly massified subject: "Only as parts of a mass, not as individuals who believe themselves to be formed from within, are human beings components of a pattern." And like the Tiller Girls, Hilberseimer's mass ornament is an end in itself. According to Kracauer, the mass ornament—unlike military demonstrations, say, whose aesthetic order is a means to an end, or in any case, tied to feelings of patriotism, loyalty, and morality, or gymnastic configurations that have a functional and hygienic dimension—has neither aesthetic nor functional meaning. "In the end there is the closed ornament, whose life components have been drained of their substance."[35] Nevertheless, in a series of passages remarkable for their relation to what we have seen in Hilberseimer's work, Kracauer takes a position against a cultural pessimism that might well result from his analyses and attempts to redeem the mass ornament, precisely because of its structural relationship to the cultural totality.

The ornament, detached from its bearers, must be understood *rationally.* It consists of degrees and circles like those found in textbooks of euclidean geometry. Waves and spirals, the elementary structures of physics, are also included: discarded are the proliferations of organic forms and the radiations of spiritual life. Hereafter, the Tiller Girls can no longer be reassembled as human beings. Their mass gymnastics are never performed by whole, autonomous bodies whose contortions would deny rational understanding. Arms, thighs and other segments are the smallest components of the composition. The structure of the mass ornament reflects that of the general contemporary situation. Since the principle of the *capitalist production process* does not stem purely from nature, it must destroy the natural organisms which it regards either as a means or as a force of resistance. Personality and national community [*Volksgemeinschaft*] perish when calculability is demanded; only as a tiny particle of the mass can the individual human being effortlessly clamber up charts and service machines. A system which is indifferent to variations of forms leads necessarily to the obliteration of national characteristics and to the fabrication of masses of workers who can be employed and used uniformly throughout the world. Like the mass ornament, the capitalist production process is an end in itself. . . . It is conceived according to rational principles which the Taylor system only takes to its final conclusion. The hands in the factory correspond to the legs of the Tiller Girls. . . . The mass ornament is the aesthetic reflex of the rationality aspired to by the prevailing economic system. . . . I would argue that the *aesthetic* pleasure gained from the ornamental mass movements is *legitimate.* They belong in fact to the isolated configurations of the time, configurations which imbue a given material with form. The masses which are arranged in them are taken from offices and factories. The structural principle upon which they are modeled determines them in reality as well. When great amounts of reality-content are no longer visible in our world, art must make do with what is left, for an aesthetic presentation is all the more real the less it dispenses with the reality outside the aesthetic sphere. No matter how low one rates the value of the mass ornament, its level of reality is still above that of artistic productions which cultivate obsolete noble sentiments in withered forms—even when they have no further significance.[36]

For Kracauer, as for Hilberseimer, capitalism is a stage in the process of demystification (*Entzauberung*) by which history, through unsentimental rationalization, continually dismantles those superstructural and naturalizing myths whose regressive effect is to prolong the notion of some unchanging and proprietary human essence.

However, the rationale of the capitalist economic system is not reason itself but obscured reason. . . . *It does not encompass human beings.* The operation of the production process is not set up to take them into consideration, nor is the formation of the socio-economic organization based on them. There is not one single instance where the system is based on human essences. . . . Capitalism does not rationalize too much but *too little.*[37]

The sign of capitalist thought is abstraction, but the present state of abstractness is ambivalent; its alternative poles are the growth of abstract thought or the decline into false concreteness. All of which means that the process of demystification and demythologizing is incomplete. In this context, Hilberseimer's constant reassertion of the cube, the sphere, the prism, the cylinder, the pyramid, the cone, and the cell—all depleted, austere, abstract pictorial and architectural hieroglyphs—should not seem surprising, and neither should his ambivalence be understood as an unresolved or illegitimate mode of architectural thought. The mass ornament *just is* this abstraction and this ambivalence, and the recognition of the ornament is the recognition that the possibility for a more concrete, articulate, private figure of redemption for the present has been foreclosed by modernity itself.

But to dwell only on ambivalence, abstraction, and distraction is to miss the other, paradoxically related side of the *Weimar-stimmung.* Initially this could be characterized as a kind of pleasure or euphoria uniting the act of architectural re-presentation (in the sense that Hilberseimer's projects are readings, interpretations, and reproductions of the cultural codes of a preexisting cultural order) with experiences of orgasmic pleasure, death, and the moment of self-obliteration. Roland Barthes describes this as an act of reading—or better, of rewriting—the doxologies of culture: a simultaneous pleasure of repeating what already exists (the enjoyment of cultural identity) and bliss of aesthetic disruption.

Text of pleasure [*texte de plasir*]: the text that contents, fills, grants euphoria; the text that comes from culture and does not break with it, is linked to a *comfortable* practice of reading. Text of bliss [*texte de jouissance*]: the text that imposes a state of loss, the text that discomforts (perhaps to the point of a certain boredom), unsettles the reader's historical, cultural, psychological assumptions, the consistency of his tastes, values, memories, brings to a crisis his relation with language. Now the subject who keeps the two texts in his field and in his hands the reins of pleasure and bliss is an anachronic subject, for he simultaneously and contradictorily participates in the profound hedonism of all culture . . . and in the destruction of that culture: he enjoys the consistency of his selfhood (that is his pleasure) and seeks its loss (that is his bliss). He is a subject split twice over, doubly perverse.[38]

An architecture of pleasure is a transaction between a bounded inventory of units, preexisting elements lifted out from the cultural sediment and redeployed; jouissance is the experience of the abyss that such transactions open up. This is the same "perverse" coupling of affirmation and negation, of reproduction and disruption, that we find in Hilberseimer, whose projects are invaded by the ideologies and repetitions of the Weimar "code" even as he issues exhortations against them. Barthes on the code:

The code is a perspective of quotations, a mirage of structures; we know only its departures and returns; the units which have resulted from it (those we inventory) are themselves, always, ventures out of the text, the mark, the sign of a virtual digression toward the remainder of the catalogue . . . ; they are so many fragments of something that has always been *already* read, seen, done, experienced; the code is the wake of that *already*.[39]

These two passages strikingly reveal the extreme, outer limits of modern subjectivity and, at that border line, the implacable closure of modernism's signifying economy whose only (impossible) escape is a kind of death wish. Hilberseimer's *texte de jouissance* takes a quasi-erotic pleasure in accomplishing the death of its subject in two senses: the

Ludwig Hilberseimer, Hochhausstadt project, 1924, perspective of an east-west street. Published in *Groszstadtarchitektur.*

groszstadtarchitektur and *weimar-stimmung*

dissolution of its content (subject matter)—the transaction
within an enclosed field of signs creates nothing, changes
nothing in the existing cultural order, for everything has
been done already—and its agent (the author or reader)—the
signifying economy conceals all traces of its production.
Thus a textual solution is created in which the death wish
is driven into the very aesthetic reflexivity of his modernism. Hilberseimer himself announced as much in his
famous recantation of the Hochhausstadt: "the result was
more a necropolis than a metropolis . . . , inhuman in every
respect."[40] But if his text is nihilistic, it contains at the
same time a trace of an affirmation. For as his work of dissolution is continued—penetrating the abstract and ambivalent mass-ornamental sign, and threatening modern
representational knowledge itself—we witness, first, the
vision of the humanist subject seared hard, brittle, and
transparent to the exterior forces of which it is an effect,
and then the final breakup of the subject in midair. This is
the euphoria of self liquidation through mechanization once
again perhaps, but now, unlike with dadaism or Meyer, with
no resistant materiality left as residue.

           Hilberseimer projects his
analyses of present culture toward a utopian future. But
here we must recall that, to the extent that the mass ornament and the code, including Hilberseimer's architectural
version of each, present themselves as a fetishization of
existing psycho-physical culture, and to the extent that the
consumption of the ornamental figures, or the mere redistri-
bution of the elements of the code, distract from concrete,
material action toward *changing* the current social system,
it becomes comprehensible how fascism, in the future that
actually came, would be able to reinvest such mass orna-
ments that lay bleached out and devoid of substance with
an altogether unintended and horrifyingly different meaning; so that the masses would ultimately come to claim to
see their own triumph of the will in the megalomania of the
ciphers and spectacles of Naziism. And here we can recol-
lect my earlier claim that the disintegrating ambiguity of

Hilberseimer's work stands in uneasy parallel to the disintegration of Weimar Germany and its passage into fascism.[41]

Hilberseimer's utopian neutralization of capitalism ends up making a contribution, beyond its value as an instrument of urban analysis, to the production of a version of the mass ornament, and it projects a form, more properly ideologically determined than most architectural critics have allowed, according to which it is proposed that society be organized. Understood in this way, the Hochhausstadt comes to constitute something like a *Vorbild* (a model, an "image before")[42] that attempts to resolve the objective demands of the social with psychosubjective existence: the project registers and anticipates the subjective oscillation between massification, critical individual agency, dispersion into a postindividual collective framework, and the reactionary capitulation of individuality to the suprahistorical forces of technology, blood, and nation.[43] In this sense, the Hochhausstadt itself can still be described as a mediation on the order of Simmel's concept of style or Meyer's Co-op form, as an architectural production standing between subject and object. And yet, another structure, which can now be specified, overlaps that of *Groszstadtarchitektur* as an effect of metropolitan actuality, as production of *Spuren,* and as mass ornament. Hilberseimer's conflictual model of subjectivity—the recognized loss

Ludwig Hilberseimer, industrial building, 1922. Published as the cover of *Der Wille der Architektur.*

groszstadtarchitektur and weimar-stimmung

of an authentic relation with the external world coupled with the hope to recapture a relation by building a world up again—is stretched out across the topography of paranoia, in which something outside, some inexorable exteriority, is felt to be closing in, and in which conflictual anxieties then become projected forms. Of course, the passage from (or even coincidence of) the radical desire for resistance and change to the increasingly cynical self-resignation is not unfamiliar, especially, perhaps, on the political left.[44] And given our analysis in this section, Hilberseimer's affirmational internalization of the schizophrenic dissolutions of capitalism—his Nietzschean choice—may correctly, I think, be interpreted as a point of contact with such cynicism and with the fear of that suprapersonal system of technological modernity.

Self-liquidating bliss notwithstanding, for Hilberseimer some postindividual artistic subject must still be the principal agency of mediation between the nonsynchronous spheres of production and form. Though he recognizes that the individual subject in modernism is ineluctably dispersed, his Nietzschean conception of the heroic artist still requires a unifying principle of agency to do the work of transfiguring mundane facticity into an inwardly appropriated law. Hilberseimer's solution, however, is not to reassert the now discredited forms of individual unity or transcendental subjectivity, but to totalize the disunifying components of the real with an entirely different conception of the subject. The amalgam of Riegl's supraindividual *Kunstwollen* and Nietzsche's will to power— and here we circle back to the central importance of what Hilberseimer termed "der Wille zur Architektur"—replaces the individual subject in a construction that can totalize capitalism as the socioeconomic force of modern society, Fordism or Taylorism as its logic of instrumentalization, cellular repetition and seriality as its architectural form, and dispersion as the subjective condition of everyday life. The very concept of the subject is thus prized loose from the embodied individual and catapulted into some ontological sphere, and there the *Kunstwollen*, suitably ambiguous, can play its totalizing role. The fundamental category under which Hilberseimer's thought operates is that of the latitudinal *whole*: we oscillate back and forth between the cellular and structural, molecular and molar, local and global, between euphoria and distraction, until a totality of "will" is reached. As the *Kunstwollen* becomes a kind of field phenomenon, it appears to operate as a virtual subject, accountable to no one while seeming to account for everything, and thus resolving the tension between the impacted closure of the present structural matrix and that impossible, free-floating, and inchoate future to be installed in its place. But the form of that utopia is, to say it once again, already presignified as a possibility, as a possible category, by the chaotic reality of the present—out of that we must tool the psychic effectivity and social actuality of the future. Hilberseimer's totality is, in this way, an *affirmational tautology*—an ecstatic surrender of the subject to the very force that assures its dissolution.

This particular inscription of the subject that I have been trying to articulate—a posthumanist subject at once subjected to material forces and systems of signification beyond its control and at the same time capable of mediating or totalizing those external forces and systems with the internal economy of architectural form—this "doubly perverse" subject is not constructed for nothing. It is an "enunciative" attempt to compensate for the loss of figurability that I have already mentioned—the loss of signification, the loss of the paternal fiction of humanist thought—to the inauthenticity of mass technological culture. It is an attempt to insert into an imposed order an alternative space of action, itself an "effect produced by the operations that orient it, situate it, temporalize it, and make it function in a polyvalent unity of conflictural programs."[45] It is an attempt to salvage, within the modality of architecture, some vestige of artistic agency that might replace a dysfunctional and discredited humanism.

The duplicity of humanism lies in its claim on behalf of individual rights to a reality that does not permit alternative constructions—indeed, a reality that does not even know itself as a construction—*as well as* the insistence on the subject's innocence of reality's formation: the confident, controlling apparatus of self-affirmation.[46] In contrast, what seems to structure Hilberseimer's punctually felt urge to totalize is, as I have said, a kind of paranoia: a paranoia that is all too cognizant of distraction as the fundamental condition of everyday life, all too aware of a world out of control, and that consequently tries to fend off the threatening and destructive identification between the discursive formations of architecture and social reality in favor of some more affirmational construction of the same. The totalization is fundamentally *imaginary* in Lacan's sense, which is to say it is illusory with respect to the chaotic reality of the city and the body (Lacan's *corps morcelé*), *and* it is essentially visual, for it is only before a visual image, a *Vorbild*, that the subject constructs its "beautiful totality," even at the same time that that image "prefigures its alienating destination; [the image] is still pregnant with the correspondences that unite the *I* with the statue in which man projects himself, with the phantoms that dominate him, or with the automaton in which, in an ambiguous relation, the world of his own making tends to find completion."[47] The paranoia arises from Hilberseimer's ideological and epistemological imperative to maintain that a correspondence continues to exist between the speculative and specular architectural discourse and the social world, and that there is a supraindividual artistic-heroic subject, reenfranchized and aggrandized, that resides in and mediates that correspondence.

And so that correspondence between subject and object must be maintained through the production and affirmation of some *object*. This much we have already seen. But how can Hilberseimer's simultaneous production of object and subject be called paranoid? According to Freudian psychoanalysis, there are two

primary factors involved in paranoia. First is the withdrawal
of the cathetic relationship of the subject with the outside
world, a divestment of the subject's mental and emotional
energy in the object. Withdrawal of cathexis is the precondition of the perceptual registration (via hallucination) of the
image of the desired object. "With a reversal to unpleasure
[the libido] clings to the perceptions into which the object
has been transformed. . . . The libidinal cathexis heightens
the images that have become perceptions, transforming
them into hallucinations."[48] Second, the withdrawn libido
returns to and aggrandizes the ego, becoming autoerotic and
narcissistic; this is a regression to an earlier functional
mode of the ego. At this point the world is perceived as
hostile to the subject and the subject becomes aggressive
toward the previously desired object. Paranoia, then,
emerges as the delusional reconstruction of a world, the
attempt to recapture a relation with the world. The paranoiac analysand constructs, from the start as it were, "in a
distorted form precisely those things which neurotics keep
hidden."[49] The paranoiac projects onto external objects anything perceived as threatening and destructive within the
ego. The perception of external reality is entirely produced
by an internal psychic economy but is imagined as outside
the body. Paranoia itself, then, is already an interpretation.
Unlike in neurosis, in paranoia there is no internal tension
between subject and object to be overcome through a process of analysis, all disturbances in the subject-object relationship having been expelled into a set of images, signs,
and identifications that already guarantee a resolution in
totality. The paranoiac's delusional conceptions of reality
"make demands on the thought-activity of the ego until
they can be accepted *without contradiction.* . . . [These are]
interpretive delusions."[50] Such interpretive strategies constitute the real lifeworld of the paranoiac.

        The return of libidinal
attachment to the ego in paranoia parallels the return of
artistic energies to an aggrandized *Kunstwollen* in Hilberseimer's theory. And the production of external signs by a

Paul Klee, *Uncomposed in Space,* 1929.

wholly internal psychic economy in paranoia parallels the projection of architectural *Spuren* by a purely formal mechanism (what I earlier called Hilberseimer's system of simulacra, which is also his *plaisir*). What is important about these paranoid symptoms here is that they are the consequence of the effort to maintain the fiction, exactly, of a wholeness in the self-engendering economy of the subject-object-producing mechanism in the face of a perceived loss of boundaries and significations. This projective, interpretive mechanism is thus both a production of and a defense against reality, an objectifying apparatus that produces coherence but entails closure. And its structure can be found in the architecture of Hilberseimer, in his search for a total system operative in the gap above the subject and its experience of everyday reality. Through the hypostatization of *Wahrheitsfanatismus*, paranoia and distraction replace humanism and mimesis in the ambiguous space of Weimar culture.

Perhaps what I have been describing is the transition from a failed idea or possibility of sustaining a critical enterprise to an order of an altogether different kind—a totalizing set of relationships among an institution of artistic production, an emergent economic and political authority, and their constituencies and audiences. Perhaps it is simply an example of how an architecture, produced by the accidents of a certain history, can be dislodged and pressed into the service of a quite different one, reinvested with new and unexpected content, and adapted to unsuspected ideological functions. But more important, what I have been describing illustrates, I believe, the way authority is revalidated, however unwittingly, by intellectuals operating by rational consent to articulate, maintain, or elaborate some prior idea or world view. Authority is maintained by the *consensus* of cultural agents—by affirmation of what exists—as well as by repression: in the final evaluation of Hilberseimer's work, this is what must be constantly confronted.

conclusion: posthumanism and postmodernism

Every time there's been a revision of the discourse of man, we have difficulty imagining what happened, because the gist of each of these revisions is always deadened, attenuated, with time, in such a way that today, as always, the word humanism is a bag in which the corpses of these successive disclosures of a revolutionary point of view on man very slowly rot, piled one on top of the other.

Jacques Lacan

Since the 1960s the discourse of the subject has taken an explicitly posthumanist turn, which has come to be thought of as definitively *post*modern, in both philosophy and architecture. In the philosophy of this period—or more acurately, in theory, this postmodern practice having displaced philosophy—the deconstruction of the humanist tradition is based on a radicalization of the texts of modern thinkers such as Marx, Nietzsche, Heidegger, and Freud. A few examples will be enough evidence of a general tendency: from Louis Althusser's reading, in *For Marx*, of humanism as pernicious bourgeois ideology and his praise of Marx's "theoretical anti-humanism" based on "the absolute precondition that the philosophical (theoretical) myth of man is reduced to ashes";[1] to Jacques Lacan's reaffirmation of "the truth discovered by Freud" of "the self's radical ex-centricity to itself";[2] to Michel Foucault's systematic interpretations of the subtly repressive expulsions and reductions of intellectual, psychological, and sexual alterities by modern reason,[3] and his meditations on the "death of man" in *The Order of Things*;[4] to Jacques Derrida's sustained critique of the metaphysics of humanism and logocentric thought[5]—throughout the work of such writers, the modern ideology of "man" as the subjective origin and interpretive limit of all sense and reality is confronted with a resolutely antihumanist effort to remove what Jean-François Lyotard has called "the humanist obstacle"[6] from philosophy.

Parallel to the discourse of the subject in post-1960s theory, and to a certain extent drawing from it, recent work in architecture has reopened what might be called a postmodern posthumanist project. Certain experiments by Peter Eisenman (who is explicit about his Derridean affiliations and nonanthropocentric intellectual position) and Bernard Tschumi (who was an early and attentive reader of post-1960s French theory),[7] as well as much of the work of a second generation of architects and architectural theorists (I am thinking of Stanley Allen, Jennifer Bloomer, Elizabeth Diller, Jeffrey Kipnis, and others), all attempt in one way or another to operate against

the received, orthodox modernist conception of architecture
that has tended to maintain an idealist distinction between
the immanent, infrangibly internal operations of architecture and the potentially disturbing, multiple externalities—
such as conditions of object distribution and audience reception, ideological enframing devices, exclusionary disciplinary conventions, and the like. In the projects of these
architects, the identification of the architectural object is
shifted away from a distinctive, uniquely visual, or even
generally aesthetic mode of perception and valuation—
whereby the object is isolated in a purely abstract and idealized realm, freed from the molestations of ideology and circumstance, and its meaning thereby fixed—and toward the
multiple and differentiated "intertextual" structures, resonances, and plays of signification in excess of the object's
abstractable visual meaning. Of course, in the most rigorous
sense of the concept, textuality does not imply a written
text at all, and if projects like Eisenman's *Arrows, Eros, and
Other Errors* or Tschumi's *Manhattan Transcripts* are perhaps most explicit about, and insistent upon, the more literal textual nature of their meaning-engendering strategies,
much of recent architectural production can best be understood as object-texts—sites for the multiple and aleatory
crossings of signifying systems—in contradistinction to
autonomous, aesthetic works, understood in Roland
Barthes's formulation where "work" denotes an aesthetic,
symbolic whole connected to an origin, author, and meaningful end, and "text" denotes "a multidimensional space in
which a variety of writings, none of them original, blend
and clash. The text is a tissue of quotations, drawn from the
innumerable centers of culture."[8]
        Now a theory of signifi-
cation that emphasizes (over and against immanent aesthetic value) the external factors that overdetermine the
object-text's potentials of meaning construction, and
stresses (over and against compositional unity and singularity) the multiplicity of readings latent even in its internal
structures, is continuous with the project of deconstructing

the humanist subject of classical bourgeois thought and orthodox high modernist art. And so, in contrast to the portrayal of the heroic modernist artist as the magisterial creator of an original and unified individual language, the author, in many of these works, is presented as mere conduit for the giddy flickering of "meaning effects,"[9] registering and repeating systems of signification whose provenance lies beyond the control of the individual writer or designer. Thus Peter Eisenman, the architect, becomes himself a kind of *pretext*, operating only to set in motion or channel the processes of assembling codes already formed in the sublanguages of topology or genetic biology; or Jennifer Bloomer, the architect cum performance artist, juxtaposes in spoken presentations fragments of texts from diverse occasions in an attempt to figure a "minor architecture"; or Stanley Allen charts the contradictory mappings of the city given by discourses such as airline flight control, subway transit, and sexual marketplaces. It is worth emphasizing, also, that many of these recent projects, like those of Meyer and Hilberseimer, attempt to negotiate the various topographies of mass culture—advertising, mechanization, mass transit, mass media, pornography, etc.—declaring themselves in and of that culture rather than the high culture of the art world. For while it is true that traffic between modern art and mass culture has a long tradition (and that certain practices like dadaism and constructivism have thematized their commerce with mass culture even more explicitly than Meyer), it is equally true that modernist critics have, for the most part, sought to deny it. Recent architectural projects, as much as recent historiographical revisions, make such critical subterfuge henceforth impossible.

Duplication, heterogeneity, schizophrenia, alterity, and difference are the *Leitworte* of the postmodern posthumanist subject revealed by these projects, a subject now splintered not merely by modernist reification but by utterly new and heretofore unimaginable desires and acts of consumption. As such, certain recent architectural programs may have occurred to the reader

283

as progeny of the posthumanist projects analyzed in the
preceding pages of this study, though now bound to the
historical modifications of the present totally reified and
administered lifeworld. And surely, in addition, the reader
will have already queried the interpretive vantage ground of
this study, marked off as it is by developments in critical
theory and architectural practice that are nonsynchronous
with its primary subject matter, even if one allows that the
earlier interpretations of Adorno, Benjamin, Bloch, Kracauer,
Lukács, et al. treat a problematic of modernism congruous
with that of Meyer and Hilberseimer. The inclination to
make the works of Meyer and Hilberseimer into "precursors
of postmodernism"—as the popular legitimation phrase of
much current historiography renders the subjects of its
study—must be forestalled. And the question of interpretive
anachronism must be at least touched upon, if not resolved.

Often emulating the his-
torical avant-garde, much of current architectural practice
seeks to subvert ideological hierarchies and closures through
highly developed formal means. Criticism through representations (and against representation, against representing others, against subjecting others) and confrontations between
art and mass culture: these seem to constitute a potent
starting point for returning contemporary architecture to its
social engagements. For what else do we mean by "society"
but a set of means for knowing, belonging, and practicing,
all fixed hierarchically through representations? And yet, if
the repudiation of the distinction between the aesthetic
object and the critical text has enabled these projects, theo-
retically, to blur the constructed boundaries between high
art and mass culture, and to challenge the monolithically
affirmative, humanist stance characteristic of other recent
architectures, a reluctance to treat in any *specific* way mass
cultural and ideological formations and their impact on
artistic production is still evident in much contemporary
work. While rejecting the elite seriousness of the modernist
notion of high art as redeemed matter, these projects, nevertheless, often serve up textuality as an escape from matter's

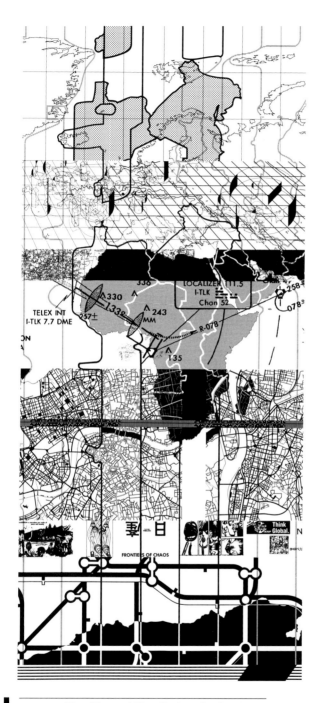

Stan Allen and Marc Hacker, *Scoring the City,* 1986: montage of urban cartographies.

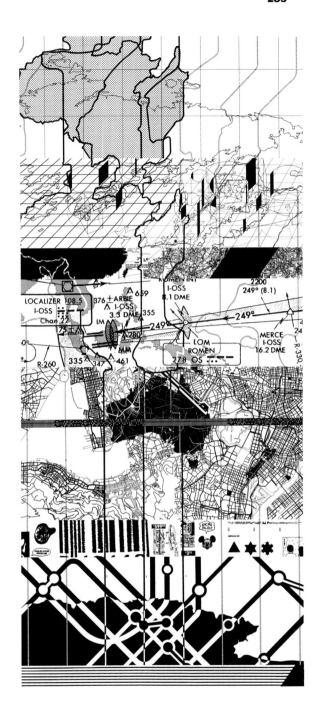

conclusion: posthumanism and postmodernism

grittier occasions; they provide spaces for retreat and contemplation, but few evince the differentiated spaces one
might ask of an architecture pitted against hegemony,
which the work of Hannes Meyer, if my analysis has been
correct, most certainly did. And if an understanding of the
affiliations between representational systems and power has
expanded our conception of architecture's domain and
responsibilities, these contemporary projects have, for the
most part, remained remarkably silent on *specific* questions
of power, class, gender, sexuality, and the actual experiences
of subjects in contemporary society. The (old) idealized,
unified, centralized subject of high art still looms large
as textuality becomes the antithesis and displacement of
materiality, circumstance, and history, and the reality principle is undermined by a principle of noninterference. With
the absorption of a critical imperative into the structure of
the object, architects themselves have, paradoxically,
assumed a self-legitimating role. Despite the intransigent
antihumanism of postmodernist deconstructionist discourse,
the practical result has often been the construction of a
canon of individual oeuvres and authors whose domain is
the gallery, the journal, and the jewelry boutique. Terry
Eagleton has made concisely, if a bit heavy-handedly, the
point I would wish to reassert: "An art which espouses the
Lebenswelt of Las Vegas is not the same as one which takes
to the streets of Leningrad; a postmodernism which
responds to local community needs, in art or architecture,
differs from one which takes its cue from the market place.
There is no automatic virtue in the 'integration' of culture
and common life, any more than there is in their
dissociation."[10]

              Most of contemporary
practice's promises of destabilization, decentering, heterogeneity, and differentiated spaces remain apolitical because
unparticularized and ahistorical. This apolitical attitude is
self-imposed, and stands in clear contrast to both the actual
and the implicit claims of radical architects in the first
decades of this century for urgent and active interventions,

and to the more recent conciliatory calls for affirmation of the social and physical contexts as found. One suspects it is a symptom of the general and profoundly felt loss of the once-dominant tradition we now call the modern movement, of the prevalent cynicism about architecture's reforming and communicative powers, and of the general confusion about what it is that critically conscious architects, at this moment in history, should be doing. Of course, whether the turn to textuality is considered an expansion of architectural practice into new critical realms, a closing down of the practice into new forms of formalism, or (perhaps most positive and fruitful) an emerging attempt to construct a countermemory of the architectural avant-garde's radical but failed past, will depend on one's construction of the ideological trajectory of modernism into the present as much as the personal politics of these practitioners or their critics. And whatever their shortcomings, the merit of these recent projects, it seems to me, lies in their forcing of just that fact: that at this moment, it is to discussions of the politics of practice, of the ideological refractions within the various modalities of architecture, past and present, that we must turn. This study of a particular trajectory of modernism has attempted, among other things, to begin to establish some of the possible terms of that discussion.

I have insisted throughout this study that architecture is in the world—in history, in ideology, in the sensuous facts of everyday existence— and that it also has a degree of autonomy and irreducibility. This is neither an original nor a difficult proposition. And yet questions concerning the precise nature of the reciprocal influences between architectural form and material life— matter and its irreducible heterogeneity in relation to subjects—bring opposing theories of architecture and its interpretation into forceful play. In fact, in the context of architectural theory, positions have tended to reduce themselves to opposing valuational poles along the same line of content, when that line is thought in terms of the category of the subject: one pole defined by the happily dehistoricized, schizophrenic subject of postmodernism, the other by the maintenance of humanist values of quality, propriety, and continuity. And it is, finally, for this reason that I have felt well advised to bring both critical theory in its more materialist (not to say Marxist) moments *and* poststructuralist theory to bear on the architecture in question, whose complexity seems to demand this sort of methodological plurality, even this sort of interpretive anachronism. The supreme, free play of unleashed signifiers, and the ecstatically schizoid, morcelated, deracinated, laughing subject it engenders, are the affirmational recto of poststructuralist formalism. But the sensuous, historical subject and the resolutely partisan, instrumental, and negational practice of the Marxist materialist verso always threaten to bleed through, disturbing the disinterestedness and undecidability of disintegrated consciousness, questioning the historical, social, and ideological frames of the very subject that claims to be free of all situating frames. This opposition traces many of the historiographical problems one encounters in the posthumanism of Hilberseimer and Meyer as well as contemporary (postmodernist, if you will) design practice. The poststructuralist and materialist analyses of the subject seem to be perpendicular cuts through the same phenomenon, namely architecture in a totally reified, postindividualist world. Both inflict a stigma on humanist ideology by insisting on the heteronomy of architecture and the inexorable externality of the factors that enable its becoming. It seems doubtful to me that a critical theory, history, or practice that forgets, as humanism does, the theories, histories, or cultural politics that overdetermine architecture's production, use, and even its understanding, will ever succeed in constructing conditions and subjectivities truly human.

notes

Introduction

Epigraph: Louis Althusser, "Marxism and Humanism" (1965), in
For Marx, trans. Ben Brewster (London: Verso, 1979), 229.

1. Siegfried Kracauer, *Schriften* 1 (Frankfurt: Suhrkamp, 1971), 13.

2. One of the most thorough studies of subjectivity and strategies of resistance is Paul Smith, *Discerning the Subject* (Minneapolis: University of Minnesota Press, 1988).

3. "'Subject'. . . may refer to the particular individual as well as to general attributes, to 'consciousness in general'. . . . The equivocation is not removable simply by terminological clarification, for the two meanings have reciprocal need of each other; one is scarcely to be grasped without the other. The element of individual humanity . . . cannot be thought apart from any concept of the subject; without any remembrance of it, 'subject' would lose all meaning. Conversely, as soon as we reflect upon the human individual as an individual at all, in the form of a general concept—as soon as we cease to mean only the present existence of some particular person—we have already turned it into a universal similar to that which came to be explicit in the idealist concept of the subject." Adorno, "Subject and Object," in *The Essential Frankfurt School Reader*, ed. Andrew Arato and Eike Gebhardt (New York: Continuum, 1982), 497–498.

4. "The individual *is interpellated as a (free) subject in order that he shall submit freely to the commandments of the Subject, i.e. in order that he shall (freely) accept his subjection*, i.e. in order that he shall make the gestures and actions of his subjection 'all by himself.' *There are no subjects except by and for their subjection*. This is why they 'work all by themselves.'" Louis Althusser, "Ideology and Ideological State Apparatuses," in *Lenin and Philosophy and Other Essays* (London: New Left Books, 1971), 182; emphasis in original.

5. A note on terminology: *Alienation* derives from the division of labor, the splitting of life into separate activities in which the individual worker's experience of a unified and self-contained process is destroyed. *Commodification* is the organized process whereby the work of art, like all objects, is alienated from its primary and traditional status as an object of use value and of aesthetic experience, and becomes an object of exchange value, one whose character is determined first and foremost by its relation to the market. *Reification (Verdinglichung)* names the penetration of commodificaton into the very core of personal experience, a condition in which the relations between persons is reduced to that of an illusory, impersonal relationship between things (i.e., "thingified," *verdinglicht*). Unlike the concept of alienation—a process that pertains to activity, and in particular to the dissociation of workers from their labor, their products, their fellow workers, and ultimately from their entire experience—reification is a process that affects our cognitive relationship with the social totality. Reification thus becomes a conceptual category by which we can explain certain transformations of the art object.

6. Althusser, "Ideology and Ideological State Apparatuses," 174.

7. For an excellent and detailed discussion, see, above all, Peter Dews, *Logics of Disintegration: Post-Structuralist Thought and the Claims of Critical Theory* (London and New York: Verso, 1987).

8. In particular, see Fredric Jameson, *The Political Unconscious* (Ithaca: Cornell University Press, 1981).

9. The concept of affiliation is from Edward Said. Said sees the relationship of affiliation as replacing the continuity, community, and legitimacy provided by biological relations or filiations. "Thus if a filial relationship was held together by natural bonds and natural forms of authority—involving obedience, fear, love, respect, and instinctual conflict—the new affiliative relationship changes these bonds into what seem to be transpersonal forms—such as guild consciouness, consensus, collegiality, professional respect, class, and the hegemony of a dominant culture. The filiative scheme belongs to the realms of nature and 'life,' whereas affiliation belongs exclusively to culture and society." *The World, the Text, and the Critic* (Cambridge: Harvard University Press, 1983), 19–20.

10. *In the Shadow of Mies: Ludwig Hilberseimer, Architect, Educator, and Urban Planner* (New York: The Art Institute of Chicago and Rizzoli, 1988); *Rassegna* 27 (September 1986).

11. Francesco Dal Co, "Hannes Meyer e la 'venerabile scuola di Dessau,'" introduction to Hannes Meyer, *Architettura o rivoluzione* (Padua: Marsilio, 1973); Claude Schnaidt, *Hannes Meyer: Buildings, Projects and Writings* (Teufen: Verlag Arthur Niggli, 1965).

12. Most notably, *Hannes Meyer 1889–1954: Architekt, Urbanist, Lehrer* (Berlin: Ernst & Sohn, 1989) and Martin Kieren, *Hannes Meyer. Dokumente zur Frühzeit Architektur- und Gestaltungsversuche 1919–1927* (Heiden: Verlag Arthur Niggli, 1990).

13. Above all, see Peter Bürger, *Theory of the Avant-Garde* (Minneapolis: University of Minnesota Press, 1984).

14. Manfredo Tafuri, *Theories and History of Architecture* (New York: Harper and Rowe, 1980), 141.

15. Sigfried Giedion, *Space, Time and Architecture* (Cambridge: Harvard University Press, 1974; original lectures 1938–1939), 18.

16. "The third space conception set in at the beginning of this century with the optical revolution that abolished the single viewpoint of perspective. This had fundamental consequences for man's conception of architecture and the urban scene. The space-emanating qualities of free-standing buildings could again be appreciated. . . . Just as at its beginning, architecture is again approaching sculpture and sculpture is approaching architecture. At the same time the supreme preoccupation of the second space conception—the hollowing out of interior space—is continued, although there is a profoundly different approach to the vaulting problem. New elements have been introduced: a hitherto unknown interpenetration of inner and outer space and an interpenetration of different levels (largely an effect of the automobile), which has forced the incorporation of movement as an inseparable element of architecture. All these have contributed to the space conception of the present day and underlie its evolving tradition." Giedion, *Space, Time and Architecture,* lv–lvi.

17. Giedion, *Space, Time and Architecture,* 434–436.

18. "[This model] presupposes in principle that the whole in question be reducible to an *inner essence,* of which the elements of the whole are then no more than the phenomenal forms of expression, the inner principle of the essence being present at each point in the whole, such that at each moment it is possible to write the immediately adequate equation: *such and such an element. . . = the inner essence of the whole.* Here was a model which made it possible to think the effectivity of the whole on each of its elements, but if this category—inner essence/outer phenomenon—was to be applicable everywhere and at every moment to each of the phenomena arising in the totality in question, *it presupposed that the whole had a certain nature, precisely the nature of a 'spiritual' whole in which each element was expressive of the entire totality as a* 'pars totalis.'" Louis Althusser, *Reading Capital* (London: Verso, 1979; original French 1968),186–187; emphasis in original.

19 Giedion, *Space, Time and Architecture*, 13–14.

20. I borrow this general formulation from Jameson, *The Political Unconscious*, 220ff.

21. Cf. Jameson, *The Political Unconscious*, 63ff.

22. Giedion, *Space, Time and Architecture*, 437–438.

23. The quotation left in Italian by Giedion is from the first manifesto of futurism.

24. Giedion, *Space, Time and Architecture*, 5–6.

25. Jameson, *The Political Unconscious*, 39–40.

Hannes Meyer and the Radicalization of Perception

Epigraph: Walter Benjamin, "Paris, Capital of the Nineteenth Century," in Reflections *(New York: Harcourt Brace Jovanovich, 1978), 148. I have modified the translation slightly to restructure certain phrases and have rendered* Wunschbilder *as "wish-images,"* aufzuheben *as "sublate." The original 1935 essay, "Paris: Die Haupstadt des XIX Jahrhunderts," is in Benjamin,* Gesammelte Schriften, *vol. 1, ed. Rolf Tiedemann and Hermann Schweppenhäuser (Frankfurt am Main: Suhrkamp Verlag, 1972); the passage cited is on p. 408.*

Co-op Vitrine and the Representation of Mass Reproduction

1. Oskar Schlemmer would call the word Meyer's favorite, in a letter to Tut Schlemmer, 1 December 1927, in *The Letters and Diaries of Oskar Schlemmer*, ed. Tut Schlemmer (Middletown: Wesleyan University Press, 1972), 216.

2. Such a condition is not unique to Meyer, of course, and can be detected perhaps most emphatically in the work of the Russian avant-garde. But in the West Meyer's work stands as perhaps the key example of the dialectic of modernism and mass culture.

3. See especially Francesco Dal Co, "Hannes Meyer e la 'venerabile scuola di Dessau,'" introduction to Hannes Meyer, *Architettura o rivoluzione* (Padua: Marsilio, 1973); and Jacques Gubler, *Nationalisme et internationalisme dans l'architecture moderne de la Suisse* (Lausanne: L'Age d'Homme, 1975). Some critics also perceive a definite shift in Meyer's design strategy around the time of his appointment as director of the architecture department at the Bauhaus. For example, Manfredo Tafuri writes, "In the works of Meyer designed between 1926 and 1930 . . . the categorical imperative of 'construction as thoroughly thought out organization of the vital processes' was expressed in a contradictory manner. On the one hand, in the Petersschule and the Geneva building, we have Constructivist mechanistic metaphors not unmindful of what was being done by the Soviets at that time; on the other, in the Bernau school and even more in the five blocks Meyer added to the Törten-Dessau Siedlung begun by Gropius, form was reduced to a tendentially scientific process approaching pure technique and function." In Manfredo Tafuri and Francesco Dal Co, *Modern Architecture* (New York: Abrams, 1979), 173.

4. "I shall call signifying practice the establishment and the countervailing of a sign system. Establishing a sign system calls for the identity of a speaking subject within a social framework, which he recognizes as a basis for that identity. Countervailing the sign system is done by having the subject undergo an unsettling, questionable [sic] process; this indirectly challenges the social framework with which he had previously identified, and it thus coincides with times of abrupt changes, renewal, or revolution in society." Julia Kristeva, *La Traversée des signes*, trans. in Kristeva, *Desire in Language*, ed. Leon S. Roudiez (New York: Columbia University Press, 1980), 18.

5. My use of the term *performative* is adapted from J. L. Austin, *How to Do Things with Words* (New York: Oxford University Press, 1962), which is concerned with speech acts and communication. I will substantially modify this term.

6. Kristeva, *Desire in Language*, 32, 33.

7. Hannes Meyer, "Die neue Welt," *Das Werk* 13, no. 7 (Bern, 1926): 205–224; trans. in Claude Schnaidt, *Hannes Meyer: Buildings, Projects and Writings* (Teufen: Verlag Arthur Niggli, 1965), 223. Page references are to the original; some translations are modified.

8. Meyer, "bauhaus und gesellschaft," in *bauhaus* 1, 1929; trans. in Schnaidt, *Hannes Meyer.* Original is in lower-case letters; my emphasis.

9. Meyer, "Education of the Architect," a lecture to the San Carlos Academy, Mexico, 30 September 1938; partial transcript in Schnaidt, *Hannes Meyer,* 53.

10. Althusser, in his "A Letter on Art in Reply to André Daspre," *Lenin and Philosophy and Other Essays,* trans. Ben Brewster (New York: Monthly Review Press, 1971), states that he does *"not rank real art among the ideologies"* (emphasis in original). His attempt here is to discriminate, following a traditional form/matter relation, between two different modes of apprehending the world: aesthetic practice and ideology. For Althusser, art gives form to the materials of ideology. But neither is ideology wholly external to art. Works of art may become the raw materials for ideological practice. Then, their aesthetic modality is subordinated to their ideological function, but the irreducibly artistic structure will enable its utilization as an ideological instrument.

11. There were, in fact, two different Vitrines, or arrangements of the Vitrine, the second, of Basel 1925, being the one under consideration here.

12. Georg Simmel, *Philosophie des Geldes* (Leipzig: Duncken und Humbolt, 1900); references are to the English translation *The Philosophy of Money,* trans. Tom Bottomore and David Frisby (London: Routledge & Kegan Paul, 1978), 454–456; some emphasis added.

13. Althusser, *Lenin and Philosophy and Other Essays,* 162.

14. The term "representation" has been charged in many and often contradictory ways in much recent poststructuralist and postmarxist theory, but has usually been taken to name the mirage of organic realist unification, with all of the bad ideological consequences that follow. Here I understand representation to be synonymous with "figuration" or "imaginary construction of a world" and will assume, therefore, that what follows in any form of aesthetic production is some sort of representation. In Meyer's case, representation is a kind of conductivity among multiple images and texts.

15. "In order to describe the dialogism inherent in the denotative or historical world, we would have to turn to the psychic aspect of writing as trace of dialogue with oneself (with another), as a writer's distance from himself, as a splitting of the writer into subject of enunciation and subject of utterance. By the very act of narrating, the subject of narration addresses an other; narration is structured in relation to this other. . . . Consequently, a dialogue between the *subject* of narration (S) and the *addressee* (A)—the other. This addressee, quite simply the reading subject, represents a doubly oriented entity: signifier in his relation to the text and signified in the relation between the subject of narration and himself. This entity is thus a dyad (A1 and A2) whose two terms, communicating with each other, constitute a code system. The subject of narration (S) is drawn in, and therefore reduced to a code, to a nonperson, to an *anonymity* (as writer, subject of enunciation) mediated by a third person, the *he/she* character, the subject of utterance. . . . The subject of utterance, in relation to the subject of enunciation, plays the role of addressee with respect to the subject; it inserts the subject of enunciation within the writing system by making the latter pass through emptiness. . . . The *subject of utterance* is both representative of the subject of enunciation and represented as object of the subject of enunciation. . . . The subject of utterance is 'dialogical,' both S and A are disguised within it." Kristeva, *Desire in Language*, 74–76. One should note that the issue of performatvity is already embedded in this dialogical relationship.

16. "What then is the reality to which *I* or *you* refers? It is solely a 'reality of discourse,' and this is a very strange thing. . . . There is thus a combined double instance in this process: the instance of *I* as referent and the instance of discourse containing *I* as the referee. The definition can now be stated precisely as: *I* is 'the individual who utters the present instance of discourse containing the linguistic instance *I.*'" Emile Benveniste, *Problems in General Linguistics*, trans. Mary Elizabeth Meek (Coral Gables: University of Miami Press, 1971), 218.

17. "A subject of enunciation takes shape within the gap opened up between signfier and signified that admits both structure and interplay within." Kristeva, *Desire in Language*, 127–128.

18. Roland Barthes, *S/Z*, trans. Richard Miller (New York: Farrar, Straus and Giroux, 1974; original French 1970), 21.

19. Benjamin Buchloh has analyzed this shift toward iconicity in the work of Soviet photomontage and factography in "From Faktura to Factography," *October* 30 (Fall 1984): 82–119.

20. Raoul Hausmann, "PREsentismus gegen den Puffkeismus der Teutschen Seele," in *De Stijl* 4, no. 9 (September 1921), reprinted in Hausmann, *Am Anfang war Dada*, ed. Karl Riha and Günter Kämpf (Giessen: Anabas-Verlag, 1980), 31.

21. A. V. Babichev, cited in Hubertus Gassner, "Analytical Sequences, " in *Alexander Rodchenko*, ed. David Elliot (Oxford: Museum of Modern Art, 1979), 110.

22. Johannes Molzahn, "Economics of the Advertising Mechanism," *Die Form* 1 (new series) (Berlin, 1925–1926), 141–144; translation in *Form and Function: A Source Book for the History of Architecture and Design 1890–1939*, ed. Tim and Charlotte Benton (London: The Open University Press, 1975), 224–226.

23. Hannes Meyer, "Die neue Welt," 222.

24. Simmel, *The Philosophy of Money*, 454.

25. Meyer, "Die neue Welt," 221.

26. Hannes Meyer, "Das Theater Co-op," *Das Werk* 11, no. 12 (Bern, 1924): 329–332.

27. And behind Freidorf lay his work on housing projects in Essen in Krupp's welfare office, his study of town planning in Berlin, and of the English cooperative, syndicalist, and garden city movements. For a brief biography of Meyer, see Schnaidt, *Hannes Meyer.* The best commentary on the Siedlung Freidorf is Jacques Gubler, *Nationalisme et internationalisme dans l'architecture moderne de la Suisse* (Lausanne: L'Age d'Homme, 1975). The original documentation and commentaries on the project are in Johann Friedrich Schär, Henri Faucherre, and Hannes Meyer, *Die Siedlung Freidorf* (Basel: Buchhandlung VSK, 1921); a second, enlarged edition, which appeared in 1943 as *25 Jahre Siedlungsgenossenschaft Freidorf;* and also Hannes Meyer, "Die Siedlung Freidorf," in *Das Werk* 12, no. 2 (1925): 40–51.

28. Henri Faucherre, "Vom inneren Aufbau der Siedlungsgenossenschaft Freidorf," in *25 Jahre Siedlungsgenossenschaft Freidorf.* Pestalozzi's pedagogy involved a rejection of catechesis and teaching based on religious aims and memorization, in favor of studies based on observation, discovery, and experimentation designed to enhance and guide the development of the natural instincts and capacities of the growing child.

29. Gubler, *Nationalisme et internationalisme dans l'architecture moderne de la Suisse*, 87. Gubler points out that part of the reason for the promotional efforts of the founders was, indeed, to make the idea of Freidorf palatable to the larger public, and, thereby, to make the Siedlung possible.

30. Georg Lukács, *History and Class Consciousness,* trans. Rodney Livingstone (Cambridge: MIT Press, 1971; original German 1923).

31. Lukács, *History and Class Consciousness,* 193.

32. Fredric Jameson, *The Political Unconscious* (Ithaca: Cornell University Press, 1981), 188.

Contra the Bourgeois Interior: Co-op Zimmer

1. Georg Simmel, "Die Mode," in Simmel, *Philosophische Kultur* (Leipzig: W. Klinkhardt, 1911), 31–64; translated as "Fashion," in *American Journal of Sociology* 62 (May 1957) and reprinted in *Georg Simmel on Individuality and Social Forms,* ed. Donald N. Levine (Chicago: University of Chicago Press, 1971), 294–323; page references are to original. "Das Problem des Stiles," *Dekorative Kunst* 11, no. 7 (1908): 307–316. *Philosophie des Geldes* (Leipzig: Duncker und Humbolt, 1900); translated as *The Philosophy of Money,* trans. Tom Bottomore and David Frisby (London: Routledge & Kegan Paul, 1978); page references are to the English translation.

2. Simmel, "Die Mode," 57.

3. Simmel, "Die Mode," 39.

4. Simmel, *The Philosophy of Money,* 484.

5. Simmel, *The Philosophy of Money,* 460.

6. Adolf Loos, "Die Überflüssigen" (1908), in Loos, *Sämtliche Schriften* (Vienna and Munich, 1962).

7. Theodor Adorno, "Functionalism Today" (1965), *Oppositions* 17 (Summer 1979): 35.

8. Adolf Loos, "Architektur" (1910), in *Sämtliche Schriften.*

9. Karl Kraus, in *Adolf Loos. Festschrift zum 60. Geburtstag* (Vienna, 1930), 27.

10. Adolf Loos, "Das Prinzip der Bekleidung" (1898), in *Sämtliche Schriften.*

11. For a discussion see Beatriz Colomina, "Intimacy and Spectacle: The Architectural Production of the Modern Subject," manuscript, S.O.M. Foundation, Chicago, 1988.

12. A characteristically laconic comment by Loos reads, "Adolf Loos, my wife's bedroom, white walls, white curtains, white Angora sheepskin." Cited in Benedetto Gravagnuolo, *Adolf Loos* (New York: Rizzoli, 1982), 102.

13. Adorno, "Functionalism Today," 35.

14. See Stanford Anderson, "Critical Conventionalism in Architecture," a lecture of 1982 published in *Assemblage* 1 (October 1986), esp. pp. 13–16.

15. Walter Benjamin, "Karl Kraus," in Benjamin, *Reflections* (London: Harcourt Brace Jovanovich, 1978; original German 1955), 247; emphasis added.

16. Simmel, *The Philosophy of Money*, 474.

17. Adolf Loos, "Kultur" (1908), in *Sämtliche Schriften*.

18. In the article "Die neue Welt," Meyer lists phonographic recordings "appropriate for the times." The excerpts of Meyer that follow are from that article unless otherwise noted (published in *Das Werk* 13, no. 7 [1926], 205–224; trans. in Claude Schnaidt, *Hannes Meyer: Buildings, Projects and Writings* [Teufen: Verlag Arthur Niggli, 1965]; some translations are modified).

19. Simmel, *The Philosophy of Money*, 484.

20. Gilles Deleuze and Félix Guattari, *A Thousand Plateaus*, trans. Brian Massumi (Minneapolis: University of Minnesota Press, 1987; original French 1980).

21. The locution "winning of a world" is from Stanford Anderson. See especially his "The Fiction of Function," *Assemblage* 2 (February 1987).

22. Boris Arvatov, *Iskusstvo i klassy* (Moscow, 1923), 83; cited in Christina Lodder, *Russian Constructivism* (New Haven: Yale University Press, 1983), 74.

23. Fredric Jameson, "Of Islands and Trenches: Neutralization and the Production of Utopian Discourse" (1977), in Jameson, *The Ideologies of Theory: Essays 1971–1986*, vol. 2 (Minneapolis: University of Minnesota Press, 1988), 81.

24. Jameson, "Of Islands and Trenches."

25. See A. J. Greimas and François Rastier, "The Interaction of Semiotic Constraints," *Yale French Studies* 41 (1968): 86–105.

26. Jameson, "Of Islands and Trenches," 91.

Co-op Building between Avant-garde and Instrumentalization: The Petersschule.

1. Ernst Bloch, "Die Bebauung des Hohlraums," in Bloch, *Das Prinzip Hoffnung* (Frankfurt am Main: Suhrkamp, 1959), published as "Building in Empty Spaces" in Bloch, *The Utopian Function of Art and Literature*, trans. Jack Zipes and Frank Mecklenburg (Cambridge: MIT Press, 1988); passages cited are on pp. 187, 196, 190; emphasis in original. It is interesting to note that Meyer, too, referred to Ledoux as a kind of predecessor. Ledoux "decided to throw away his aristocratic notions and to take an active part in the bourgeois revolutionary movement. . . . On the square base of these modest houses he placed a pyramidal stone roof. In all architectural periods the pyramid had symbolized the dominant power of king or priest. This architect deliberately handed over the pyramid to the new dominant class and placed it at the service of the liberated and revolutionary bourgeoisie. . . . Shall we, the architects of the democratic countries, be found ready to hand over the pyramids to the society of the future?" Hannes Meyer, "The Soviet Architect," in *Task* no. 3 (Cambridge: Harvard University, Graduate School of Design, 1942): 32.

2. There are actually two versions of the project that will be of concern here, the original competition entry of 1926 (entry number 72, motto: "compromise") and the revised presentation of the project in *Bauhaus* 2 (Dessau, 1927): 5. Both were designed with Hans Wittwer.

3. Hannes Meyer, "Wie ich arbeite," *Architektura CCCP* 6 (Moscow, 1933); manuscript in German; partial translation in Claude Schnaidt, *Hannes Meyer: Buildings, Projects and Writings* (Teufen: Verlag Arthur Niggli, 1965), 19–21; my emphasis.

4. Letter from Meyer to Graf Dürckheim, 24 August 1930, in *Hannes Meyer. Bauen und Gesellschaft. Schriften, Briefe, Projekte* (Dresden: VEB Verlag der Kunst, 1980).

5. See the chapter "Reproduction and Negation" on the League of Nations project.

6. Adolf Behne, paraphrasing Meyer in a review of Meyer's ADGB school, *Pädagogische Beilage zur Sächsischen Schulzeitung* 20, no. 5 (June 1928): 41.

7. Hannes Meyer, "Freidorf Housing Estate, near Basle, 1919–21," trans. in Schnaidt, *Hannes Meyer*, 7, 13.

8. Theodor Adorno, *Aesthetic Theory,* trans. C. Lenhardt (London and New York: Routledge & Kegan Paul, 1984), 160–161.

9. Hannes Meyer, "Die Siedlung Freidorf," *Das Werk* 12, no. 2 (1925): 40–51. But see Jacques Gubler's discussion in *Nationalisme et internationalisme dans l'architecture moderne de la Suisse* (Lausanne: L'Age d'Homme, 1975), where he argues that significant lessons of the Freidorf experience can be traced throughout Meyer's later work. Gubler's argument is consistent, I think, with the trajectory I am constructing here.

10. Adorno, *Aesthetic Theory,* 21.

11. Hannes Meyer, "Curriculum vitae," in *Hannes Meyer. Bauen und Gesellschaft,* 10–14.

12. Boris Arvatov, cited in Christina Lodder, *Russian Constructivism* (New Haven: Yale University Press, 1983), 106. Meyer would have known of such pronouncements through publications and contacts with El Lissitzky.

13. Lenin's New Economic Policy of 1921 reestablished a limited market economy and fostered the reemergence of a wealthy bourgeois patronage for art.

14. El Lissitzky, "Nasci" (1924), in *El Lissitzky: Life, Letters, Texts,* ed. Sophie Lissitzky-Küppers (London: Thames and Hudson, 1983), 330.

15. Boris Arvatov, *Natan Al'tman* (Berlin, 1924), 34; cited in Lodder, *Russian Constructivism,* 105.

16. Lissitzky, "Our Book," in *El Lissitzky: Life, Letters, Texts,* 357.

17. When Anatolii Lunacharsky undertook to review the Erste Russische Kunstausstellung, he confirmed this, citing with approval there a passage by the German critic Fritz Stahl: "There is no doubt that a particular harmony exists between the revolutionary art of these painters and the revolutionary character of the Soviet power itself. This power, in fact, wants to create new and extraordinary forms by destroying everything old, but in painting this revolutionary spirit is expressed in completely abstract forms, which go to extremes and end up as simply absurd, *forms that the people are not likely to accept.*" Fritz Stahl, "Russische Kunstausstellung Galerie van Diemen," *Berliner Tageblatt,* 18 October 1922; cited in Anatolii Lunacharsky, "L'esposizione russa a Berlino," *Rassegna sovietica,* no. 1 (1965): 110–116; original edition in *Izvestia,* no. 273 (1922). For further discussion, see my essay "Photomontage and Its Audiences, Berlin, circa 1922," in *Harvard Architecture Review* 6 (1987), and Benjamin H. D. Buchloh, "From Faktura to Factography," *October* 30 (Fall 1984).

18. Buchloh, "From Faktura to Factography," 103.

19. Meyer wrote to the painter Willi Baumeister in October 1926 that he and the journal *Werk* had received letters against his article "Die Siedlung Freidorf." "'The New World' in Switzerland has 'denounced' me, and the obstacles to the coming realization are for us greater than ever." The letter is published in *Hannes Meyer 1889–1954: Architekt, Urbanist, Lehrer* (Berlin: Ernst & Sohn, 1989), 75.

20. Ernst Kallai, "Lissitzky," in *El Lissitzky: Life, Letters, Texts;* my emphasis.

21. Meyer wrote, "El Lissitzky's 'Story of 2 Squares' is still an illusion of a spatial excerpt conjured up by the draughtsman's art." Hannes Meyer, "Die neue Welt," in Schnaidt, *Hannes Meyer*, 93.

22. El Lissitzky, "The Blockade of Russia Moves toward Its End," in *Veshch*, 1922; reprinted in *El Lissitzky: Life, Letters, Texts*, 340–341.

23. Meyer, "Curriculum vitae," 13.

24. Other works published were by W. Baumeister, N. Gabo, K. Malewitsch, G. Vantongerloo, P. Mondrian, L. Moholy-Nagy, V. Servrankx, W. Dexel, L. Kassak, O. Nerlinger, and El Lissitzky (the Prounenraum, 1922, and Proun, 1925).

25. Jacques Gubler, ed., *ABC. Architettura e avanguardia, 1924–1928* (Milan: Electa, 1983), 128.

26. Lest this assertion seem overly facile, the reader may recall Mikhail Tarabukin's remark that the artist's task is that of "linking the very process of work with that of creativity," of creating "real objects" that have no prototype in the real world but are "constructed from start to finish outside lines which could be extended from it to reality." For a discussion, see Lodder, *Russian Constructivism*, 101ff.

27. The caption in *ABC* reads "Gestaltung der technischen Möglichkeiten moderner Materialien und Konstruktionen. Studium der Funktionen von Treppen, Plattformen und Aufzügen." The project was from Ladovsky's course of 1922 for the design of a building of a functionally specific task and the demonstration of mass and balance.

28. Francesco Passanti, in a lecture to the Graduate School of Design, Harvard University, 4 April 1990, has pointed out that the terms under which the Maison Citrohan was introduced by Le Corbusier—*les standards, type*, and *machine à*—were already understood to convey a sense of collectivity. This was continuous with the concerns of some members of the Werkbund (such as Hermann Muthesius) for the expression of a collective experience of existing, German society. But it could also have been understood by Meyer as an international collective.

29. Le Corbusier, "The New Spirit in Architecture" (1924), in *L'Almanach d'architecture moderne* (Paris: Editions Crés, 1925): 21–23; translated in *Form and Function: A Source Book for the History of Architecture and Design 1890–1939*, ed. Tim and Charlotte Benton (London: The Open University Press, 1975), 134–136.

30. Hannes Meyer, "bauen" (1928), trans. in Schnaidt, *Hannes Meyer*, 97; ellipsis in original.

31. *ABC* 4, vol. 2 (1927–1928); translation in Ulrich Conrads, *Programs and Manifestoes on 20th-Century Architecture* (Cambridge: MIT Press, 1970), 115–116.

32. In fact, the illustration for the lighthouse beacon did not arrive in time for publication. On page 108 of *L'Art décoratif*, Le Courbusier noted: "Entire page reserved for illustration of a lighthouse beacon by ANCIENS ETABLISSEMENTS SAUTER-HARLÉ, 16 Avenue de Suffren, PARIS." The illustration is reproduced in *Assemblage* 4 (1987): 5.

33. Le Corbusier, *L'Art décoratif d'aujourd'hui* (Paris: Editions Crés, 1925); translated as *The Decorative Art of Today*, trans. James Dunnett (Cambridge: MIT Press, 1987), 109–110.

34. Le Corbusier, *The Decorative Art of Today*, 57.

35. Hannes Meyer, "Die neue Welt," *Das Werk* 13, no. 7 (1926), 224; trans. in Schnaidt, *Hannes Meyer*.

36. Hannes Meyer, "Biografische Angaben," in *Hannes Meyer 1889–1954: Architekt, Urbanist, Lehrer*, 357.

37. Meyer, "Wie ich arbeite" (see citation in note 3).

38. Hannes Meyer, "Über marxistische Architektur," manuscript of 1931; reprinted in *Hannes Meyer. Bauen und*

Gesellschaft; partial English translation in Schnaidt, *Hannes Meyer.*

39. Hannes Meyer and Hans Wittwer, "Erläuterung zum Schulhaus von heute," typescript, Basel 1926 (GTA Archives 28–1926–1–1), published as facsimile in *Hannes Meyer 1889–1954: Architekt, Urbanist, Lehrer,* 81.

40. Meyer and Wittwer, "Erläuterung zum Schulhaus von heute."

41. Terry Eagleton, "Ideology, Fiction, Narrative," *Social Text* 2 (1980): 75.

42. Meyer, "Die neue Welt," 222.

43. Meyer, "bauen," 95. Original is in lower case.

44. Hannes Meyer, "Projekt für die Petersschule, Basle, 1926," in Schnaidt, *Hannes Meyer,* 17.

45. Gilles Deleuze and Félix Guattari, *A Thousand Plateaus,* trans. Brian Massumi (Minneapolis: University of Minnesota Press, 1987; original French 1980), 141. Sanford Kwinter pointed me to this concept, though he should not be held responsible for my use of it here, where Deleuze's abstract machine is perhaps wrongly conflated with the almost Brechtian, propagandistic potential for negation and resistance I believe is at work in Meyer's project. But see the next chapter on the ADGB building for a modification of that practice of resistance.

46. Gilles Deleuze, *Foucault,* trans. Seán Hand (Minneapolis: University of Minnesota Press, 1988; original French 1986), 37.

47. Deleuze and Guattari, *A Thousand Plateaus,* 142.

48. Geoffrey Scott, *The Architecture of Humanism* (1914; London: Constable and Company, 1924), 213, 218; emphasis in original. See also Heinrich Wölfflin, *Renaissance and Baroque,* trans. K. Simon (Ithaca: Cornell University Press, 1966); and Georg Simmel, "The Aesthetic Significance of the Face" (1901), trans. Lore Ferguson, in *Georg Simmel, 1858–1918,* ed. Kurt H. Wolff (Columbus: Ohio State University Press, 1959), 276–281. For a preliminary sketch of the notion of physiognomy in architecture, see Anthony Vidler, *The Writing of the Walls: Architectural Theory in the Late Enlightenment* (Princeton: Princeton Architectural Press, 1987), 118ff.

49. I have not been entirely careful here in my criticism of these architects. For a more balanced and nuanced analysis of the problematic of Italian modern architecture, the state, and the regime, see Giorgio Ciucci, "Pagano und Terragni: Faschistische Architektur als Ideal und als Staatsstil," in Hartmut Frank, ed., *Faschistische Architekturen: Planen und Bauen in Europa 1930 bis 1945* (Hamburg: Hans Christian Verlag, 1985), 123–138; and "Italian Architecture during the Fascist Period: The Many Souls of the Classical," *Harvard Architecture Review* 6 (1987): 76–87.

50. See Jacques Lacan, "The Mirror Stage as Formative of the Function of the I," in *Ecrits: A Selection*, trans. Alan Sheridan (London and New York: W. W. Norton, 1977).

51. I borrow this formulation from Fredric Jameson, "Pleasure: A Political Issue," in Jameson, *The Ideologies of Theory: Essays 1971–1986*, vol. 2 (Minneapolis: University of Minnesota Press, 1988), 71–72.

52. O. Birkner, J. Herzong, and P. DeMeuron, "Die Peterschule in Basel (1926–1929)," *Werk/Archithese* 13–14 (January-February 1978).

53. Paul Klee, *Tagebücher*, ed. Felix Klee (Cologne, 1957), 323ff. The diary entry is from 1915. For a discussion, see O. K. Werkmeister, "Walter Benjamin, Paul Klee, and the Angel of History," *Oppositions* 25 (Fall 1982): 102–125.

The Bauhaus and the Radicalization of Building.

1. Hannes Meyer, "bauhaus and society" (1929), in Claude Schnaidt, *Hannes Meyer: Buildings, Projects and Writings* (Teufen: Verlag Arthur Niggli, 1965). Original is written in lower case; my emphasis.

2. Walter Gropius, who has set the tone for most subsequent criticisms of Meyer's work at the Bauhaus, condemns Meyer in a letter to Tomás Maldonado: "I cannot allot to [Meyer] the importance with which you credit him during the years of the Bauhaus. His strategy and tactics were too petty; he was a radical petit bourgeois. His philosophy culminates in the assertion that 'life is oxygen plus sugar plus starch plus protein,' to which Mies promptly retorted: 'Try stirring all that together; it stinks.'" Publisher's epilogue, Schnaidt, *Hannes Meyer,*123.

3. Almost every commentator on the Bauhaus follows this pattern, if they do not ignore Meyer altogether. A recent "reassessment" is one of the most balanced criticisms: "Since Meyer aroused so much controversy, on ideological as well as personal and political grounds during his two years as director of the school, it is not easy to evaluate his achievements there. There is no doubt that his policies were successful on a practical level, and that under his direction the workshops produced designs in keeping with the requirements of German industry and the domestic market: the Bauhaus did, in fact, become a competent 'trade school,' with, at last, an active architecture department. His design theory at that time, however, was so totally materialistic and reductionist that it is difficult to take it seriously; nevertheless he identified and challenged some of the uneasy assumptions about radicalism in design on which teaching at the school was based. He was politically aware, although not politically astute, and he was prepared to sacrifice the school for his convictions." Gillian Naylor, *The Bauhaus Reassessed* (New York: E. P. Dutton, 1985), 174.

4. Michael Müller's *Architektur und Avantgarde* (Frankfut am Main: Syndikat, 1984), for one, follows Bürger in supporting a definitional distinction between a modernism based primarily on issues of aesthetic autonomy and those "avant-garde" practices, in Bürger's sense. See also the collection of essays inspired in part by the English translation of Bürger's text (Peter Bürger, *Theory of the Avant-Garde* [Minneapolis: University of Minnesota Press, 1984]) in *Architectureproduction*, ed. Beatriz Colomina and Joan Ockman (New York: Princeton Architectural Press, 1989).

5. "Sublation," as I have been using the concept here, is the English approximation of Hegel's notoriously untranslatable term *Aufhebung*, which means simultaneously "negation" and "preservation" in a different, usually "redeemed," form.

6. "All of use are fully aware," Gropius wrote in 1922, "that the old attitude of *l'art pour l'art* is obsolete." In Hans M. Wingler, *The Bauhaus* (Cambridge: MIT Press, 1969), 51.

7. Arbeitsrat für Kunst circular, translated in Ulrich Conrads, *Programs and Manifestoes on 20th-Century Architecture* (Cambridge: MIT Press, 1970), 44.

8. In his 1923 review of Gropius's *Idee und Aufbau*, Le Corbusier had already criticized the waste of energy on decorative design when new industrial standards could only emerge from the masses ("le standard surgit de la masse profonde"). Le Corbusier, "Pédagogie," *L'Esprit Nouveau*, December 1923. By 1926 in the *Bauhaus Journal* itself Georg Muche, a painter and architect who taught at the school, published a critique of the implications of Gropius's slogan: "The illusion that fine art must be absorbed in the creative types of industrial design is destroyed as soon as it comes face to face with concrete reality. Abstract painting, which has been led with convincingly unambiguous intentions from its artistic Utopia into the promising field of industrial design, seems quite suddenly to lose its predicted significance as a form-determining element, since the formal design of industrial products that are manufactured by mechanical means follows laws that cannot be derived from the fine arts." Georg Muche, "Fine Art and Industrial Form," in H. M. Wingler, *The Bauhaus* (Cambridge: MIT Press, 1969), 416.

9. Francesco Dal Co, "Hannes Meyer e la 'venerabile scuola di Dessau,'" introduction to Hannes Meyer, *Architettura o rivoluzione* (Padua: Marsilio, 1973).

10. Dal Co notes that, when Tristan Tzara affirms that the informing principle of his dadaist project "is not art but disgust," and that "every pictorial or plastic art is useless," Tzara articulates a disenchantment of the present world that leads to the discovery of the structural inadequacy of this world's art. Then there comes the search for that "irrational order" Jean Arp speaks about, whose "irrationality" is determined solely by the relationship with the contingent, an order that, inasmuch as it is irrational with respect to the given historical conditions, is intended as a possible alternative to what Arp called "this sad tale of humanity." This search for an existence that is elsewhere, that is other, for a condition reachable "through a way entirely other than a reasonable way," was also, Dal Co further contends, the aim of the first surrealist manifesto of Breton. See also Manfredo Tafuri, *The Sphere and the Labyrinth* (Cambridge: MIT Press, 1987; original Italian 1980).

11. Dal Co, "Hannes Meyer e la 'venerabile scuola di Dessau,'" 43.

12. Manfredo Tafuri and Francesco Dal Co, *Modern Architecture* (New York: Harry N. Abrams, 1980), 132. The contact with neoplasticist and constructivist experiences becomes fully evident, for example, in the project of 1926 by Georg Muche and Richard Paulick for a steel house, the analytic experiments of Moholy-Nagy, the graphics of Herbert Bayer, and the furniture of Marcel Breuer.

13. See Lucia Moholy-Nagy, *Marginal Notes* (Krefeld: Scherpe Verlag, 1972), 79.

14. The author of the text is either El Lissitzky or Malevich. It was originally published in Hans Arp and El Lissitzky, *Kunstismen* (Munich: Eugen Rentsch Verlag, 1925), ix–x. For a discussion, see Yve-Alain Bois, "Malevich, le carré, le degré zéro," *Macula* 1 (1978): 28–49.

15. Along similar lines, Dal Co argues that the facts of the transfer of the Bauhaus from Weimar to Dessau also indicate Gropius's conservative vision of the role of art in society. After the announcement of the proposed transfer from Weimar, several German cities offered to host the Bauhaus, including Frankfurt, Hagen, Mannheim, and Darmstadt. In support of his choice of Dessau, Gropius cited some motivations that illuminate his vision of the architect's role, viz., that he preferred a direct relationship with the "dynamic" Burgermeister Hesse (who would later oust Meyer from the Bauhaus), whose "courage" and "spirit of initiative" Gropius praised, inasmuch as this would allow him to remain sufficiently *outside* the practical political problems that the settlement of the Bauhaus in other cities would have stirred up. Nor does this just indicate a wish to preserve the autonomy of the school. The refusal to transfer the Bauhaus to Frankfurt, for example, if it could be partly justified for reasons of economic convenience and the possible affiliation with big industry in Dessau, was also dictated, Dal Co argues, by a fundamental political choice: Gropius wanted to avoid a confrontation with that attempt at an overall management of the city with which the most advanced architects of German social democracy were experimenting and which in Frankfurt, with the work of Ernst May, had its most evident success. Gropius in effect demonstrated that he did not wish to take part in the possibility of an architectural intervention in the general problems of the city, and he refused to submit himself and the Bauhaus to those conditions that alone would have allowed for that greater merging of art and life that he continued to invoke rhetorically. He preferred instead to safeguard his own limited autonomy as an artist. The potential for effective intervention realized by May Gropius entrusted to the "courage" of the political forces, status quo. The history of Gropius's Bauhaus, I would assert polemically, is a history of such compromises.

16. Oskar Schlemmer, "To Otto Meyer," in *The Letters and Diaries of Oskar Schlemmer,* ed. Tut Schlemmer (Middletown, Conn.: Wesleyan University Press, 1972), 221.

17. Sibyl Moholy-Nagy, *Moholy-Nagy: Experiments in Totality* (Cambridge: MIT Press, 1969), 46, 47.

18. Oskar Schlemmer, who shared his house with Meyer when Meyer first arrived at the Bauhaus, had already perceived a tension between Meyer and Moholy as well as other main figures: "[Meyer] was not interested in Klee; he says Klee must be in a perpetual trance; Feininger does not appeal to him, either. Kandinsky [does] because of his theoretical underpinnings. In terms of character he feels closest to Moholy, although he is very critical towards much about him—his manner (officious), his false teachings (which students also see as such and reject); he was not interested in Muche's steel-construction new building, since steel is the least important element in it. Gropius can count himself fortunate to have this honest fellow as the latest feather in his cap." Oskar Schlemmer, "To Otto Meyer," 202. Tensions between them notwithstanding, Klee would support Meyer when he was threatened with dismissal, and Meyer would write to him, "You must not think that I am in any way embittered. On the contrary the events have revived powers that I have had to stifle in Dessau. I feel younger and more ready for battle than ever. . . . You know that we will always reach out our hands to each other over the barriers that divide us. I will always remain grateful to you." Hannes Meyer, letter to Paul Klee, Berlin, 23 August 1930, in Meyer, *Bauen und Gesellschaft. Schriften, Briefe, Projekte* (Dredsden: VEB Verlag der Kunst, 1980), 74–75.

19. Hannes Meyer, "Bauhaus Dessau: My Experience of a Polytechnical Education" (1940), in Schnaidt, *Hannes Meyer*, 111.

20. Hannes Meyer, "Wie ich arbeite," *Architektura CCCP* 6 (Moscow, 1933); manuscript in German; partial translation in Schnaidt, *Hannes Meyer*, 27.

21. Meyer, "My Dismissal from the Bauhaus," in Schnaidt, *Hannes Meyer*, 101.

22. Meyer, "Bauhaus Dessau: My Experience of a Polytechnical Education," 111.

23. Meyer, "My Dismissal from the Bauhaus," 103. Note that the self-help ideology can be traced back to Meyer's experience at Siedlung Freidorf.

24. Hannes Meyer, letter to Edwin Redslob, 11 August 1930, quoted in Magdalena Droste, "Unterrichtsstruktur und Werkstattarbeit am Bauhaus unter Hannes Meyer," in *Hannes Meyer 1889–1954: Architekt, Urbanist, Lehrer* (Berlin: Ernst & Sohn, 1989), 160.

25. Walter Benjamin, "The Work of Art in the Age of Mechanical Reproduction," in Benjamin, *Illuminations*, ed. Hannah Arendt (New York: Schocken, 1969), 233–234.

26. Benjamin, "The Work of Art in the Age of Mechanical Reproduction," 236–237, my emphasis.

27. Between 1928 and 1930, Meyer had continued the work already begun by Gropius on the Siedlung Törten at Dessau. Meyer brought the commission for the ADGB with him to Dessau after winning in 1927 the limited competition with invited entries from Max Berg, Alois Klement, Willy Ludwig, Erich Mendelsohn, and Max Taut as well as Meyer, judged by Adolf Behne, Otto Hessler, Heinrich Tessenow, and Theodor Leipart, chairman of the execuuive council of the Federation.

28. This and the quotations that follow are from Meyer, "Die Bundesschule des ADGB in Bernau bei Berlin," in Meyer, *Bauen und Gesellschaft*, 63ff., trans. in Schnaidt, *Hannes Meyer*, 40ff. I have modified Schnaidt's translation in places.

29. Arieh Sharon, a Bahaus student and construction supervisor for the ADGB, offers some anecdotes about Meyer's convictions: "Basically, we were even not allowed to draw elevations, which were supposed to be only a logical sequel of the windows' functional sizes and relationships. But nevertheless, I drew on the drawing edges some elevation sketches and always suspected Hannes Meyer of peeping with at least one eye. . . . My main problem was caused by the electro-mechanical installation. According to Hannes Meyer's firm architectural convictions, all the pipes and fixtures had to be exposed: this applied to the water, heating, rain, sewage pipes, the electric installation pipes and even the chimneys." Arieh Sharon, *Kibbutz + Bauhaus* (Tel Aviv and Stuttgart: Kar Krämer Verlag, 1976), 31.

30. Meyer, "Wie ich arbeite," 27.

31. Naylor, *The Bauhaus Reassessed*, 174 (quoted in note 3 above), for example.

32. See Ernst Bloch, "Nonsynchronism and Dialectics," *New German Critique* 11 (Spring 1977): 22–38.

33. Perhaps Bloch gave the better characterization of Meyer's avant-gardism when he wrote, "Today the artist can be considered avant-gardist only if he succeeds in making the new art forms useful for the life and the struggle of the broad masses; otherwise glittering alloy is nothing but old iron." Ernst Bloch, *Spuren* (1930; Frankfurt am Main: Suhrkamp, 1969), 202.

34. Walter Benjamin, "The Author as Producer," in Benjamin, *Reflections*, ed. Peter Demetz (New York: Harcourt Brace Jovanovich, 1978), 228.

35. A cogent articulation of this position using the linguistic metaphor is given by Alan Colquhoun: "The development of the avant-garde marks a radical break with the form of artistic language which existed until the latter part of the nineteenth century. Traditionally, language was always thought of as describing something outside itself, in the 'real' world. The difference between natural language (considered as an instrument rather than a poetics) and artistic languages was merely that in the latter the form was an integral part of the message—the 'how' was as important as the 'what.' At whatever date we put the moment when the epistemological foundations of this 'rhetorical' world began to disintegrate, it was not until the end of the nineteenth century, in the context of avant-garde art, that the content of a work began to be indistinguishable from its form. External reality was no longer seen as a *donné* with its own preordained meanings but as a series of fragments, essentially enigmatic, whose meanings depended on how they were formally related or juxtaposed by the artist. In modern architecture this process took the form of demolishing the traditional meanings associated with function. But these were replaced by another set of functional meanings, and architecture was still seen in terms of a functional program which was translated, as directly as possible, into forms." Colquhoun, "From Bricolage to Myth, or How to Put Humpty-Dumpty Together Again," *Oppositions* 12 (Spring 1978): 4.

36. Hannes Meyer, "Flucht ins Leben," in *Bauen und Gesellschaft*, 185.

37. Hannes Meyer, interview in *Sovremennaya architektura* 5 (Moscow, 1930); cited in Schnaidt, *Hannes Meyer*, 27. Like many radical artists and architects, Meyer would remain optimistic about the possibilities for the Soviet Union long after such optimism was warranted. See, especially, "Antworten auf Fragen der Prager Architektengruppe 'Leva Fronta'" (1933), in Meyer, *Bauen und Gesellschaft*, 121ff. The problem of Meyer's affiliation with Stalinism and those raised by his move to Mexico in 1939 cannot be dealt with here. Yet the point of such an analysis would be the same: to interrogate the politics *of* form as well as politics *and* form.

Reproduction and Negation: The Cognitive Project of *Neue Sachlichkeit*

Epigraph: Theodor Adorno, "Commitment," in Aesthetics and Politics, *ed. Perry Anderson et al. (London: Verso, 1977), 191–192.*

1. Hans Sedlmayer already lamented this "loss of center" in his *Verlust der Mitte* (Salzburg, 1948).

2. I am adapting Edward Said's analysis of the literary establishment (see his *The World, the Text, and the Critic* [Cambridge: Harvard University Press, 1983]) to architecture in suggesting that humanist ideology has produced a profession of specialists, usually called historians of architecture, who have claimed as their domain a limited field of affirmative formal connoisseurship. Operating entirely within this domain, their formal analyses validate the work of architecture, the work validates the culture that produced it, and the culture validates the humanist historian. My point is that authority is maintained by such consensus as well as as by repression.

3. Throughout this essay I will follow the convention of referring to the author of the League of Nations project as Hannes Meyer, even though Hans Wittwer surely played an important role in the design. Meyer and Wittwer received one of nine third prizes in the controversial competition. Hilberseimer's project was first prepared in 1928 and published in 1930 in *Die Form.*

4. Colin Rowe and Robert Slutzky, "Transparency: Literal and Phenomenal," in *The Mathematics of the Ideal Villa and Other Essays* (Cambridge: MIT Press, 1976), 170, 174; reprinted from *Perspecta* 8 (1963).

5. Rosalind Krauss discusses the at once liberating and tendentious imperatives of Rowe and Slutzky's formalism in "Death of a Hermeneutic Phantom: Materialization of the Sign in the Work of Peter Eisenman," *Architecture and Urbanism* (January 1980): 189–219. I am indebted to her reading of the Rowe and Slutzky text for my analysis here.

6. The phrase "practice of negation" was suggested by T. J. Clark's "More on the Differences between Comrade Greenberg and Ourselves," in Benjamin H. D. Buchloh, Serge Guilbaut, and David Solkin, eds., *Modernism and Modernity* (Halifax: University of Nova Scotia Press, 1983). I have modified Clark's concept according to the differences in the practices that he discusses and those of Meyer and Hilberseimer, but I wish to reconfirm his assertion that negation is a constitutive part of modernism.

7. Benjamin Buchloh, "From Faktura to Factography," *October* 30 (1984): 87, n. 6.

8. Hannes Meyer, "Die neue Welt" (1926), trans. in Claude Schnaidt, *Hannes Meyer: Buildings, Projects and Writings* (Teufen: Verlag Arthur Niggli, 1965), 95.

9. Hannes Meyer, "bauen" (1928), trans. in Schnaidt, *Hannes Meyer*, 95. Original is in lower-case letters.

10. Hannes Meyer, "Projekt für den Völkerbundpalast, Genf, 1928," in Schnaidt, *Hannes Meyer*, 25.

11. Cf. Kenneth Frampton, "The Humanist versus the Utilitarian Ideal," *Architectural Design* 38 (1968): 134–136.

12. Meyer, "Projekt für den Völkerbundpalast, Genf," 29.

13. Walter Benjamin, "Surrealism: The Last Snapshot of the European Intelligentsia," in *Reflections*, ed. Peter Demetz (New York: Harcourt Brace Jovanovich, 1978), 180.

14. Frampton, "The Humanist versus the Utilitarian Ideal," 135. This is an early formulation; Frampton implies some revision in his later publications.

15. "[The principle of exteriority] holds that we are not to burrow to the hidden core of discourse, to the heart of the thought or meaning manifested in it; instead, taking the discourse itself, its appearance and its regularity, that we should look for its external conditions of existence, for that which gives rise to the chance series of events and fixes its limits." Michel Foucault, "The Discourse on Language," translation of *L'ordre du discours* (Paris, 1971) by Rupert Swyer, reprinted as an appendix to Foucault, *The Archaeology of Knowledge* (New York: Irvington Publishers, 1972), 229.

16. Walter Benjamin, "The Work of Art in the Age of Mechanical Reproduction," in *Illuminations*, ed. Hannah Arendt (New York: Schocken, 1969), 238.

17. Ludwig Hilberseimer, *Groszstadtarchitektur* (Stuttgart: Verlag Julius Hoffmann, 1927), 98–100.

18. Hilberseimer, *Groszstadtarchitektur*, 103.

19. The Berlin application was published in *Die Form*, 1930. The tower model was exhibited at the Ausstellung der freie Wohlfahrtspflege in Düsseldorf in May-October 1926, and in Stuttgart in May-June 1927.

20. For this analysis of the nonoriginality of origins, I am indebted to Rosalind Krauss's discussion of the pictorial grid in "The Originality of the Avant-Garde: A Postmodernist Repetition," *October* 18 (1981): 47–66.

21. I was led to this understanding of Hilberseimer through a reading of Theodor Adorno's analysis of Schoenberg in *The Philosophy of Modern Music,* trans. Anne G. Mitchell and Wesley V. Blomster (New York: Seabury, 1973; original German 1958).

22. Cf. Clark, "More on the Differences between Comrade Greenberg and Ourselves," 185.

23. See the section "Reconciliation and Mimetic Adaptation to Death," in Theodor Adorno, *Aesthetic Theory* (London and New York: Routledge & Kegan Paul, 1984), 193–195.

Ludwig Hilberseimer and the Inscription of the Paranoid Subject

Epigraph: Bertolt Brecht, "Mann ist Mann," Erste Stücke, vol. 2 (Frankfurt am Main: Suhrkamp-Verlag, 1953), 229–230.

The Crisis of Humanism, the Dissolution of the Object

1. Though the revelation of the steel structure of the skyscraper has often been emphasized, Mies himself verifies the importance of viewing the shimmering glass wall and the registration of the contingencies of the site over the demonstration of the building's skeleton. He writes, "My efforts with an actual glass model helped me to recognize that the most important thing about using glass is not the effects of light and shadow, but the rich play of reflection. . . . A superficial examination might suggest that the curved outline of the plan is arbitrary. This was determined, however, by a concern for the illumination of the interior, for the massing of the building as viewed from the street, and for the play of reflections. The only fixed points of the plan are adjusted to the needs of the building and designed to be carried out in glass." Mies van der Rohe, "Hochhaus Projekt für Bahnhof Friedrichstrasse in Berlin," *Frühlicht* 1 (Summer 1922): 122–124.

2. Georg Simmel, "Die Grosstädte und das Geistesleben" (Dresden, 1903); translated as "The Metropolis and Mental Life," in *The Sociology of Georg Simmel,* trans. and ed. Kurt H. Wolff (New York: The Free Press, 1950), 409–424.

3. Theodor Adorno, in a letter to Walter Benjamin of 1935, in Adorno, *Über Walter Benjamin* (Frankfurt am Main: Suhrkamp Verlag, 1970), 112.

4. Theodor Adorno, *Negative Dialectics*, trans. E. B. Ashton (New York: The Seabury Press, 1973; original German 1966), 28.

5. Adorno called "an exact fantasy" of reality a "fantasy that abides within the material that the sciences present to it, and reaches beyond them only in the smallest aspects of their arrangement: aspects, granted, that fantasy itself must originally generate." Theodor Adorno, "Die Aktualität der Philosophie" (1931), in Adorno, *Gesammelte Schriften*, vol. 1, ed. Rolf Tiedemann (Frankfurt am Main: Suhrkamp Verlag, 1970), 341. An exact fantasy is "scientific" in its refusal to remove itself from the technical logic of the medium of architecture, yet, as an active rearrangement of that logic, it is a controlled effort to split open the real by striking its elements against each other with the force of the imagination.

6. For a close reading of Schwitters's Merz-column in the context of emergent Weimar culture, see Dorothea Dietrich, "The Fragment Reframed: Kurt Schwitters's *Merz-column*," *Assemblage* 14 (1991).

7. Theodor Adorno, "Thesen über die Sprache des Philosophen," in Adorno, *Gesammelte Schriften*, 1:369.

8. Here I invoke an Althusserian understanding that architecture is not simply a free-floating object in its own right, nor does it mirror some base, context, or ground and simply replicate the latter ideologically; but that the object possesses some "semi-autonomous" force with which it can also be seen as negating that context. See Louis Althusser, "Ideology and Ideological State Apparatuses," in Althusser, *Lenin and Philosophy*, trans. Ben Brewster (London and New York: New Left Books, 1971). I must gloss over some problems with my use of the Althusserian term "mediation." For a discussion see Jameson's introduction to his *The Political Unconscious* (Ithaca: Cornell University Press, 1981), 23ff.

9. Mies's radical engagement with irrationality and chaos, his framing of circumstance, at once anguished and exhilarated, perhaps begins and ends here in the skyscraper projects: his later work emphasizes again and again its ambition to salvage the purity of high art from the encroachment of urbanization, mass production, technological modernization, in short, of modern mass culture. Mies's contact, at this time in his career, with the *G* group, the expressionists, and the Berlin dadaists including Raoul Hausmann, Hannah Höch, and Kurt Schwitters may account for his momentary plunge into particularity in postwar Berlin.

10. Ludwig Hilberseimer, *Groszstadtarchitektur* (Stuttgart: Verlag Julius Hoffmann, 1927), 62, 61.

11. Jean Baudrillard, *Simulations* (New York: Semiotext(e), 1983), 136.

12. It is interesting to note that in 1919 Hannah Höch had used the same illustration of the Pennsylvania Hotel in her *Cut with the Dada Kitchen Knife.*

13. Baudrillard, *Simulations,* 11; emphasis in original.

14. Ludwig Hilberseimer, "The Berlin School of Architecture of the Twenties," manuscript of 1967 (Ludwig Karl Hilberseimer Archives, Art Institute of Chicago, series 8/1, box 7/10), 49–51; published in German as *Berliner Architektur der 20er Jahre* (Mainz: Florian Kupferberg Verlag, 1967).

15. Ludwig Hilberseimer, "Grosstadtarchitektur," *Der Sturm* 15, no. 4 (1924): 177–178; my emphasis.

16. Jean Baudrillard, "The Ecstasy of Communication," in Hal Foster, *The Anti-Aesthetic* (Port Townsend: Bay Press, 1983), 126–127.

17. Gilles Deleuze and Félix Guattari, *Anti-Oedipus: Capitalism and Schizophrenia,* trans. Robert Hurley, Mark Seem, and Helen R. Lane (Minneapolis: University of Minnesota Press, 1983; original French 1972), 365.

18. Hilberseimer's articles for *Der Einzige,* all published in volume 1 (1919), were: "Schöpfung und Entwicklung," Jan. 19, pp. 4–6; "Umwertung in der Kunst," Jan. 26, pp. 24–25; "Form und Individuum," Feb. 2, pp. 30–31; "Der Naturalismus und das Primitive in der Kunst," March 9, pp. 88–89; "Kunst und Wissen," March 30, pp. 127–128. I shall also frequently refer to a longer work, also entitled "Schöpfung und Entwicklung," manuscript of c. 1922 (Hilberseimer Archives, Art Institute of Chicago, series 8/3, box 1/10). This 41-page manuscript synthesizes many of Hilberseimer's earlier articles and is the source for many later ones. The strategy of repetition extends to Hilberseimer's writings: yet another version was published with the same title in *Sozialistische Monatshefte* 28 (1922): 993–997. Translations are mine unless otherwise noted.

Hannes Meyer referred to Hilberseimer as a "socialist architect." See *The Bauhaus*, ed. H. M. Wingler (Cambridge: MIT Press, 1969), 164. Hilberseimer would teach at the workers' school, the Kollektiv für sozialistisches Bauen, in 1931–1932. Yet there is no evidence in his writings that his socialism is anything more than routine for the times.

19. Friedrich Nietzsche, *The Will to Power* (1886–1888), trans. and ed. Walter Kaufmann and R. J. Hollingdale. (New York: Random House, 1968), 853.

20. Hilberseimer, "Schöpfung und Entwicklung" (manuscript), 4, 11. Walter Benjamin criticized the emphasis on creativity over the properly destructive task of the artist in a way that suggests a comparison of Hilberseimer and Meyer. "For too long the accent was placed on creativity. People are creative to the extent that they avoid tasks and supervision. Work as a supervised task—its model: political and technical work—is attended by dirt and detritus, intrudes destructively into matter, is abrasive to what is already achieved, critical toward its conditions, and is in all this opposite to that of the dilettante luxuriating in creation. His work is innocent and pure, consuming and purifying masterliness. And therefore the monster stands among us as the messenger of a more real humanism. He is the conqueror of the empty phrase. He feels solidarity not with the slender pine but with the plane that devours it, not with the precious ore but with the blast furnace that purifies it. The average European has not succeeded in uniting his life with technology, because he has clung to the fetish of creative existence. One must have followed Loos in his struggle with the dragon 'ornament,' heard the stellar Esperanto of Scheerbart's creations or seen Klee's New Angel, who preferred to free men by taking from them, rather than make them happy by giving to them, to understand a humanity that proves itself by destruction." Walter Benjamin, "Karl Kraus," in Benjamin, *Reflections*, ed. Peter Demetz (New York: Harcourt Brace Jovanovich, 1978), 272–273.

21. Hilberseimer, "Schöpfung und Entwicklung" (manuscript), 32.

22. Hilberseimer, "Schöpfung und Entwicklung" (manuscript), 9, 31.

23. Hilberseimer, "Schöpfung und Entwicklung" (manuscript), 13, 11. Riegl emphasized art works as "evidence not only of man's creative struggle with nature, but also of his peculiar perception of shape and color." Alois Riegl, "The Modern Cult of Monuments: Its Character and Its Origins" (1928), trans. Kurt W. Forster and Diane Ghirardo, *Oppositions* 25 (Fall 1982): 47.

24. Hilberseimer, "Schöpfung und Entwicklung," *Sozialistische Monatshefte*, 996.

25. Hilberseimer, "Mexikanische Baukunst," *Das Kunstblatt* 6, no. 4 (1922): 163.

26. Hilberseimer, "Schöpfung und Entwicklung" (manuscript), 14.

27. Ludwig Hilberseimer, "Kirchenbauten in Eisenbeton," *Zentralblatt der Bauverwaltung* 67, no. 42 (1927): 533.

28. Hilberseimer, "Schöpfung und Entwicklung" (manuscript), 11, 14.

29. Hilberseimer, "Schöpfung und Entwicklung" (manuscript), 12, 41.

30. Hilberseimer, "Schöpfung und Entwicklung" (manuscript), 41, 34, 39, 2.

Hope beyond Chaos: Expressionism and Dadaism

1. Ludwig Hilberseimer, "Schöpfung und Entwicklung," manuscript of c. 1922 (Ludwig Karl Hilberseimer Archives, Art Institute of Chicago, series 8/3, box 1/10), 38.

2. G. W. F. Hegel, *Aesthetik*, vol. 2 (Frankfurt, 1955), 414; quoted in Georg Lukács, *Studies in European Realism*, trans. Edith Bone (New York: Grosset and Dunlap, 1964), 155.

3. Ludwig Hilberseimer, "Schöpfung und Entwicklung," *Sozialistische Monatshefte* 28, no. 26 (1922): 993, 995–996.

4. Hilberseimer, "Schöpfung und Entwicklung," *Sozialistische Monatshefte*, 993.

5. Ludwig Hilberseimer, "Der Naturalismus und das Primitive in der Kunst," *Der Einzige* 1, no. 10 (1919): 89. Hilberseimer draws somewhat on Carl Einstein, *Negerplastik* (Leipzig: Verlag der Weissen Bücher, 1915).

6. Ludwig Hilberseimer, "Schöpfung und Entwicklung," *Der Einzige* 1, no. 1 (1919): 5–6.

7. Ludwig Hilberseimer, "Konstruktivismus," in *Sozialistische Monatshefte* 28, nos. 19–20 (1922): 831. Hilberseimer, however, praises the work of the constructivists as properly elementary form.

8. Herbert Marcuse, *Counterrevolution and Revolt* (Boston: Beacon Press, 1972), 108. Also see Martin Jay's chapter "Anamnestic Totalization: Memory in the Thought of Herbert Marcuse," in *Marxism and Totality* (Berkeley and Los Angeles: University of California Press, 1984), 220ff.

9. Hilberseimer, "Schöpfung und Entwicklung" (manuscript).

10. Wilhelm Worringer had already linked primitive art to the "synthesists and expressionists" in France in his "Zur Entwicklungsgeschichte der modernen Malerei," *Der Sturm* 2, no. 75 (August 1911). Hilberseimer also knew Einstein's *Negerplastik*. But Hilberseimer characteristically conflated primitive art with a more Nietzschean sense of "primitivism."

11. Ludwig Hilberseimer, *Berliner Architektur der 20er Jahre* (Mainz: Florian Kupferberg Verlag, 1967), 30. The project Mies submitted was that for the Kröller-Müller Museum in The Hague. The projects by Hilberseimer are probably those later published in Max Wagenführ, "Architektonische Entwürfe von L. Hilberseimer," *Deutsche Kunst und Dekoration* 22 (July 1919). (See next chapter, note 19.) Wagenführ confirmed that Hilberseimer's projects should be understood as antidotes to expressionism.

12. On the expressionists and, in particular, Heckel, Pechstein, and Schmitt-Rottluff of Die Brücke, see Hilberseimer's "Der Naturalismus und das Primitive in der Kunst," but key concepts and phrases recur throughout the 1919 articles. (See previous chapter, note 18, for a full listing of these articles.)

13. Fredric Jameson, "Postmodernism, or The Cultural Logic of Late Capitalism," *New Left Review* 146 (July-August 1984): 63–64.

14. Wolgang Pehnt, *Expressionist Architecture* (London: Academy Editions, 1973), analyzes the categories of tower and cave as tropes of expressionism.

15. From the catalogue of the group Rih, Karlsruhe, in Helga Klieman, *Die Novembergruppe* (Berlin: Gebr. Mann Verlag, 1969), 59; cited in Manfredo Tafuri, *The Sphere and the Labyrinth* (Cambridge: MIT Press, 1987; original Italian 1980), 122.

16. I have learned here from Fredric Jameson's analysis of the philosophy of Herbert Marcuse as "a profound and almost platonic valorization of memory, anamnesis, in human existence. . . . The primary energy of revolutionary activity derives from this memory of prehistoric happiness which the individual can regain only through its externalization, through its reestablishment for society as a whole." Fredric Jameson, *Marxism and Form: Twentieth-Century Dialectical Theories of Literature* (Princeton: Princeton University Press, 1971), 112–113.

17. Ludwig Hilberseimer, "Anmerkungen zur neuen Kunst," Sammlung Gabrielson Göteburg 1922–23 (Hilberseimer Archives, Art Institute of Chicago, series 1/1, box 1/4); reprinted in the pamphlet *Zehn Jahre Novembergruppe*, 52–57; English trans. in Manfredo Tafuri, "USSR-Berlin 1922: From Populism to the 'Constructivist International,'" in Joan Ockman et al., eds., *Architecture Criticism Ideology* (Princeton: Princeton Architectural Press, 1985), 179–183; my emphasis.

18. Jean Granier, "Nietzsche's Conception of Chaos," in David B. Allison, ed., *The New Nietzsche* (Cambridge: MIT Press, 1985), 135–141.

19. Friedrich Nietzsche, in *Nietzsches Werke, Grossoktavausgabe*, vol. 7 (Leipzig: Alfred Kröner Verlag, 1901–1913), § 121; cited in Granier, "Nietzsche's Conception of Chaos," 136.

20. Michel Haar, "Nietzsche and Metaphysical Language," in Allison, *The New Nietzsche*, 17.

21. Friedrich Nietzsche, *The Will to Power* (1886–1888), trans. and ed. Walter Kaufmann and R. J. Hollingdale (New York: Random House, 1968), §§ 767, 333.

22. Nietzsche, *The Will to Power*, § 481.

23. Nietzsche, *The Will to Power*, § 583.

24. Friedrich Nietzsche, *The Gay Science* (1882), trans. Walter Kaufmann (New York: Random House, 1974), preface, 4.

25. Nietzsche, *The Will to Power*, § 481.

26. Friedrich Nietzsche, *Thus Spoke Zarathustra* (1883–1884), in *The Portable Nietzsche*, trans. and ed. Walter Kaufmann (New York: Viking Press, 1968), "The Seven Seals."

27. Hans Richter defined *G* as being "born from the need to say what we could not tolerate and, at the same time, from the need to create a forum for the ideas that, after the dada period and with constructivism, were characterized as representing the cultural tendencies of the new era." Hans Richter, *Köpfe und Hinterköpfe* (Zurich: Verlag der Arche, 1967), 75. Die Kommune was a dissident faction of the avant-garde whose members overlapped with other groups. See Klieman, *Die Novembergruppe*.

28. Interestingly, Carl Einstein's novel *Bebuquin oder die Dilettanten des Wunders* (1912) characterizes the ego as a constantly shifting constellation of sensations whose very composition changes with time. Einstein's notion of perception itself (*Sehen* in his teminology) is a dissolution of subject-object oppositions that Hilberseimer may have learned from.

29. Hans Richter, letter to Raoul Hausmann, 16 February 1964, quoted in Hausmann's letter to the editor, "More on Group G," *Art Journal* 24 (Summer 1965): 350–352.

30. Hans Richter and Werner Graeff, *G* 1 (July 1923): 1.

31. Richter, *Köpfe und Hinterköpfe*, 75.

32. The essay also appears as Hilberseimer, *Groszstadtbauten* (Hannover: Aposverlag, 1925).

33. Kurt Schwitters, *Kunst und Zeiten* (1926), now in Schwitters, *Das literarische Werk*, vol. 5, ed. Friedhelm Lach (Cologne: DuMont Buchverlag, 1981), 236–240. Other artists listed were Braque, Boccioni, Mondrian, Van Doesburg, Malevich, Lissitzky, Moholy-Nagy, and Mies van der Rohe.

34. Kurt Schwitters, "Stuttgart die Wohnung Werkbundausstellung," *Der Sturm* 18, no. 10 (1928): 148–150; now in Schwitters, *Das literarische Werk*, 5:280–286. In this context, Schwitters's terms "basic and normal" should not be considered as preceded by an implied "merely," for the automatism, banality, and radical indifference that Schwitters, Hausmann, and others sought in conventionality and normality seem to be just what Schwitters also saw in Hilberseimer's work.

35. Various notions of elementarism were in the air among the members of the Berlin-Moscow axis. Hilberseimer would later suggest that the "new spirit" in much of the art shown in the gallery Der Sturm may have come from Nietzsche, who had written of the *Elementarphilosophie* of the pre-Socratics in contrast to Plato. See Hilberseimer's address to the Technische Universität, Berlin, 1963 (Hilberseimer Archives, Art Institute of Chicago, series 1, folder 5/7). I owe this reference to Richard Pommer.

36. Raoul Hausmann, "Présentism gegen den Puffkeïsmus der teutschen Seele," *De Stijl* 4, no. 9 (September 1921); cited in Timothy O. Benson, *Raoul Hausmann and Berlin Dada* (Ann Arbor: UMI Research Press, 1987), 205.

37. Hilberseimer, "Anmerkungen zur neuen Kunst," 180.

38. Hilberseimer, "Dadaismus," *Sozialistische Monatshefte* 26, nos. 25–26 (1920): 1120–1122. The internal quotation is Hilberseimer's.

39. Hilberseimer, "Dadaismus."

40. Edward Said, commenting on the writings of Antonio Gramsci, in his *The World, the Text, and the Critic* (Cambridge: Harvard University Press, 1983), 171.

41. Georg Grosz and Wieland Herzfelde, "Die Kunst ist in Gefahr" (Berlin, 1925); English translation in Lucy Lippard, ed., *Dadas on Art* (Englewood Cliffs: Prentice-Hall, 1971), 81. There are moments in this article in which an almost Benjaminian conception of the technological determinants of art is at work.

42. Ludwig Hilberseimer, "Dix," *Sozialistische Monatshefte* (January 1923): 66.

43. Raoul Hausmann, "L'Esprit de notre temps 1919," in Michel Giroud, ed., *Raoul Hausmann: "Je ne suis pas un photographe"* (Paris: Chêne, 1975), 30.

44. Hilberseimer, "Dadaismus."

45. Hilberseimer, "Schöpfung und Entwicklung" (manuscript), 13. Agnes Kohlmeyer, "Apollo e Dioniso: Hilberseimer critico d'arte," *Rassegna* 8, no. 27 (September 1986): 30–31, using Hilberseimer's art critical writings, asserts that Hilberseimer can be seen as part of the "formal dadaist" tendency. I can agree with her assertion but would note its incomplete formulation.

46. Hilberseimer, "Schöpfung und Entwicklung" (manuscript), 29. Hilberseimer notes that the internal quotation is from Raoul Hausmann. I have not been able to find a published source.

47. Ernst Bloch, in an interview given in 1968; Michael Landmann, "Talking with Ernst Bloch: Korcula, 1968," *Telos* 25 (Fall 1975): 178.

48. For the following summary of Bloch's thought, I have drawn especially from Martin Jay, *Marxism and Totality* (Berkeley and Los Angeles: University of California Press, 1984), 174ff., and Fredric Jameson, *Marxism and Form* (Princeton: Princeton University Press, 1971), 116ff.

49. Ernst Bloch, "Aktualität und Utopie. Zu Lukács' *Geschichte und Klassenbewusstsein*," reprinted in *Philosophische*

Aufsätze zur objektiven Phantasie, Gesamtausgabe, vol. 10 (Frankfurt, 1969), 618; cited in Jay, *Marxism and Totality,* 182.

50. Ernst Bloch, "Nonsynchronism and the Obligation to Its Dialectics," *New German Critique* 11 (Spring 1977): 31.

51. Ernst Bloch, *Das Prinzip Hoffnung,* 2 vols. (Frankfurt: Suhrkamp, 1959), 2:41; emphasis in original.

52. Jameson, *Marxism and Form,* 146.

53. Bloch, *Das Prinzip Hoffnung,* 2:110, 150; emphasis in original.

54. Hilberseimer, "Schöpfung und Entwicklung" (manuscript), 41.

55. On the concept of "foreclosure" (*Verwerfung*) and its relation to the structure of paranoia, see Jacques Lacan, "On a Question Preliminary to Any Possible Treatment of Psychosis," in *Ecrits: A Selection,* trans. Alan Sheridan (New York: W. W. Norton, 1977), especially 201ff.

Groszstadtarchitektur and *Weimar-stimmung:* The Construction of the Paranoid Subject

1. Jacques Derrida, *Positions,* trans. Alan Bass (London: Athlone, 1981), 29.

2. Peter Sloterdijk, *Critique of Cynical Reason* (Minneapolis: University of Minnesota Press, 1987; original German 1983), 385.

3. Sloterdijk, *Critique of Cynical Reason,* 195–197.

4. Sloterdijk, *Critique of Cynical Reason,* 199. The quotation of Heidegger is from *Sein und Zeit* (1927), 173.

5. Sloterdijk, *Critique of Cynical Reason,* 199, 200–201.

6. Ludwig Hilberseimer, *Groszstadtarchitektur* (Stuttgart: Julius Hoffmann, 1927), 1–2.

7. Manfredo Tafuri, for one, has made this connection. See especially his *The Sphere and the Labyrinth* (Cambridge: MIT Press, 1987; original Italian 1980).

8. Hilberseimer, *Groszstadtarchitektur,* 2.

9. Hilberseimer, *Groszstadtarchitektur,* 2.

10. Walter Rathenau, *Gesamtausgabe,* vol. 2 (1977), 52; cited in Sloterdijk, *Critique of Cynical Reason,* 434ff.

11. Rathenau, *Gesamtausgabe,* 2:93. It is interesting to compare Rathenau's cynical irony with Ernst Jünger's aestheticization of war technology and the *Fronterlebnis,* but also with the opposite reactions of recent liberal humanist evaluations of Hilberseimer's architecture. Richard Pommer, for example, remarks that "it is of course the total elimination of nature that is so shocking and deadening in Hilberseimer's city," and that his avant-gardism "does not help to explain the equally depressing absence of any visual excitement or pleasure in Hilberseimer's necropolis." Richard Pommer, "'More a Necropolis than a Metropolis': Ludwig Hilberseimer's Highrise City and Modern City Planning," in *In the Shadow of Mies* (Chicago: The Art Institute of Chicago, 1988), 34–35. My point is not, of course, to choose the aesthetic preferences of Rathenau or Jünger over Pommer, but rather to insist that aesthetic preferences *in se* can no longer be the basis of an interpretation of Hilberseimer.

12. Rathenau's striking description of the mechanization of the city is worth repeating: "Visible and invisible networks of rolling traffic crisscross and undermine the vehicular ravines and twice daily pump human bodies fom the limbs to the heart. A second, third, fourth network distributes water, heat and power, an electrical bundle of nerves carries the resonances of the spirit. . . . Honeycomb cells, fitted out with silky fabrics, paper, timber, leather, tapestries, are ordered into rows; outwardly supported by iron, stone, glass, cement. . . . Only in the old centers of the cities . . . residues of physiognomical peculiarities are still maintained as almost extinct showpieces, while in the surrounding districts . . . the international world warehouse extends." "What then is the purpose of these unheard-of constructions? In large part, they directly serve production. In part, they serve transport and trade, and thus indirectly production. In part, they serve administration, domicile, and health care, and thus predominantly production. In part, they serve science, art, technology, education, recreation, and thus indirectly . . . once again production." Rathenau, *Gesamtausgabe,* 2:22, 51.

13. Hilberseimer, *Groszstadtarchitektur,* 20, 21.

14. Rathenau, *Gesamtausgabe,* 2:67; my emphasis.

15. Ernst Bloch refers to the *Fronterlebnis*—with its community of males uncorrupted by capitalist exchange—as Ernst Jünger's "concrete utopia."

16. Ludwig Hilberseimer, "Dadaismus," *Sozialistische Monatshefte* 26, nos. 25–26 (1920): 1120–1122.

17. Hilberseimer, *Groszstadtarchitektur,* 13; my emphasis.

18. For example, Gustav Stotz, the organizer of the Werkbund Weissenhof exhibition in Stuttgart in 1927, in a review of *Groszstadtarchitektur,* declared that Hilberseimer "proceeds in his observations from the decisive formative factors—economic, social, and technical—without historical restrictions, and leaves the formal and aesthetic side of the problem as a secondary concern." Gustav Stotz, "Werkbund Gedanken," in *Stuttgarter Neues Tageblatt, Beiblatt,* 25 August 1928 (Ludwig Karl Hilberseimer Archives, Art Institute of Chicago, series 9/5, folder 5). Manfredo Tafuri is one of the few recent critics to assign more than summary importance to Hilberseimer and the Hochhausstadt project. See especially the chapter "Sozialpolitik and the City in Weimar Germany," in his *The Sphere and the Labyrinth.*

19. The date is not certain. Hilberseimer's drawing of a Palace design, published in *Deutsche Bauhütte* 10 (1906), is his first published design. The drawing for a village mentioned here may be from the same period, though it is most likely from a later group of drawings submitted to the Ausstellung unbekannter Architekten in April 1919.

20. See Heinrich Tessenow, *Die Wohnhausbau* (Munich, 1909); Paul Mebes, *Um 1800, Architektur und Handwerk im letzten Jahrhundert ihrer traditionellen Entwicklung* (Munich, 1908); and Friedrich Ostendorf, *Sechs Bücher vom Bauen* (Berlin, 1913–1922). Ostendorf was Hilberseimer's teacher at the Grand Ducal Technical University Fredericiana in Karlsruhe.

21. For example, see Hilberseimer, "Konstruktivismus," *Sozialistische Monatshefte* 28 (1922): 831–834; and "Anmerkungen zur neuen Kunst," Sammlung Gabrielson Göteburg 1922–23 (Hilberseimer Archives, Art Institute of Chicago, series 1/1, box 1/4), trans. in Manfredo Tafuri, "USSR-Berlin 1922: From Populism to the 'Constructivist International,'" in Joan Ockman et al., eds., *Architecture Criticism Ideology* (Princeton: Princeton Architectural Press, 1985), 179–183.

22. Ludwig Hilberseimer, "Cézanne," *Sozialistische Monatshefte* 28, nos. 1–2 (1922): 64.

23. Hilberseimer, "Anmerkungen zur neuen Kunst."

24. Ludwig Hilberseimer, "Archipenko," *Sozialistische Monatshefte,* May 1921 (Hilberseimer Archives, Art Institute of Chicago, series 8/3, box 5/43): 465–466. Compare Hilberseimer's analysis of Archipenko's synthesis of New York skyscrapers etc. to his own appropriation of the same in his architecture.

25. Hilberseimer, "Anmerkungen zur neuen Kunst."

26. Hilberseimer, "Berlin School of Architecture of the Twenties," unpublished translation of *Berliner Architektur der 20er Jahre* (1967) (Hilberseimer Archives, Art Institute of Chicago, series 8/1, folder 7/10), 51–52.

27. Hilberseimer, *Groszstadtarchitektur*, 99–100.

28. Hilberseimer, "Der Wille zur Architektur," *Das Kunstblatt* 5 (May 1923): 133–140; illustration is on p. 140, captioned "Entwurf zu einem Fabrikbau." The project was further developed and published in Hilberseimer, "Grosstädtische Kleinwohnungen," *Zentralblatt der Bauverwaltung* 32 (1929): 1–6.

29. Ernst Bloch, *Das Prinzip Hoffnung*, 2 vols. (Frankfurt: Suhrkamp, 1959) 2:150; emphasis in original.

30. Hilberseimer pointed out that the Hochhausstadt was at once a critique and an homage to Le Corbusier's project, which he called the only other fundamental, theoretical demonstration of the problem of giving form to the chaos of the metropolis. "Le Corbusier does not concentrate [the density of the population], as it seems at first glance, but only orders and improves. Without any change in principle. Without rethinking the problem anew." Hilberseimer, *Groszstadtarchitektur*, 13, 15.

31. Siegfried Kracauer, "The Mass Ornament," *New German Critique* 5 (Spring 1975): 69; emphasis in original.

32. Siegfried Kracauer, "Über Arbeitsnachweise," *Frankfurter Zeitung*, 17 June 1930; reprinted in Kracauer, *Strassen in Berlin und anderswo* (Frankfurt, 1964), 70.

33. Kracauer, "The Mass Ornament," 70.

34. Siegfried Kracauer, "Girls und Krise," *Frankfurter Zeitung*, 26 May 1931; quoted in Karsten Witte, "Introduction to Siegfried Kracauer's 'The Mass Ornament,'" *New German Critique* 5 (Spring 1975): 63–64.

35. Kracauer, "The Mass Ornament," 68.

36. Kracauer, "The Mass Ornament," 69–70; emphasis in original.

37. 37. Kracauer, "The Mass Ornament," 72.

38. Roland Barthes, *The Pleasure of the Text*, trans. Richard Miller (New York: Hill and Wang, 1975), 14.

39. Roland Barthes, *S/Z*, trans. Richard Miller (New York: Hill and Wang, 1974), 20–21.

40. Ludwig Hilberseimer, *Entfaltung einer Planungsidee* (Berlin: Verlag Ullstein, 1963), 22. This statement has, of course, been used by critics to absolve Hilberseimer of his crime against humanist thought. But in the present analysis, no absolution is needed or possible.

41. The idea of a dialectic of progress, of advances in society taking place through repression of individuals, is a central theme in modern social theory evident in writers from Hegel to Weber, Freud, and Marx. But Weimar's right wing intellectuals contributed to an irrationalist and nihilist embrace of technology and the eclipse of the bourgeois individual through a reactionary reading of Nietzsche, elevating the idea of the *Fronterlebnis* over effeminate normative standards, linking the concept of eroticized technological beauty to an elitist notion of the will, and finally interpreting war technology and the metropolis as the embodiment of that beauty and that will. Perhaps Ernst Jünger is the most vivid example of the fetishization of the technological that begins sounding very close to the language of Hilberseimer, but culminates in Naziism. For example, Jünger wrote, "The country and the nation . . . must come to terms with the following necessity: We must penetrate and enter into the power of the metropolis, into the forces of our time—the machine, the masses, and the worker. For it is in these that the potential energy so crucial for tomorrow's national spectacle resides. . . . It is precisely these masses who will produce a decisive and unrestricted leader, one who will have far fewer restrictions on his actions than even the sovereign of the absolute monarchy did." Ernst Jünger, "Grosstadt und Land," *Deutsches Volkstum* 8 (1926): 579–580. The self-constructing machine is also a fascination that extends across much of modernist production—perhaps most familiarly in surrealism and dadaism—and finds expression in megalomaniacal protofascisms. For example, Peter Sloterdijk recalls a 1934 description by Adrien Turel of a "total prosthesis of a technical kind" that gives us pause in relation to Hilberseimer's self-engendering machine and a possible way into its gender specificity: "This technical prosthetic system, which is a typically masculine achievement, can only be compared with the prenatal, complete enclosure in the body of the mother. All people, no matter of what sex (!), were initially, in their prenatal period, caught in the great prototype of every nourishing landscape, every protective sphere, every prision, too, i.e., they have experienced the enclosure in the body of a mother. The masculine counterpart to this is the development of technocratic prostheses, of power, of financial power and of the technical apparatuses for a complete capsule system in which individual people seem to be enclosed for better or worse." Adrien Turel, *Technokratie, Autarkie, Genetokratie* (1934), 59–60; cited in Sloterdijk, *Critique of Cynical Reason*, 459. What separates Hilberseimer from such thought, I believe, is precisely the de-aestheticization and de-eroticization of mass technology.

42. Heidegger comments, "*Bildung* means two things: first, a forming (*Bilden*), in the sense of an explicating imprinting. Yet at the same time, the 'forming' 'forms' (imprints) by anticipatory fitting to a determining view, which is thus called the *Vorbild*." Martin Heidegger, "Platons Lehre von der Wahrheit," *Wermarken* (Frankfurt am Main: Vittorio Klostermann, 1976), 217. It is of some interest, too, that Freud describes the identification with the father in terms of a *vorbildliche Identifizierung*.

43. The latter was described by Ernst Jünger as an "anonymous slavery," saying, "it is certainly our innermost will to sacrifice our freedom, to give up our existence as individuals and to melt into a large life circle, in which the individual has as little self-sufficiency as a cell that must die when separated from the body." Ernst Jünger, "Fortschritt, Freiheit und Notwendigkeit," *Arminius* 8 (1926): 8.

44. See, for example, Walter Benjamin, "Left-Wing Melancholy. (On Erich Kästner's New Book of Poems)" (1931), *Screen* 15, no. 2 (Summer 1974): 28–32.

45. Michel de Certeau, "Walking in the City," in *The Practice of Everyday Life* (Berkeley: University of California Press, 1984), 117.

46. For a recent discussion of the scientism of humanist discourse in terms of a theory of the subject, see especially Paul Smith, *Discerning the Subject* (Minneapolis: University of Minnesota Press, 1988), 83ff. Smith finds in humanism itself a "metaparanoia." I have benefited from his arguments, though my construction of paranoia here is different.

47. Jacques Lacan, *Ecrits: A Selection*, trans. Alan Sheridan (London and New York: W. W. Norton, 1977), 2–3.

48. Sigmund Freud to Carl Gustav Jung, in *Letters* (Princeton: Princeton University Press, 1974), 40.

49. Sigmund Freud, "Psychoanalytical Notes on an Auto-biographical Account of a Case of Paranoia" (1911), in Freud, *Standard Edition* (London: Hogarth Press, 1953–1974), 12:9.

50. Sigmund Freud, "Further Remarks on the Neuropsychology of Defence" (1896), in Freud, *Standard Edition*, 3:185; my emphasis.

Conclusion: Posthumanism and Postmodernism

Epigraph: Jacques Lacan, The Seminar of Jacques Lacan, book II, ed. Jacques-Alain Miller, trans. Sylvana Tomaselli (New York: W.W. Norton, 1991; original French 1978), 208.

1 Louis Althusser, *For Marx*, trans. Ben Brewster (London: Verso, 1979; original French 1965), 229.

2. Jacques Lacan, *Ecrits: A Selection*, trans. Alan Sheridan (London and New York: W. W. Norton, 1977; original French 1966), 171.

3. See, for example, Michel Foucault, *Madness and Civilization: A History of Insanity in the Age of Reason*, trans. Richard Howard (New York: Vintage Books, 1973; original French 1961).

4. Michel Foucault, *The Order of Things: An Archaeology of the Human Sciences*, trans. unnamed (New York: Pantheon, 1970; original French 1966).

5. See, for example, Jacques Derrida, "The Ends of Man" (1968), in Derrida, *Margins*, trans. Alan Bass (Chicago: University of Chicago Press, 1982).

6. Jean-François Lyotard, *Le Tombeau de l'intellectuel, et autres papiers* (Paris: Editions Galilée, 1984), 65.

7. For a preliminary analysis, see Louis Martin, "Transpositions: On the Intellectual Origins of Tschumi's Architectural Theory," *Assemblage* 11 (1990).

8. Roland Barthes, "The Death of the Author," in Barthes, *Image—Music—Text*, ed. and trans. Stephen Heath (New York: Hill and Wang, 1977), 146.

9. The term is Fredric Jameson's. See his "Postmodernism, or The Cultural Logic of Late Capitalism," *New Left Review* 146 (July-August 1984).

10. Terry Eagleton, *The Ideology of the Aesthetic* (Cambridge: Basil Blackwell, 1990), 374.

illustration credits

References are by page number.

17. Reproduced from Sigfried Giedion, *Space, Time and Architecture* (Cambridge: Harvard University Press, 1974).

26, 32, 64, 65, 70, 71, 84, 86, 89, 96, 100 left, 134, 135, 137, 138, 139, 142, 161, 163, 166–167. Deutsches Architekturmuseum, Frankfurt am Main.

30, 31, 36, 37, 88. Institut für Geschichte und Theorie der Architektur an der ETH, Zurich.

40–41, 44, 66–67, 76–77. Reproduced from Hannes Meyer, "Die neue Welt," *Das Werk* 13, no. 7 (Bern, 1926).

47. Reproduced from Hannes Meyer and Jean Bard, "Das Theater Co-op," *Das Werk* 11, no. 12 (Bern, 1924).

60, 61. Reproduced from Heinrich Kulka, *Adolf Loos* (Vienna: Verlag Anton Schroll, 1931).

72, 129. Reproduced from *Bauhaus Photography* (Cambridge: MIT Press, 1985).

94, 98, 112. Reproduced from *Bauhaus* 2 (Dessau, 1927).

95. Reproduced from *ABC*, series 2, no. 2 (Basel, 1926).

100 right. Reproduced from El Lissitzky, *Rußland, Die Rekonstruktion der Architektur in der Sowjetunion* (Vienna: Verlag Anton Schroll, 1930).

101. Drawing by Paul Hanley.

104. Courtesy of Arturo Schwartz, Milan.

117. Bildarchiv Felix Klee, Bern.

123. Reproduced from *9 Jahre Bauhaus* (Dessau, 1928).

147. Reproduced from *Tvorba* (Prague, 1931).

152, 153. Reproduced from Colin Rowe, *The Mathematics of the Ideal Villa and Other Essays* (Cambridge: MIT Press, 1976).

157. Reproduced from S. O. Khan-Magomedov, *Rodchenko: The Complete Work* (Cambridge: MIT Press, 1987).

162. Reproduced from Claude Schnaidt, *Hannes Meyer: Buildings, Projects and Writings* (Teufen: Verlag Arthur Niggli, 1965).

169. Courtesy of Philippe-Guy E. Woog, Geneva.

174–175, 176, 177, 179, 181, 198, 254, 261, 268–269, 271. Courtesy of The Art Institute of Chicago.

188, 191, 192, 195. The Museum of Modern Art, New York.

190, 201, 232, 257, 260. Copyright 1992 Estate of George Grosz, Princeton, N. J. / VAGA, New York.

193. Copyright 1992 Cosmo Press, Geneva / ARS, New York.

199, 247, 256 top, center. Reproduced from Ludwig Hilberseimer, *Groszstadtarchitektur* (Stuttgart: Julius Hoffmann, 1927).

200. Kunstmuseum Düsseldorf im Ehrenhof.

218. Reproduced from Udo Kultermann, *Wassili und Hans Luckhardt* (Tübingen: Verlag Ernst Wasmuth, 1958).

219. Staatsgalerie, Stuttgart

223. Photo Moderna Museet, Stockholm.

226. Reproduced from *G* 4 (March 1926).

231. Staatliche Museen Preussischer Kulturbesitz, Nationalgalerie, Berlin.

234. Musée National d'Art Moderne, Centre Georges Pompidou, Paris.

256 bottom. Reproduced from Ludwig Hilberseimer, *Groszstadtbauten* (Hannover: Aposverlag, 1925).

259, 262. Reproduced from *Hans Richter by Hans Richter*, ed. Cleve Gray (New York: Holt, Rinehart and Winston, 1971).

264. Reproduced from *Envisioning America: Prints, Drawings, and Photographs by George Grosz and His Contemporaries, 1915–1933* (Busch-Reisinger Museum, Harvard University, 1990).

276. Private collection, Bern.

284–285. Courtesy of Stan Allen, Architect, New York.

index

Page numbers in italics indicate illustrations.